Fried Ants and Yorkshire Pudding

Glenville Kedie

Cover by Glenville Kedie
Photography by David Kedie

Author's Note:

Except for members of my own family, many of the characters in this story are composites of several different people. With the exception of certain historical figures, most of the people's names have been changed to protect individual privacy. In places, the chronology has been streamlined for dramatic effect. I have chosen out of habit to use standard American spelling for English words such as *Colour* and *Flavour*, though in other places the English terminology and slang have been left intact because of context and idiom. I have also endeavored to capture the peculiarities of accent and speech. Please, try to *hear* the accents as you read. Any historical errors are my own, and are in places intentional; this is a *story*, albeit a true one told from the perspective of those involved. It is not intended as an accurate geopolitical treatise on the history of Uganda or British colonialism. Everything else – the Karamujong houseboy and his abbreviated trousers, the money under the carpets of the Capri, the fried ants, the sunburns, the iridescent ocean at Malindi, and the bodies, most especially the bodies – is true.

Glenville Kedie
March 2013

For Dad, who dared to rise above his station.
For Mom, who loved him enough to follow.

Introduction

I'm often asked if I remember Africa. If I remember the scenery, the animals, the last dying vestiges of England's former colonial empire. If I remember the coup in 1971 when Amin took over the country, began his purges of the army, the government, his systematic, intentional evisceration of the country. If I remember the colors, and the killings, and the mass expulsions, and the sights and smells of a nation gone mad. Remember? A better question might be, *how could I possibly forget?*

The Pearl of Africa - that's what Uganda used to be called, what it still is called in the National Anthem. It may well have been John Hanning Speke himself who coined the expression, after stumbling on the lake in 1858. He wasn't looking for the lake per se; he was looking for the source of the great and mighty Nile, river of Moses, river of Pharaohs. He had followed myths and legends, sought mountains where the moon was born, met peoples stranger than any thus far encountered in his life. Upon finding the 40,000 square mile body of water that proved indeed to be the primary source of the great river, he named it in honor of his Queen, Victoria, as was to be expected in his day.

Just by coincidence, my Father was almost exactly the same age as Speke was when, in January 1970, we left England for Uganda. By then I was five, our Queen was named Elizabeth, and the lake probably didn't look that much different than it had when Speke and Burton first saw it over a century before. However, less than a year after we got there, the country - the Pearl itself - had changed quite considerably. A few more bodies in the water, for one thing, and a damn sight more crocodiles.

When we arrived in Uganda, Apolo Milton Obote still ran the country, with the support of army commander Idi Amin. The British government, while not happy about Obote's reliance on military rule, was still actively aiding the nation, which is how we came to be there in the first place; through various agencies, England supplied contract engineers and advisors to Uganda's industry and agriculture. Britain provided air traffic controllers and airport management staff, instructors for the teaching college and medical university, experts in public works administration, sewage treatment, electrical power generation and distribution, road building and rail transportation, to name a few. In my father's case, the British government brought him in as an expert in printing, photography and lithographic reproduction, for both the newspaper and tourism industries. He was there mostly as a teacher, as part of Britain's effort help provide the infrastructure necessary for the nation of Uganda to stand freely as an independent economy. The rest of us – Mummy, Lulu and I – went along because Uganda is a bloody long way from Sheffield, which was fine with us. There was no nobility or altruism in our going; the fact is, my father would have done *anything* to get us all the hell out of the dead-end sinkhole that was the industrial north of England. England in general, and Sheffield, grimy old Sheffield in particular, with its smoke stacks and steel mills and bugger all in the way of prospects for an ambitious young chap like my Dad. He was 29 when he left England, a man moving his family to Africa, who'd never been further from home than a holiday in Devon when he was sixteen. It's bravery like that which makes him my hero.

M'zungu, they called us in Swahili. *Muzungu*. M'zungu – white person, for one; but also something strange, something marvelous, something baffling. There could be contempt in the word, or a bland, ambiguous friendliness; either way, it is what we were. Guest, strangers, but yet somehow completely at home.

So what was it like, growing up in Africa? That's the question I'm always asked. There are many images that have stuck with me; seemingly minor details, which, together, make up the palette of Africa in my mind, the palette from which I try to paint a picture for whoever is asking. The lucidity of the colors, and the crystalline quality of the equatorial sunlight, for example; or the vast openness of the place, and vistas so enormous that you could see the curvature of the earth over land and water both. The sound of insects everywhere, the click of stones being dropped into the worn wooden dimples of a *M'weso* board. The curried meat smell of samosas bought from a street vendor's greasy cardboard box and eaten hot while standing in the shade of a tin awning. The steaming spicy odor coming from the servant's quarters, of stewing goat meat and the plantain *matoké*, like stiff, green bananas, steaming away under banana leaves. The thud of *fenai* – breadfruit, or Jakfruit, as we also called it – hitting the ground outside the kitchen window; the sickly-sweet rotten banana smell of the fenai flesh itself, sticky and cloying and delicious. Or that after being shot at close range with a 7.62mm full metal-jacketed bullet and steeping in the weak-tea waters of Lake Victoria for a few hours, the skin of dead African soldiers, big blotchy patches of it around the bullet holes, turns stark white. Or that sixty thousand people can be stripped of homes, businesses, jewelry, cash, the clothes off their backs and even their own country almost overnight, and not a single person in the world will lift a finger to stop it. Or that three hundred thousand people can simply disappear, and the word *genocide* is never even mentioned. Strange, but these aren't things that most people can't even conceive of, but all of them, together, make up the Uganda where I grew up, and which I loved.

I was only young when we arrived, but still, I remember it all. What I didn't know, at the time, was that since its discovery, Uganda had been under the control of Great Britain, but on October 9, 1962, independence was granted and she was on her own. To ensure a smooth transition to self-governance, England tried to make sure Uganda was equipped for its new responsibilities. To that end, the British government built an enormous hydroelectric dam over Ripon Falls at Jinja – the very spot where Speke first saw the Nile flowing out from the lake. British engineers constructed the Makerere University teaching hospital; they built schools, and roads; railways were erected, extended and improved. Prime Minister Obote was set up to share power with the *Kabaka*, the traditional Baganda king, Edward Mutessa, whose family had ruled the region for generations, whose ancestors had been Speke's hosts and sometime captors, nearly a century and a quarter before.

Where Britain failed in this plan was in their failure to note that the cultural and religious differences between the peoples of Uganda ran deep. To see them all simply as *African* was a mistake, let alone to see them as uniformly *Ugandan*. Tribes like the Baganda and the Bunyoro had cultivated animosity between themselves for centuries. The Kabaka was hardly respected by Muslims from the north, who in turn struggled with Christians from the south. Add to this the descendants of the Indian servants and laborers brought in by the British in the 1800s, now prosperous merchants and citizens for three and four generations; all these vying groups wanted a voice in the new government, and it soon became clear why, in 1966, the power sharing arrangement collapsed. By '67, King Freddy was king in name only, and Obote, with the army as his good right arm, ran the country as sole dictator.

Yes, but what was Uganda *like*? That one's easy; in spite of the killings and the deportations and the dead bodies floating daily in the water off the beach – or possibly, *because* of those things – it was like any other childhood, anywhere. Sure, most people can't say that they've sat with their friends next to a corpse washed up on a beach, daring one another to be the first

4

touch it, or being able to say that *No, I was the first to touch the last one. Now it's* your *turn*.

But at the time, without something against which to compare, without a point of reference, these things were, for lack of a better word, *normal*. Commonplace, everyday. All I can really say for sure is that by comparison, as childhoods go, overall it was a damn sight better than England. Details, like what happens to the skin of African soldiers when they get shot to death, will stay with me always. As to the rest of it, the man I am now sees the boy that I was then, and what that boy sees is, to him, all perfectly, perfectly *normal*. Even the coup, when it happened, seemed normal, at the time, or at least not entirely unexpected – Unable to keep all groups working together, Obote, with increasing frequency, looked to the army to maintain control. A poorly educated but ambitious young officer served as his personal liaison; Idi Amin, a massive, solid, charismatic Kekwa from the north. Obote's rivals were greatly troubled by Amin. It was alleged that he'd illegally led Ugandan troops on raids across the border into the Congo; large sums of money began turning up in Amin's personal bank accounts, and after investigations revealed Amin's involvement in illegal arms sales, the government began demanding Obote's resignation.

In early 1967, rather than yield power, Obote called on Amin and his troops and staged a *coupe d'état* against his own government. When the Baganda and their Kabaka objected and demanded that Obote disband his new, non-elected government, Obote turned the wrath of Amin against the Kabaka's Palace. The palace, more a large house than a fortress, was quickly overrun, but not before King Freddie managed to slip past the soldiers in a rainstorm and flee to Great Britain in exile. He escaped his own execution, despite the absurdity of the fact, by hailing a passing taxi – just one more thing that in Uganda, came to be seen as normal.

5

In January of 1971, Idi Amin staged a coup of his own and took over Uganda, the country that had become my home. When history books speak of how someone "Took over" this or that country, I find the phrase almost comical – the average human mind can only relate to such lofty ideas as the "taking over" of entire countries on a minuscule scale. All the events; the planning, the secrecy, the horror and the danger and the dying – especially the dying – all the subtlety and nuance of revolutionary upheaval, all of these get lost in a nice, sterile idiom. *Took over the country* – the phrase makes it sound like the country was a classroom which the teacher has left, and the biggest boy moves to the front of the room, bars the door, and rearranges the seating chart. He eats his fill of the other boys' lunches and deals with the boys he doesn't like as he sees fit. But when it happens, when a whole country gets "taken over," what it *really* looks like is a little more serious.

January '71, a week before my sixth birthday and nearly a year to the day since we arrived, Milton Obote, who had been our President, was in Singapore attending a conference of commonwealth leaders. While he was away, Colonel Amin, whom our President had left in charge, decided he could do a better job of running the country himself. So after shooting a couple of chaps who disagreed with him –- quite a few of them, it turned out later, when all was said and done – he declared himself President and promoted himself to General. Obote – well, he was lucky to have been out of the country at the time. He had to just like it or lump it, with 'lump it' being a bullet in the back of his head. Before the coup, every shop, every house, every business, had a photograph of a smiling Doctor Obote on a prominent wall. The following morning, within hours, in fact, the photo of a big, toothy giant of a man had replaced them; Amin, with more gold braid and medals on his uniform than I'd known they'd been wars enough to win them in.

Looking back, I don't remember when I saw the first one. The first body, that is. Of a Ugandan, soldier or otherwise, shot at close range with a 7.62mm FMJ bullet. Full Metal Jacket, that is, meaning the copper-clad slug passes clean through the body with minimal expansion. There's less tissue damage that way, you see, meaning there's more of a chance for survival, at least in theory according to the concerned humanitarians who wrote that bit into the Geneva Convention. Though I imagine that when standing in the back of a three ton army lorry idling gate-first over the edge of a cliff, or while being marched out into the moonlit surf fronting a quiet fishing village on Lake Victoria, if *you* were one of the poor buggers looking up the muzzle of a poorly maintained Fabriqué National rifle, you probably couldn't spare much gratitude to such lofty humanitarian concepts. The soldiers with the guns laugh, the man next to you wets his trousers in fear, and the last thing you hear before the world goes dark is the *rat-a-tat-tat* of automatic gunfire.

The next afternoon, an English family – *my* family – will watch, puzzled and not fully comprehending the seriousness of what we're seeing, from the window of a VW beetle, as what's left flops, patchy and white, in the surf off Bugonga village.

But that was all still to come, later on.

Chapter 1

The word *ENTEBBE* is cut into the earth at the side of the runway as we pass, raised letters ten feet high and tilted forward on a high berm of red dirt, the letters filled in with chalky white stones. Six years from now, 103 future Israeli hostages will look out the window of Air France flight 139 and see those same raised letters. A week later, the Israeli commandos sent in to rescue the hostages may have seen the inscription as well. Today, it's still only February, 1970; no Israelis have been thrown out of the country yet, the Indians still own all the businesses, and I am five, just coming home for the very first time.

"*Uganda*?" Mummy had said, her brow furrowed and her eyes narrowed suspiciously. "Where the bloody hell is Uganda?" Daddy shrugged and smiled.

"I've got no idea," he said, walking to the bookcase and taking out an ancient atlas. "But it's got to be better than bloody *Sheffield*." Looking at the book after he puts it down, I see that Uganda is in pink, and I know that all the pink bits are England's – it says so, right at the beginning of the book.

Daddy had just come home from his meeting at the Crown Agency; they'd asked him to come in to talk about a job. A job far, far away in a place called Africa. I'm four, four and a half, five, nearly, and I know exactly where Africa is. It's full of jungles and elephants and tigers and monkeys, and Tarzan lives there, and next to Daddy and Drandrad, my Grandfather, there's nobody I like better than Tarzan.

We left England hours ago, centuries ago; I'm five, now, and I tell everyone who asks I'm nearly five and a half. But it's a fib – I'm not quite really, not just yet. It was my birthday, just last week. Drandrad had knelt in front of me, and I looked him in the eyes, held his hands, and told him,

"Drandrad, when I've gone to Africa, don't go to Gentle Jesus." That's where people go when they get old, I know, they go to heaven to be with Gentle Jesus. I have no real idea where either of these two places are, Africa or heaven... they could both be the same distance from Drandrad, as far as I can tell. "Promise me you won't go to Gentle Jesus." I squeezed his big hands so he knew to listen carefully. "If you feel yourself going to Gentle Jesus, get a stick," I said, looking at him as earnestly as I know how.

It sounds comical now, as an adult, but to my young mind, it made perfect sense. People got old. Old people needed a stick to walk with. Then they got poorly. Then they had to go to hospital, and after they'd been in hospital for a while, they died and went to Gentle Jesus. The stick, I was sure, must be an important step, a way to prolong the space between getting old and getting poorly, a way to stay away from wherever it was that people went when they left, forever, to go and be with Gentle Jesus. "Get a stick," I said again. I had to make sure he understood that I was telling him something important, something that he might not have known.

Drandrad laughed through his own tears at my leaving, and held me tight to his chest. To this day, I still recall how hard and strong his massive, gentle hands, his big butcher's hands, felt around my little-boy self. The weave of his coat, pressed close to my wet face, the green plaid trilby on his head; he smells of cigarette smoke and Polo mints.

"I will, my darlin', ah promise. Go on, now," he says, turning me by my shoulders towards Mummy. "Go on. 'Night G'bless," he says, touching his fingers to his lips, blowing a kiss like he's putting me to bed, like this is any other night when he comes to tuck me in, but I see him sniffling his own tears away into a hanky. He kisses me, kisses Mummy, kisses Lulu. Nannan kisses

9

me too, everyone kissing each other goodnight, goodbye, Mummy kissing Nannan, everybody kissing everybody and everybody blessing everybody and everybody crying. A horrible longing ache hangs everywhere, enclosed and surrounded in the sterile new airport smell.

"Y'will write, won't y'? Write to us as often as y'can." Writing is all anybody will be able to do for a while; Nannan and Drandrad don't have a telephone yet. Nobody else on their street does yet, either.

"I will, I promise," everyone says, all of us promising each other, all of us meaning it.

We are out on the tarmac, walking towards the aeroplane, and I'm struggling to pull my hand free from Mummy's, but not with any conviction. I want to go back, I just don't know where *back* is, exactly. Through the row after row of sliding glass doors we'd just come through– sliding glass doors were still a novelty in 1970, something space-aged and delightfully modern, and they'd captivated me just an hour before when we'd first arrived. Then, even though I knew we were going to be leaving, that we were going to get on a plane and fly to Africa, I still hadn't grasped the finality of what *leaving* really meant.

Through those sliding doors, I'd watched Drandrad waving as we walked away, toward the waiting BOAC plane. That's when it had dawned on me; *leaving* meant that my Drandrad wouldn't be there anymore.

Daddy's already gone to Africa, two months ago now, to find us a house and get everything ready for our arrival. It's just Mummy, Lulu and me. Lulu is three, still a baby, almost, not sure what all the fuss is about, seeing but not remembering. Me, between my tears, I see everything, remember all of it, and fold every detail into the pages of the wet grey scrapbook between my ears. The sucking *gulp* sound of the sliding glass doors we'd just come through, the dizzying tilt of the linoleum flooring disappearing into the distance in the airport concourse viewed from my five year old perspective, the disorienting lines of fluorescent fixtures that stretched away overhead. Outside, there's the shooshing skreel of planes in the distance, the bite of the wind as we walk out to the aeroplane. And of course, the sight of Drandrad, Nannan, Mummy's sister, my Uncle, all holding each other and crying as we'd walked away.

Here I must explain the concept of what *leaving* meant to our family, and define the terms of distance in which this family thought: My Mummy had lived with her parents until she'd married at age 19. She'd then moved, with Daddy, into the house next door. And by *next door*, I'm referring to houses that were built in row after terraced row, squat adjoining brick boxes, two rooms downstairs, two rooms up; a steep narrow staircase separating front room from kitchen. Each room was a uniform ten by ten feet, with an outside lavvy in an asphalt yard, a brick wall between your house and the one next door, another brick wall between your yard and the house the next street over. Brick boxes built to accommodate steelworkers, cattle-like, at the turn of the 19th century. These were houses built when Her Majesty had still been named Victoria. *Next door* in her case meant the thickness of two courses of brickwork that made up the one wall separating the two families, new and old.

I was born in that house – well, almost. I was born in Hillsborough General Hospital, just down the road, a place built of the same red bricks from the same kilns as the houses, the same bricks as the steel works and railway bridges and schools. The hospital was the same one Mummy had been born in, the same place Drandrad had been born in the early years of The Great War. House, hospital, church and school – all build of the same brick, each with its coal-fire to keep out same chill, to ward off the same damp.

Daddy's wanting to move away was something Drandrad couldn't fathom. The year after Lulu was born, Daddy had found us a new house – a real house, a real *detached* house, in Dronfield.

11

It was only five miles away, but Drandrad thought we were moving to the backside of the great beyond, to the dark winking arsehole of the moon. And a mortgage; *was he insane?* Drandrad had asked of his daughter's husband – tying himself to a *bank,* signing away his future for a *house,* when he could keep on renting one of these perfectly fine terraced houses that the city council owned, and offered for a few bob a week to anyone who wanted one?

"What, y'mean like the one we've been living in, with an outside loo that freezes solid in the winter and a tin bath hung on the wall outside the kitchen door? Not bloody likely. I want something better than that for my family," said Daddy.

I'd heard their arguments, Daddy and Drandrad. About the Unions, and how they were helping, or paralyzing, the country, depending upon who was making the argument. The distribution of wealth. *This Government…*

"This Guv'm'nt…" was how Drandrad started so many sentences, and he usually went on with something about its concern for the working man, or its lack thereof, depending on his point of view in the argument. He was my hero, so I listened earnestly to just about anything he said.

"Rubbish!" Daddy would shout, to Drandrad's insistence that it had been the unionization of British industry that had raised the standard of living of the common man, or had increased foreign imports, or whatever point he'd been defending. Fingers would jab at the air on both sides of the dinner table, and sweeping statements of rhetoric would be made, and eyes would flare wide and frog out in disbelief, and I'd have to stop listening.

"They still love each other," Mummy would tell me. "Just because they argue doesn't mean they don't love each other." And they did. An hour later, they'd both be out at the causeway edge in front of one of our houses, leaning over the open bonnet of whatever rattletrap car one of them considered himself lucky enough to be driving that week. I'd stand out there with them

12

and pass them tools while they talked and laughed about chokes and manifolds and carburetors, of past disasters with ancient worn-out gearboxes exploding and rust holes patched with cellophane tape and house paint. Daddy just wanted different things for his family, that's all. Daddy wanted what no Englishman of his working class station was supposed to want – *More*. More opportunity, more money, more than a six day workweek and a council house and a landlord and a few pints at the pub every night, more than a cobbled-together old car and weekends spent out on a freezing cold beach at Skegness or Cleathorpes drinking tea from thermoses and calling it a holiday. But most of all, he wanted more than that for his wife, for his children, for his family.

He had come through these same corridors at this same airport just a few weeks before, heading out to his own aeroplane. Twenty-nine years old and never having been outside England in his life, he'd set off to prepare a place for us in Africa. Going on ahead, he'd called it. In my mind I pictured him being led through the bush by native porters like the Great White Hunter in a Tarzan film, bundled camp goods on their heads, a bush hat pulled down over his eyes, sweat staining an otherwise spotless safari suit while he chopped at grasses and vines with a machete.

When he announced that we'd be moving to Africa, Mommy, after her initial shock, was happy to follow Daddy anywhere, but Drandrad wasn't exactly thrilled with the idea – or about the fact that I, his only grandson, would be taken away from him. But he knew Daddy well enough to know that once he'd made up his mind to try something, there was no getting around the fact. From that day until the day we left, Drandrad never missed an opportunity to tell me how much he loved me.

I can still smell his cigarettes, his Polo mints, when I see the aeroplane swimming adrift and indistinct through my tears. I'm surrounded by unfamiliar noises and smells, the shouts of men loading suitcases, the smell of paraffin and rubber. The man I love most, next to Daddy, is now back somewhere behind me, down a warren of corridors, through walls of moving glass. At this moment, I know nothing but my own thick, heavy grief, pails and floods and curtains of it

A light dusting of snow begins to fall just as I'm walking through the curved door onto our aeroplane. I stay close to Mummy, walk head down and sniffling miserably past the smiling lady in the dark serge uniform who points us to our row. The plane is warm after the chill wind on the tarmac, and the air has the bite of stale cigarettes. I remember how the sound of my quiet crying echoed, and the shaky feeling under my feet, like I'm walking down the aisle of an over-wide bus.

The summer before, an American man had walked on the moon. I saw him do it, on the television. Walking through the airport, down towards the plane, up the aisle, being strapped into my seat, I'm wearing Moon Shot shoes, my connection with that American man. Moon Shot shoes came out a few weeks after the Apollo 11 landing. They have a tread pattern molded to replicate the cratered surface on which Neil Armstrong had walked, and inside each shoe, a secret compartment contains a small round magnet. It's the magnet that makes them special; given enough speed, if I could just run fast enough... we begin to move, hurtling down the runway, and I know, *know* with the certainty only a five year old can muster, that it's my shoes, or at least the secret hidden magnets in my shoes, that lift us into the air. Moon Shot shoes can make me fly, I'm sure of it.

And fly we do. The noise and the shaking of the plane settle to a single note of background thunder. Mummy stares straight ahead at the crown of the man's head in front of her, squeezing my hand and Lulu's, one in each of her own. Lulu sits upright in her seat, her little legs straight out in front of her, her doll Ellie clutched tight against her tummy. Lights whiz past the window, yellow ones and blue ones, watery and wavy though my tears or the rain on the window, I can't tell which.

14

When Mummy tells us that it's all right to take off our safety belts, I slide to the floor, kneel facing backwards, towards where I think Drandrad is, and lay my head on the seat, still crying. Perhaps, I think miserably, my Moon Shot shoes are the only thing holding the aeroplane up off the ground.

As the plane rises, a darkened, sleeping England moves slowly underneath. Still trying to cry, I look at the comics I've brought for the trip, but none of the bright pictures can hold my attention. I push the buttons on the arms of my chair, stabbing at them, trying to find the one button that will turn us around and take us back. I try to see how far down I can slide in my seat without touching my Moon Shot shoes to the floor; but eventually, I settled instead for pressing my face to the window and simply watching the night fly past.

It's a clear evening and below is unbroken blackness speckled with the occasional pinpoint of light. The many little towns and villages between London and the coast, I assume, though I'm as unfamiliar with the geography of England as I am with Africa and Heaven. By the time sleep drifts up under me, we're in the middle of the black nothing that is the English Channel.

When I wake the sun is up. I can smell butter and hot tea, and jovial kind of brilliant daylight comes through the small round aeroplane windows, which through the cigarette smoke seems just a little too bright, far brighter than any kind of overcast sunlight I'm used to in Sheffield. I'm not crying anymore; I want to, and I know I will, but I have nothing left in my head to cry with.

Looking out the window all that I can see, as far as I can see, is an aching blue sky above, so bright I can almost taste it, and below, close enough to skip over and roll in, are stinging white clouds like the curly carved top of a dreamy white cream-cake.

"Kneel up on your seat," says Mummy, "Look out of the window for a bit." I do. I'm utterly speechless. There are no

15

words for this. Up until this time the biggest space I'd ever seen was the sea at Mablethorpe, all horrid grey and fishweed smelly, always moving, always cut over with the serrated breadknife of North Sea wind, and covered with a sky like scorched tinfoil. Or the hilly fields on the drive to Clumber Park or Yarmouth, behind walls of stone and thick privet hedgerows, walls between me and the field, hedgerows between the fields and each other.

But this bigness goes on forever; no matter how hard I crane to look ahead, or how much I fidget to see underneath or behind, my eyes just strain and cross at my own startled reflection. The world is nothing but blue above and white, rolling, below. I watch for God, breathing the cold air off the window, until sleep slips up under me again. God, I'm sure, looks a lot like Drandrad, and he's hiding, somewhere behind one of those clouds.

A change to the thunder of the aeroplane wakes me. I hadn't even known I'd stopped noticing it until the sound shifted, drifted, grew again, and when I look out the window, the sky is still that brilliant blue but clouds below have been replaced with greens, lots and lots of greens; water green and flower green and grassy, leafy, living-thing green, and it's all so much closer.

A nappy yellow grass-green is punctuated by the tops of black-green acacias sliding along below; moldy waterweed pond green passes as streams and lakes and rivers. On the ground, dark here and bright there and fluid everywhere, are more shades of yellow and green than I knew there were numbers. There are colors I've never even seen before, even in my biggest, bestest paint box, and over it all, occasional scoops of low hanging cloud-cream drift lazily past at eye level.

A yellow scurf of grass covering the spaces between the green patches is cut here and there with sharp-etched roads of dark brown-red dirt. Even from up here, I can see each road rutted into stripes of umber murram, two light lines waving slightly down the middle where the wheels go.

16

"Look, lovie, that's Africa," says Mummy. "We're here. We'll be landing soon. Look!" she exclaims, pointing down at the enormous buff-colored land below us; something is moving, an animal of some sort, with horns, big and wide. There are three more of them, the... *horned animal thingies* ahead of it, a tiny human figure behind, moving slowly. I want to ask, what is it, what are they, but instead I ask,

"Will we see Daddy soon?"

"Yes," she says. "Y'Daddy'll be waiting for us at the airport. Are you excited?" She looks excited herself, and nervous, like she's trying not to be frightened. She looks like she needs us to know she's not frightened, but I can see it anyway. I nod and don't say anything. Lulu just smiles; we are her world, me and Mummy, and we are both here with her – what does she need to be frightened of? Light catches on the silver chain across the front of the bright red dress that she loves so much, the dress which barely covers her knees. Her little white shoes are unbuckled on her feet, her short, red-blond hair hangs in ringlets, a fringe over a face even more freckly than my own. She twirls Ellie's hair with her finger. The dolly sits in her lap, and she sings to it softly, hardly interested in the huge green world outside the window.

"And Drandrad?" I ask. Mummy flinches.

"No, pet, y'Drandrad's back at 'ome." I knew he wouldn't be there, and yet I asked anyway. I had to. I didn't know until I heard the way Mummy's voice hitch a little as she answered, that I'd asked on purpose. To punish her, for taking me away from him.

The aeroplane comes in low over a huge ocean the color of tea, mashing in a wide green open-topped pot. The sea of tea reflects the clouds, and the plane banks sharply and sweeps around as though it's trying to dunk a biscuit-wing, sinking lower all the time. There are small open boats on the water, and we're low enough that I can see people, dark, dark people, waving up at us. We cross a rocky red shore and the land comes

17

up quickly now, green and enormous, to meet us. I know at once from the shape of the sky and the color of the air that this place is different from the place I've left, wholly different, in ways I never knew two places could be so unalike.

I see the word *ENTEBBE* at the side of the runway, and trace the letters against the window with my finger as we taxi slowly by. In the background, beyond the spindly stick-trees and fields of grass the color of Weetabix, is the lake. That's what Mummy calls it, anyway – a lake, but I'm sure she must be wrong. A lake is something small, like the pond at Millhouses where Drandrad takes me to ride in the little paddle boats, pedaling to spin the propeller and waving to Mummy and Daddy on the shore until the man with the megaphone shouts our number, tell us we have to come in, that our time is up. *That's* a lake; this *has* to be the sea. It seems bigger, and smoother, even, than the sea at Mablethorpe, and longer, wider, as though there's more of it hiding somewhere, just out of sight, like God behind his cloud.

"That's Lake Victoria," says Mummy, seeing me puzzling over its size. "Daddy's letters say y'can see it from our 'ouse!"

The aeroplane noises slow down all at once as I stare out the window, at the light glinting off the Lake Victoria sea, and I look down at the ground rolling by so close, scared for a minute that something had happened to my Moon Shot shoes, not realizing that this is what's supposed to happen, that we've landed.

The plane rolls along, bouncing, slowing, again feeling just like a great big rattley old bus. Men in dark uniforms, or mismatched parts of uniforms, move around on the ground under the plane. Black men, dark black men in black uniform trousers and ties, and white shirts with short sleeves and damp patches on their backs. Three over here roll a moving staircase, two over there drive an open-topped tractor with a trail of carts behind it like a little fun-park train; two others just walk around, pointing, stopping, pointing, talking with animated gestures.

"Are they Africans, Mummy?" I've never seen a sky so blue, or air so bright, or men quite so black.

"There you are, young man," says the smiling lady in the dark serge uniform, her accent very posh, very proper, not all broad and Yorkshire like Mummy. "These are for you. You're now a Junior Pilot." She kneels next to my seat and pins a badge on my shirt, little golden metal wings. I pull at the badge, turn it for a better look. BOAC, it says across the top, in big letters, and underneath, JUNIOR JET CLUB. Ready them I burn with pride - of all the boys in the world (and little girls too, of course, since Lulu is wearing a pair as well,) they picked *me* to be a member of the Junior Jet club, which must be a pretty special and exclusive club. After all, they have a special pin, shiny enameled gold, with a special club identity card I can write my name on so everyone will know who I am, and a stewardess to make a fuss over me as the plane sits the tarmac. I am sure that no one will ever look at me the same way again.

"Nem winds," says Lulu, touching my enameled pin. "Ulu winds," touching her own. She grins up at me, holds Ellie tighter against her tummy like she does when she's happy. She's only three, still a baby. She still can't say my name. A Drink is *Nitnit*, a biscuit is *Tibida*, chewing gum is *Pimp*. All her words are still something else. Mummy has to ask me what she's saying, sometimes; I'm the only one who seems to be able to understand her. I am Nem, and now both Nem and Ulu have winds.

"Follow Nem, duckie," says Mummy, "Follow y'brother," as I walk ahead of them down the aisle of the plane, towards the hot breeze blowing in through the open door.

Outside, the air is like breathing in a steam-filled room, when I take a bath in the tin tub in front of the hearth with Drandrad in the winter, the windows closed, the steam from the kettles of water that Nannan boils for the tub filling up the kitchen. But here it doesn't smell like a paraffin heater, it smells like fruit and

19

flowers and an odd sweet sourness that drifts off all the people and makes smelling seem almost as real as chewing.

The Africans below move around slowly but purposefully, opening doors under the plane, standing, waiting, and smiling at the bottom of the stairs. I'm already too hot, and my good English clothes begin to feel awful, tight and wet, thick and heavy like layers of toilet paper soaked in warm clotted cream.

The arriving passengers are separated from the people waiting at the airport by a simple wooden lattice under a cement roof, like the awning over a bus shelter. Daddy is standing on the other side of it. He looks different; bigger, for one thing, than I remember him, with boxer's arms that are tanned and thick as axehandles, his black hair unkempt, his black beard long and shaggy. He waves to us as we file past a stern African man in a dark uniform wearing a peaked cap. The man thumps a rubber stamp into Mummy's passport. The passport man is so black that it scares me when he suddenly smiles, a bright flash of white teeth suspended between two rows of splotchy blue and pink gums. His gums look like he's been chewing on a leaky ball-point pen.

"Welcome to Uganda," he says. *Welkam to Yuganda.* His words sound as hard as pebbles bounced off the concrete roof. I clutch at Mummy's skirted leg in surprise, but she hasn't taken her eyes off Daddy.

"Look at you, y'scruffy bugger," Mummy says though her smile, as she throws her arms around Daddy's neck. "Who's been at your hair?" They kiss for a long time; Lulu and I pull faces to each other, make kissy fish-lips, bobble our heads and smirk up at them. They look down at us, and laugh. Daddy is wearing nothing but tan shorts and a short-sleeved safari shirt, untucked, and flip-flops. There's a cigarette in his hand, cupped away from Mummy's hair, which is piled on top of her head in her customary bun, and stiff with hairspray. His arms and legs are tanned brown as beef gravy from the sun, his nose peeling and red. He has a watch on his left wrist and on his right, two knotted black bracelets. It's these that startle me most of all.

"They're elephant hair," he says, putting the cigarette between his lips and taking them off, handing one to each of us. "Look," he says, squinting through the smoke, "They fit like this." He slides the knots away from each other, and the bracelet shrinks down around my wrist, the thick black fibers glossy and smooth. I stare at it in wonder. Lulu rolls hers around and around her writs, showing it to Ellie.

As Daddy picks both Lulu and I up to squeeze us and kiss us, I remember him all over again, his prickly mustache and the smell of cigarettes and Brut in his beard. Suddenly I don't care where we are, as long as he's there.

As he holds me, I am stunned by the size of the world behind him – mountains, or maybe clouds, so far away that I can't tell the difference. The air is bright and heavy at the same time, thick and hanging, and it makes seeing feel like breathing underwater. There are colors – so many colors! We walk off into a sea of color, the African women moving about us wearing fabrics dyed in a hundred shades of red and yellow and black in complex, overlapping patterns, with brilliant batik scarves on their heads. Vendors sell fruit and gaudy, child-like paintings, and the trees are covered in bright green leaves and flowers in red, yellow, and white.

Outside, soldiers in drab army green and linty black berets lean indolently against a dusty jeep parked across the road. One soldier stands with a tin helmet strapped tightly to his head, despite the sun beating down on it, holding a rifle straight up and down in front of him with both hands. An African man walks past the soldiers, watching all of us, the new arrivals. He's carrying speckly red chickens by their ankles, two in each hand. The only thing not brightly colored are the men; the men wear clean white shirts, or ragged dirty ones, tan shorts like Daddy's, or black trousers, some with the knees missing, and as they stand next to each other none of them seems to pay the other's clothing any mind at all. Except the beggars, the wretched beggars, like sacks of rag the color of the dirt they sit on, who are propped up against the walls with their palms outstretched to the passersby.

Further down from the beggars, closer to us, a man sits cross-legged on the ground next to a faded red blanket laid out with carved wooden animals, and ugly squatting daemon-gods, and colorful beaded amulets, and polished soapstone boxes. I follow Daddy past him without taking my eyes off the brightly colored beadwork. The colors make me hungry, make me want to taste the beads and slip them under my tongue. Behind the beaded pendants and decorated wooden sticks there are carved black elephants with straight ivory tusks, standing in ranks of descending size. Some are as small as my fist; others, bigger than a man's head. There are giraffes, pale tan mottled with dark brown, and rhinos, paused in mid-stride, and dozens of the knotted black bracelets like the ones on my wrist. The man on the blanket sees my hungry eyes and picks up a beaded stick with a long tuft of hair hanging off one end, like a big floppy paintbrush. He waggles it at me and smiles, beckoning. I don't go to him, but I ask Daddy,

"What's that thing do?"

"*Hapana, hapana. Asante sana.*" Daddy says, waving his hand dismissively at the carvings man, shaking his head. To me he says, "It's a horsehair whisk. They use them for keeping flies off. Don't worry about that *takataka*. I told him no, we didn't want one." But I *do* want one, I think to myself. I want one very badly, one of everything, the elephant hair bracelets and the carved wooden rhinos and the bright beaded pendants that look good enough to eat. Daddy says. "You'll see that kinda stuff everywhere." He turns to Mummy excitedly. "C'mon then, let me show you y'new house." He flicks his hand to a crowd of boys clustered by a wall, and two of them rush over to pick up the suitcases. Mummy looks shocked, hesitates a moment behind

22

Daddy as the boys struggle to half carry, half drag, the heavy cases. One of the boys looks at Mummy, smiles shyly.

"Jambo, Memsah'b," he says softly. Embarrassed, Mummy looks away. Daddy, though, is unconcerned.

"Jambo, toto," he say. "Habari musuri?" He boys laugh, and nod, and cover their mouths with their hands. I am stunned, stunned that these boys are carrying our bags, stunned by the colors and the smells and the heat, stunned that my Daddy speaks African, just like Tarzan. Ahead of us, Daddy leads the way out through the crowds of Africans, across a narrow tarmac road.

With the two boys following, he walks us out to a car park with perhaps a dozen vehicles lined up on packed raw earth the color of ground nutmeg. The cars are all dusted halfway up their doors with the same spice-rack color. He hands Mummy a key.

"If you can guess which car it goes to," he says with a cheeky grin, "You can have it." In the car park there's a rusty old Vauxhall with a cracked windscreen, two or three Volkswagen beetles all turned pale orange by the dirt. Near the back is a Land Rover painted with zebra stripes, over there another in faded green dusted down with red, next to it an Austin with big round headlamps, a Ford with odd asymmetrical windows and sharp creased angles like a badly pressed shirt.

"What's *takataka*?" I ask Daddy. "And who's *Jambumamsub*?"

"Takataka? Where d'you hear that?"

"From you. You just said it. You said that the beady fly whip thingy was a takataka."

"Did I?" Daddy laughs. "It means rubbish, in Swahili."

"What's Sa... Sa... weeli?" I ask.

"Swahili. One of the languages they speak here. *Jambo* means hello. Memsah'b what you call a lady. He was just sayin' 'ello to y'Mummy." I am suddenly afraid.

"Don't they speak English?"

"Don't worry. Most people speak English just fine."

Ahead of us, Mummy walks up to a low, dark blue two-door car, long and sleek though the bonnet, with a high ridge down the outside edges of each fender. The fenders end at headlamps sitting like the eyes on either side of a gaping oval maw. From the front, the car looks like some kind of scoop-feeding sea creature I've seen in my animal books. There's a medallion above the wide yellow license plate, ragged-edged wings like a Junior Jet Club badge, but bigger. The car is low to the ground and appears to be moving at high speed, even while sitting here at a dead stop. When Mummy tries it, the key slips cleanly into the lock, the button pops up, the catch opens with a hollow click.

"It had to be," she says, shaking her head. "This one had to be yours."

"Yours, y'mean," Daddy corrects her. "Jensen 541," says Daddy. "Only about 200 of them ever built. Isn't it lovely?" He strokes the bonnet.

"Yes," she says, "I'm sure it is, but where are we going to put the bags? That back seat would cramp a midget."

"Don't worry," he says, smiling easily. "It's not far. We'll manage all right." He drops some strange coins in the boys' outstretched hands, that land with a tinny clink, not sounding like real money at all.

"Asanti, B'wana," says one. "Asanti sana!" They look older than me, but they seem smaller, lither, more compact. I watch as they run back to their fellows, each comparing what he received with the other.

Daddy begins putting the luggage into the car. Two small suitcases are tucked onto each of the back seats so that Lulu and I sit up high. Another is propped up on end, on the floor behind the passenger seat. The rest of the bags just manage to fit in the boot, though it won't close all the way and Daddy has to tie it down with a piece of string.

"Good job the rest of our things're comin' on later," he says. "Might have had to leave the kids here and come back for them tomorrow." He winks at me, but I stick my tongue out at him anyway. "You drive," he says to Mummy, once Lulu and I are in the back. "I'll hold this other case on my knee." He's all the way up against the dashboard so his seat will tip back properly against the suitcase sitting behind it. Lulu's short legs just touch the back of Daddy's seat, but I have to curl mine under me, and sit looking out of the tiny side window. Mummy starts the car.

"Bloody hell," she says as the engine growls to life. The sound causes one or two of the passing Africans to stop, even back up a pace, either out of caution or to get a better look. Mummy lifts gingerly off the clutch, moves out onto the road. The car lurches forward like a toy shoved roughly across a well-polished floor. All the soldiers turn to look at the sound of the car's approach. "Ooh, Davie, I don't know about this," she says. Her foot barely twitches over the accelerator pedal and the car races forward as if kicked from behind. Daddy has a great big smile on his face.

"Bloody thing sucks up petrol." He raps on the roof with his knuckle. "But it's fast. Body's made of fiber-glass," he says, "Even then, it still weighs a ton." Mummy offers him an indulgent smile, but she's clearly not as impressed as he'd like her to be. "What d'you think?" he asks proudly.

"How much did y'pay for it?" At this, Daddy's grin spreads wide all over again.

"Next to nothing," he says. "There was this bush pilot, bloke called Frasier, he'd take tourists out on safari in his plane, away up north of here in the game parks. On his way back he liked to buzz this army camp near the airfield. The soldiers there all knew him, and this was his signal, like, that he needed a lift. He'd land at the airstrip and an army lorry would come by, pick 'im up, give 'im a lift to the nearest village.

"Anyway, Frasier'd apparently buzzed the camp again, not knowing that the Colonel in charge of the army had rotated all the soldiers on the post with some of his own private troops.

25

These chaps didn't know anything about Frasier or his tourists, all they knew was there's this plane making low passes right over their barracks. Scared the sh..." He glances over his shoulder. It's been a while since he's had children in the car, obviously. "Scared the *daylights* out of them. They're not a bright lot, most of 'em. They thought they were being invaded by the Sudanese. So when he lands and sees the army truck coming, same as usual, he hops down out of his plane and goes over to collect his lift. Instead, about a dozen soldiers proceeded to kick the living you-know-what out of him and leave him unconscious by the plane." Daddy is laughing while he tells this story. Mummy looks even whiter than she did when we landed, but says nothing. This is definitely not England anymore.

Outside, the red dirt road has opened onto a narrow two-lane strip of tarmac, a white line down its middle and red dirt ditches on either side. The country slopes down to the right at a slight angle towards the lake that has to be a sea, a mile or so away.

Along the roadside walk African women with wide bottoms wrapped tightly about in patterned kitangi dresses carry bundles on their heads, and occasionally men in black trousers, loose white shirts and dark narrow ties, walking or pedaling clattery black bicycles. Some of the bicycles carry huge bundles, of sticks or wicker cages or unidentified doughy lumps wrapped in sacking tied to the handlebars, or even the seat, so they have to pedal standing up. Everywhere past the road is grass, tall and dull yellow, and everywhere in the grass, a high-pitched whining screech. Daddy sees me craning to get a better look at it all through the little triangular window.

"Grasshoppers," says Daddy. He sees my puzzled look. "That noise? Grasshoppers, about this big." He holds his finger and thumb as wide as my palm. "The Africans cook them up and eat them. Termites as well," he says. "They call them fried ants. Yum!" I crinkle my nose, disgusted.

26

"Will we see any lions?" I ask him. He smiles. "Not many, I don't think. At least not on our street."

"What about lizards?"

"Now lizards, definitely. I can promise you lots of *them*." He turns back to Mummy. "This Frasier, who I got the car off, he came into the Lake Vic... The Lake Victoria Hotel, just up ahead on the right... he comes in a couple of weeks ago with two black eyes, his lip all fat and split wide open..." He interrupts himself. "That's where I work, by the way, there on the left, Government Printing." He points to what looks like a large compound of wooden barrack behind a high wall, with big gates guarded by two oddly tall black men in faded khaki uniforms. Sunlight glitters off the tops of the walls; I see a line of broken bottles embedded along the top of the wall. I immediately think of a song Drandrad taught me; *ten green bottles, hanging on a wall, ten green bottles, hanging on a wall, and if one green bottle should accidentally fall..* Daddy sees me looking.

"To keep the *kondos* out," he says. "Most of the government buildings and a few of the bigger houses have glass cemented into the walls like that."

"What's a kondo?" asks Mummy.

"Thieves, burglars. Some of the buggers'll nick anything that's not nailed down." He turns to the back seat. "That reminds me, we've got a dog, kids." I look up, excited.

"A dog? Is it a big one?" Daddy nods.

"Bigger than you! His name's Bruno, he's a great big Rhodesian ridgeback, with a bit of Alsatian in him. Great dog, old Bruno, and really good at keeping the kondos away at night." He turns back to Mummy. The bottles, and the idea of us having a great big dog, don't really seem as exciting to her as much as they do me. Mummy is listening, but she's clearly having trouble taking it all in, glancing between her familiar but strange husband, and the alien countryside she's driving through; Daddy's untrimmed beard and shaggy hair, his loose casual

27

clothes, the heat, everything around so green that it stings the eyes, bush pilots and army trucks, broken bottles and enormous dogs and robbers, whatever language they're in... it's all a bit much for her, so soon after leaving the cold predictability of England.

"That's the hotel," Daddy says, oblivious.

A long white building glistens behind a high wall, a central tower rising above the two wings. It seems bigger than its two stories, simply because all the other buildings around it are so much smaller. The wall is overgrown with flowers the most insane shade of purple-magenta I've ever seen. A driveway leads up from the gates to a red-roofed entryway, and as we pass, I catch the briefest slice of pale blue from the pool, a tall diving tower at the far end of it.

"Can we swim here?" I blurt. Daddy turns, surprised.

"Swim? 'Course we can. We'll go tomorrow." *Tomorrow?* That's practically forever, I think to myself. Daddy doesn't notice my disappointment. He turns back to Mummy, picking up his story about the car. "Anyway, he decided he'd had enough. Next day he flew back here, drove up to the British Consulate in Kampala – that's the capitol, about twenty-odd miles straight up this road we're on here – where they gave him a ticket out of the country the next day, since he was in fear for his life if the soldiers ever got hold of him again. He stopped in at the hotel on his way to the airport."

"And sold you a car that sticks out like a sore thumb right before he left the country in fear of his life?" says Mummy, but Daddy doesn't catch the sarcastic tone in her voice.

"Yeah, it was the only thing he had of any real value. Do you like it?"

"Oh, it's very nice," says Mummy, "But I think it's a bit more car than I'm going to need, don't you?" Daddy shrugs, enjoying the sound of the engine, even though Mummy is still creeping

28

cautiously along the road as though the accelerator pedal might be wired to a stick of dynamite.

The sky out of my side window is an unbroken gemstone blue, all the way to a high horizon, where it vignettes into fluted white above smoky purple hills.

"That's our golf course," Daddy says, pointing to the manicured sea of rolling green just past the hotel.

"*Our* golf course?" says Mummy. In our part of England, only the very rich can afford to play golf. And there aren't many of them, not that *I've* seen.

"Don't worry, you'll meet everyone. I go golfing every night now. I'll take you out."

There are more cars on the road now, Volkswagen beetles and combi vans, green Land Rovers, lorries with African men sitting with their legs hanging off the back, and more black bicycles, some being ridden by men in white shirts and black trousers, some by impossibly small boys, not much older than me, shoeless, standing up at an angle with one leg through and under the crossbar to reach the pedals, and both hands stretching *up* to reach the handlebars.

We pass a row of single-story cinderblock buildings, some with battered tin awnings in front. Some of the buildings have a slightly scorched look, like they've had fires built against their walls. One or two bear traces of whitewash, and those that do show an ochre stain creeping from the ground a few feet up the wall. Posters, some tattered, some bright and garish, are pasted to walls, and in the window of one of the buildings, metal signs advertising VIM cleaner and Lifebuoy soap.

"Go straight, here," says Daddy, "We're just going to take a little tour through town. The house is back that way. I just thought you might like to see a bit of Entebbe first."

"So how far is it, then?" asks Mummy. Daddy looks at her, puzzled for a moment.

"How far is what?" he asks.

"Entebbe."

"This *is* it," he says, gesturing out the window. "The hospital's down that way, you've already seen the Lake Vic, the golf course…" he points back, out of Mummy's side window.

"So where are the shops?" Mummy asks. Daddy points casually at the battered, metal-awninged buildings, at the low mud-stained walls.

"Right here. Most of what we'll need you can get here, like sugar and bread and stuff. The market is down here, on the right, and the butcher's is just past it." He points to a dilapidated series of sheds as we drive past, not even sheds, really, just corrugated tin roofs over wooden posts.

"Butchers?" Mummy says, quizzically. Everyone knows what a butcher's shop looks like; sterile white tile, a big plate glass window, angled trays of ice and artificial grass, today's best cut's laid out with white signs on them, their price in red letters; a glass cabinets, a row of hooks, a big wooden slab for cutting, sawdust underfoot, the butcher in a white apron and wellington boots. Daddy points.

"Right here," he says, pointing at a mud hut just off the road. There's a scrawny, wide-horned cow tied to a tree out front, a red, crusted tree-stump on a tamped-earth floor, no ice or tile or sawdust in sight. Mummy is about to say something, but Daddy interrupts. "The Entebbe marketplace," he says, pointing at a mismatched cluster of corrugated awnings supported by rough-hewn poles. On the open ground between the patches of shade, dark skinned African women stack fruits and vegetables on dusty red blankets, their wares piled in little pyramids. They weigh things on hand-held scales, make change, talk to their neighbors. Aubergines are stacked next to pineapples, big ones fat as a rugby ball and little ones not much bigger than a mango. "That's matoké," says Daddy, pointing to piles of stumpy green bananas sticking straight out of their hand-like bunches. "They boil it, and eat it like mashed potatoes."

I see sacks stiff with repeated use, folded down tidily at the top, with metal scoop-shovels stuck down into them, full of speckledy beans, red and white and brown. A woman sits next to several piles of mysterious brown crusty stuff in different shades of orange and red and tan, which could be curry spices or sea salt or clumps of clotted dirt, for all I know. The air smells of sweat and smoke and of split green wood, like rotting fruit on the boil. The smell is sour but not exactly unpleasant.

Daddy says, "Kirefu's is back there, we just passed it. It's indoors; they have all tinned stuff and washing soap, things like that. Anything they don't have, we can go up to Kampala for." He points up the road we're on. "Kampala's a big city, they've got everything up there."

Mummy has gone oddly quiet, and her knuckles are very white on the steering wheel. She clenches, Unclenches her jaw.

"What's wrong?" Daddy asks. He can tell she doesn't like it already. "What's the matter with you? Y'just got here. Give it a chance, for Christ's sake." Mummy doesn't say anything, and Lulu simply looks out the window. Even in Sheffield, even in shitty old Attercliffe, there are proper shops. Drandrad's butcher shop, with its steel trays of meat in the window, the clean metallic smell of blood and sawdust, Drandrad in his white apron smeared pink at the waist. The tobacconist down the road, smelling like fresh newspapers and Uncle Hugh's pipe, with row after row of thick glass jars full of sweets, and a scale on the counter for weighing them. These... *takataka* buildings don't look anything like shops to me. I'm suddenly very angry at Daddy, for bringing us to this place, even if there *are* lizards, even if we own the biggest dog in the world.

31

Chapter 2

But soon I learn that Uganda is everything England was not. England was cold, wet, miserable, dark, the sky a boiled dishrag – and not just the weather, but the people as well. And the food. Cold, wet, and miserable, all of it. Africa, *my* Africa, is bright, teeming with the overlapping smells of life, life beginning and life coming to an end. But we had a lot to learn about life on the equator.

I'm in the hospital, the uneven light from the door at the far end of the hallway reflecting off the polished concrete floor like frozen muddy water. I sit on a hard wooden bench outside the doctor's office, my skin like ice, playing a game with myself where I try very hard not to move, because if I move, my shoulders feel like they're being cut with glass. The air smells like Dettol and antiseptic and boiled bandages, and in the concrete hallway all the sounds I hear are like they're coming up the inside of a toilet-roll tube.

On the walls are posters, pictures, mostly, very few words, showing some of the horrible African diseases that people should watch for. Pictures of men with huge, swollen legs, people with faces completely covered in tiny pale blisters, each blister the nesting sight of some insect's larvae; children with bellies distended to the point of bursting from tapeworms; random, anonymous open sores from untreated wounds, from infection, from untreated animal bites. The pictures are terrifying, and I try desperately not to look.

The doctor comes out to where I'm sitting. I lean forward, a dampened cotton shirt draped around me, and thick, pillowy white blisters across my arms and back. A continuous fluid cape of them stretches from shoulder to shoulder, from the middle of my back and up my neck to the line of my straight sand-blond hair, not individual pustules, but large, puffy; blisters like jellyfish, big as my hand. From the tops of both arms, from shoulder to elbow, and again from elbow to wrist, the whole upper surface of both arms, is swollen tight over firm pockets of clear salty fluid under taut, pale, dead-white skin. My arms look like puddings, like pieces of cold boiled chicken.

The doctor is an Indian man with skin the color of a new leather shoe sole, and he smiles in a way I'm sure he must practice, a special smile to reassure children.

"Follow me please, young man," the doctor says, his voice all Bombay and Calcutta and Oxford and Cambridge. I stand, and walk into his office.

It never occurred to Mummy and Daddy how much hotter the sun is here than in England, where the sun isn't ever very hot at all. Drandrad would tie knots in four corners of a hanky to keep the sun off the top of his balding head; Daddy might open the first two buttons of his shirt, maybe roll his trousers up to the knee if he went to the seaside – that was how Yorkshiremen dealt with the English sun. Daddy worked indoors all day; he golfed in the late afternoon, where the sun was enough to tan his skin, redden his nose, leave his forehead peeling, his arms a little red. On the weekends he might sail, but only for an hour or so; then it was in the bar, or under the shaded verandah at the Lake Vic with a gin and tonic for the afternoon. But until we'd arrived, he'd never thought about the sun, midday, all day, bright and fierce and relentless, while his children played in the pool.

When the doctor sees my arms under the shirt, he stops smiling, and looks hard for a moment at my parents. "Does this hurt?" he says gently. "What about this?" He touches the blisters with the end of a pen, gently poking the watery pillows with the tip of a finger. He peels the damp shirt slowly from my back and I wince.

33

He prods gently at the white dumplings on my shoulders. No, it doesn't hurt to touch them, I tell him, if he doesn't touch too hard. "What about here?" he says, brushing the lacy pink edge where the blisters meet the rest of my skin, and I flinch away, cry out, my eyes stinging. "I'm sorry," he says, and I can tell that he really means it.

He turns to the door. "Could you come in here please?" he says out into the hallway.

He takes Mummy and Daddy into an adjoining office. I can't see them, but I can just see his face in profile through the doorway. He's quiet for a moment, then suddenly he very nearly shouts at Mummy; he is incensed, rage flaming in his eyes, though his voice is trying to hide it. I'm only five, but I'm not stupid. I can see how angry he is, but I don't know why.

"What have you been doing to this boy?" the doctor hisses. "My God, what have you done to him?" His anger is startling, and Mummy starts to cry, turning to Daddy.

"What do you mean?" says Daddy, defensive anger of his own rising in his voice, anger thrown back in the doctor's face. He too can't understand why the doctor is so hostile. "We told the nurse what happened! It's a bad sunburn!"

"Rubbish! Rubbish! I've never seen anything so bad! It looks like he's been dipped in scalding water! Look at him!" He jabs his finger through the open door, and is surprised to see me looking back at him. I don't want him to be cross, so I smile. I hear the anger truly rise in Daddy's voice then. He's on his feet, eyes blazing, shouting back in the Indian doctor's face.

"You think *we* did that? He's not used to the heat here. My wife and children, they just arrived from England a few days ago. He was playing too long in the swimming pool at the hotel and he got too much sun. It's from the sun, it's a bloody sunburn!" Daddy is horrified at what he thinks the doctor might be suggesting. "Jesus, you don't think we could do that to our own son, do you?" Daddy says, suddenly quiet. I can hear in his voice that he's almost crying himself at the thought. The doctor pauses, looks again at me kicking my legs against the bench and smiling at him, back at Daddy's questioning face. He takes a breath, lowers his voice.

"You'd be surprised at the things I see. You'd be surprised at the things people can do to one another, especially in a place like this. A sunburn? I don't believe it. I've never seen anything like it." But he's calmer now, and it looks like he might believe it, after all. He looks thoughtful for a moment, glances back up at Mummy and Daddy.

He reaches into a drawer, takes out a pad, writes something on it. "Take this to the dispensary," he says softly, handing Daddy a sheet of paper. He relents, places a hand on Daddy's shoulder. "And for God's sake, keep him out of the bloody sun."

The medicine is thick, green-white, handed to Mummy in a sterilized salad cream bottle – it may well *be* salad cream for all I know, a pale unpleasant glop that is to be smeared on my arms and back morning and night, then covered with a damp shirt.

Walking back to the car, all I can feel is a tingle on the hairline at the back of my neck, like a cut that only just happened and hasn't yet started to bleed; the anticipation of it hurting, of it being touched or bumped or scraped, is worse than the hurt itself. But from the hospital car park, I think I see the roofline of the Lake Victoria Hotel, and all I can think about is how I just can't wait to get back out into the pool again.

Chapter 3

We were surrounded by a vastness of space that none of us had ever before conceived of, but my world in Uganda became small and familiar, as does that of every child. Entebbe was a village, in the sense of being a small town – but it was also a *collection* of villages. In addition to the few buildings that would with varying degrees of accuracy be described as *western*, it was also made up of disparate gatherings of thatched, mud-wattled huts built around a common area, each a half-hour's walk from the other. In my mind I can still paint a map of the place, and walk its streets as I used to back then. Life, for me, was mostly home, and school, and going to town with Mummy or Daddy. There was my African life - walking the dirt lanes with friends, riding bicycles to the youth hostel to buy Danish chocolates and hard sweets, playing in the fields and plantations that lay between our house and the lake. And then there was my M'zungu life – swimming at the swimming pool, films and crisps and lemonade at the golf club, sailing, and skiing, and picnicking at the sailing club.

Picture it; Lake Victoria School sits parallel to and up the hill from our house on Bugonga Road; turn left at the top of our driveway, down a hundred yards, cut right, up over the beaten dirt bank, through the tall grass, through the cleared field between the crumbling and abandoned brick mission hospital and the last house on the uphill side of the road. I cross my fingers and try not to look at the mission as I pass. It is dark there, the windows empty and hollow, as I walk past it up the steep goat path, through the wet moldering banana patch.

At the top of the hill, turn right on Circular Road, across from the Morton's house; two of their daughters are the same age as me and Lulu, the third, Scrotty Grot we call her, because she always manages to get so scruffy, is a few months younger. The school is just past the house, where the tarmac of Circular Road swings left towards Government Printing and Airport Road. Lower School sits next to the murram tracks that run along the back boundary of the school grounds, the grounds tapering up in a widening wedge to the Upper School, which I'll not be old enough to attend yet for another two years.

Mr. Shelley is our headmaster. He's a heavy, thickset Englishman in tweed suits that don't match the weather, up on the stage each morning as we file in to the assembly hall, me and the other children standing in rows to face him. A sea of small, bright black faces stare up at him, and three, five, maybe a dozen whites – English, Danish, Israeli. Of the Africans, some faces are a lighter coffee brown, though most are a darker Nilotic blue-black. Then there is the pale half-way color of the Indians, like white children dipped in treacle, like black children bleached with Vim.

Mr. Shelley stands on the stage, at the podium. Next to and fanned out behind him are Mr. Trotter, Mr. Peters, Miss Llewellyn – white, all English except for Miss Llewellyn, with her Welsh chapel-bell voice that makes me blush and twist and want her to touch my hair, a voice that doesn't fit her stern earnest face and plain straight skirts, wool in grey herringbone, and brown, thick-soled shoes. With them are Mr. Njoki, Mr. Mkembe, Mrs. Ambatembe, all with skin like burnished chocolate, sparkling white teeth and eyes flashing in shadow on the stage. All the teachers sit together in a row of folding metal chairs, while we children stand and wait. The doors to the assembly hall are left open to the bright clear morning sunshine outside, but the curtains along the opposite side stay drawn for shade.

Mr. Shelley says, "Good morning, children!" Every morning it's the same greeting, him looking over the tops of his glasses.

37

We respond, turning our heads slightly as we do, so as to encompass the whole school in our expanding circle of welcome,

"Good morning, Mr. Shelley. Good morning, teachers. Good morning, everyone!" To the headmaster, to the teachers, to each other; it is given – in my mind, at least – a solemnity of ritual, each syllable paced precisely, each diphthong drawn out and lingered over, delivered in the sharp cadence of African speech; the hard *A* at the end of *Meesta,* and *teacha,* the way the mouth has to be held just so to side-slip around the *R* in *moh-ning* without missing the hard *O,* the three distinct beats of *e-va-ry.*

Picture it; their manner of speech seemed strange for the first few days, but now it is easier, I find, to speak the greeting the way they say it, my friends, the other children with whom I play. Outside the house, it's easier to speak the greeting – to speak at all, for that matter – with the thick Ugandan accent of the group, than to try and talk the way Mummy and Daddy might, the way an English person might. *Good moh'ning e-va-ry wan.*

The piano rings out, a descending prelude that cues us all that it's time to sing, and we do, standing with hands on hearts, all together we sing;

> *Oh Uganda*
> *May God uphold thee*
> *We lay our future in thy hands*
> *united, free,*
> *for liberty*
> *together we all will stand.*

And then we sit. "Cross-leg sit," Mr. Shelley calls out, and each line of boys and girls moves down a little to allow the extra room that all our splayed knees take up, sitting cross-legged on the floor. He gives a homily – about cleanliness, or obedience, or using our *talons* in the service of God. At least that's what I think he said, which makes me think of the fish eagles crying mournfully from the treetops by the lake, swooping down to carry off large fish or small children, at least that's what my

38

friends tell me. If God wants me to use my talons in his service then I decide that it's my job to find out where mine are. Either that or stop paying attention to Mr. Shelley, who is plump and sweats a lot and whose lower lip seems floppy and unattached in the middle.

Another time he tells us about an American war going on in a place far away called *Vee-et Narm*, and has us all bow our heads and pray for the brave American soldiers fighting there. And another, he tells us about some men in space, who were on their way to the moon but got stuck in their spaceship and might not be able to get home. He has us pray for them too, pray for their safe return, but I think, like using our talons for God, he might be making some of these stories up. Mr. Armstrong already walked on the moon, and it looked fairly dull and grey on the tele. I can't think of any reason we'd want to go back.

In the playground after assembly, we all drink our milk, lukewarm, from thick triangular plastic bags (ours have blue writing, though a few boys, the ones from Israel, have special bags with red writing on them, which they means it's been blessed by the Israeli God.)

In the playground, I can run fast and my Moon Shot shoes can make me run faster, climb higher, swing further, jump longer. Wearing Moon Shot shoes clearly makes me superior to these little African boys and girls. I show Miss Llewellyn how fast I can run in them.

"Watch me," I shout to her, and I run, up to the thick hedge bordering Circular Road, along towards the Tamarind tree, down past the tilted ocean of grass which is the playing field separating our red stained buildings from the Upper School and the big boys. Through the beaten dusty ground behind the old swing frames that have no swings, up to the drinking fountain – I leap that final step, land square in a puff of moon dust, panting, and I exclaim, "Moon Shot shoes!" just like the boy in the advert did, the advert that I saw on television right before we left England. My, how impressed she seems!

She's engaged to marry Mr. Peters – they've become friends with Mummy and Daddy, and come over to our house sometimes – but I know she's impressed by how well, and fast, I ran. We know so many things, when we're young.

The African children talk in words that I don't understand yet, and the ones that I do understand they say in a way that's hard to follow, and hard to imitate, though I feel I must imitate it, if they're going to be able to understand me. They have this in common, more so than the color of their skin – they belong here, and I am new. But they don't have Moon Shot shoes. In the playground I'm an oddity, at first. I can imitate their manner of speech, but I often don't understand it. It's too rapid, too harsh, like words made of stone clanking into one another, too un-English, too African, and filled with words that I think they must be saying wrong.

"How many brothers do you have?" a bigger boy asks. *How meny brothas?*

"I haven't got any," I say. There's a murmuring among the children.

"How many sisters?" *Sistas*, he says, two rapid, hissed syllables.

"I've got one sister," I say, proudly, but the boys all look stunned.

"Only one! Is your Father not strong?" *Yo-wa Fa-tha*, he says, breaking up the words distinctly against his plump muscular lips, knocking them apart. I don't know what to say to this, so I ask him his name, hoping he'll ask mine, hoping he'll be my friend.

"I am Alastair Amin," he says. "I have twelve brothers and sixteen sisters!" *Twelve brothas, six-tin sistas*. At this, there's a murmur of approval. Sixteen sister! And I thought one was bad enough.

"How many cocks does your Father have?" a bigger boy asks. There are peals of laughter at this question, which I don't understand. I try to guess at the other word, the word he's asking how many of which *yo-wa Fa-tha* has, must have been some other word; *corks*, perhaps? Drandrad uses corks for floats when he goes fishing. Daddy's an angler too; surely he had some corks of his own, but how many to tell this boy? Most of these boys are sons of fishermen, the men I'd seen from the air in their open boats – did they use cork floats as well? But they had nets, which were different. So how many corks – or cocks – *did* my Father have? Three? Ten?

"Five," I say, mimicking the posture of the boy asking, my chin thrust forward, my eyes challenging and unblinking, unsure why he laughs so hard at my response. Another boy asks,

"How may cocks does your Mother have?" *Yo-wa Motha*. Again with the corks. They must *all* be the sons of fishermen, I think to myself.

"Twelve," I say, and the boy laughs harder, and the boys next to him, and before long there are a dozen of them gathered around, frightening, arrogant and condescending, some bigger than me but not by much, most smaller, with thin legs and small round bellies, their shorts frayed at the cuffs, their shirts laundered in lake water. They scare me, but I can tell they're not yet ready to hit me or push down me onto the grass to fight, as I can see some of them want to do, as they do with one another. The teacher is watching, and the teacher will beat boys who push other boys down, beat them with their hands and sometimes with a stick. I know this, and these black boys, even the little ones, littler than me who laugh too but clearly don't know what they're laughing about, they know this also. So they stand there and sneer past their up-thrust little chins and *tsk* with scorn and derision at me and my Father's many cocks, and still I don't know why.

"How may cocks does your sister have?" the boy called Alastair asks. *Yo-wa sista.* I try to think of a big number. I try to impress them with the number of corks my family can afford, hoping to frighten them away.

"A hundred," I say, and the boys fall on the floor laughing, clutching their bellies, pointing, explaining the joke to each other in rapid burst of something not English.

Alastair isn't laughing like the other boys, but watches me, sizing me up. I've seen his type since, easy on the give when he has an advantage and quick to turn ugly when the mood suits him, to try and make a littler one cry – he pokes his finger at my chest, the other boys suddenly quiet.

"Do you know what is fucking?" he asks. *Wat is facking*? I'm five, five and a half, nearly six next year. There are many things I know – Daddy and Drandrad have tried to teach me so many things, about fishing and animals and reading words and counting numbers – but *facking* isn't a thing I've ever heard before. I yield, and shake my head.

"Look, I show you," he says generously. *Aye shoyu,* and in the dusty red earth under the swing frame that has no swings on it, he takes his finger and sketches a picture of a lady as big as himself.

And suddenly, I'm not outside the circle. Suddenly, they gather around me, fan out behind me and my new friend, and I'm one of them, just like that. Other boys gather round to get a better look at what he's drawing in the dirt. I can tell it's a lady, because he draws her boosies big and round like balloons, with an eyeball in the middle of each one. I've seen boosies of course, swelled up under ladies clothes, even glimpsed Mummy's in the changing room at the swimming pool. But he gives her something else as well, like two brackets and a dot where her legs meet and her weewee hole sits, that I don't know anything about. I'm still trying to figure this out when the boy lays down on top of his drawing, puts his tummy on her tummy and starts bouncing his

42

bum up and down. The other boys are laughing again, hooting, holding on to each other, their big teeth startlingly white, whiter than I am, and I'm laughing too – the boy on the ground is laughing, and making funny piggy noises as he bounces his bottom.

"This is fucking," he says, "They do this all the time." *Facking, Ol thi tiy'm*. Who does this, I wonder, *ol thi tiy'm*? He doesn't say.

I don't understand the point of *Facking* until a few days later when I learn a new trick, quite by accident, while climbing on those same empty swings. Wrapping my arms and legs around the sloping uprights, I begin to shinny up the pole, trying to reach the top – the top! I'll be able to see the whole world from up there, or at least all the way to England! I grip the pole tight between my thighs, cross my ankles over one another, pull with my arms and squeeze down with my legs, straining to gain purchase... And then the *Funny Thing* happens, as my legs tighten, as the pole slips up through them while I'm climbing. The Funny Thing, like being tickled in my tummy and going to the toilet when I really really have to go bad, and getting into a warm bath all at the same time. I have to look around, to make sure no one is watching – I feel sure that somehow, this has something to do with *facking*, and that something as... *nice* as this must have made everyone turn and look. But no one has noticed. The world has not stopped; no one has turned, no one is staring. This is something that I've invented, all by myself.

I slide back down the pole, forgetting completely about climbing to the top, about seeing the whole world. I'll have to remember that trick, I tell myself. I wonder, why hasn't anyone else found out about this yet? Swing sets everywhere would be *swarming* with people.

M'zungu, they call me. I practice saying the word to myself, with the long puckery *u* sound the Africans use, practice saying like I practice the hard A in *teacha* and the O in *moh-ning*. What do we speak, when we shout and play with one another? English, mostly, I think, but then language, for a child living in two worlds, becomes a very fluid thing. I don't differentiate between languages, English and Swahili, so much as learn that there are many words for different things, spoken differently at different times depending upon to whom one is talking. *Shamba*, the garden, *Aiya*, the maid, housekeeper, nanny, cook, and *Toto*, the child over whom the aiya watches. *Memsah'b*, Madame, *B'wana*, sir. Jambo! *Jambo*. Habari? *Habari musuri*! I hear the greeting on the street, from a friendly African stranger who might pass us in town. Hello, how are you? I am fine. Hello, how is the news? The news is good. *Takataka*, rubbish; *mingimingi*, many, lots, plenty. Even the grownups at the sailing club and golf club incorporate snippets of this middle language into their everyday speech. The commands we use, or the requests, when spoken politely, to Jeliati the *aiya*, the house girl; or even Mummy when I slip into the habit of forgetting to be English. *Meme nataka*, I want, *n'dio, hapana*, yes and no. *Kuja hapa*, come here, *Haraka* and *pacipaci* – Pacipaci, Haraka! barked sternly by a grownup, whenever a child or a dog or an African is moving too slowly.

My new friends – *rafiki yangu mpya* – Andrew Makay, Ferrie Sentasa, Jeccy Kiganda, whose parents can afford school books and clothes, along with the few children of other Europeans – they don't wear Moon Shot shoes. Most don't wear real shoes at all, just canvas plimsolls, painted every week with chalky white paint-polish that comes in plastic squeezy bottles with a foam rubber tip, painted on but still losing the battle with the brown-red murram dirt stains that eventually color everything. Houses, cars, plimsolls – all invariably end up the same color as the murram roads, the murram paths, the murram playground.

The children are just like me, but so different; their bellybuttons pop out through their shirts like little brown grapes, and their hair is tight, black, curly, and the only part of their skin that's the same color as mine is are the palms of their hands.

44

But as different as we look, we all dress alike; khaki shorts, and a white cotton shirt with short sleeves are all we wear every day, and black rubber flip-flops when we're not at school. There's no reason to wear anything else, anything more would simply be too hot. How long was, before my feet grew and would no longer fit into my Moon Shot shoes? Not long, surely. Weeks even, a couple of months at the most. How long before I'm wearing my own pair of plimsolls, crusty with useless chalky polish, the white rubber sides permanently rusted from murram. How long, until I out of necessity trade in my magic, magnetic Moon Shot shoes for my own pair of flip-flops?

Picture it; we live in two worlds, Lulu and I; at home we're English, at least when we're with Mummy and Daddy. With Jeliati, we become instantly little Africans, even if we are little bossy ones. We eat English food – beans on toast and boiled eggs and Yorkshire pudding smothered in gravy. But in the market, we're African again. Despite how disgusted I was when Daddy first described them to me, in the market whenever I smell fried ants I start looking around hungrily; from the chambered tunnels beneath their craggy nests, seething heaps of termites will have been scooped out and sealed into coffee cans, drizzled with groundnut oil and roasted over an open fire. On every corner there are vendors selling rolled paper cones of roasted termites – and we sniff around, trying to find the nearest one.

"Can we please have some?" I ask, and Lulu nods next to me, eager for a taste. Mummy puts some copper coins in my hand.

"Share them with your sister," which I do, each of us all the while wishing we had a whole coffee can of them to ourselves – so crunchy and salty, spicy and strong. Or we might buy a packet of grasshoppers, their legs pulled off, their heads and fat abdomens fried crisp and savory, all greasy and warm from having sat awhile in the sun. This is our treat, whenever we come to the market. Lulu and I walk a little way behind her eating our fat fried ants, salty and crispy-sweet like oily little nuts.

In the market the sharp smell of spices come up at me, and with them the pleasant sweet odor of slow decay, of flowers and the delicious greasy meat smell of dinners cooking over open flame. At the other end of the market, under the uniform shade of mismatched plywood and corrugated tin and cardboard roofs, the fish merchants call to customers and to each other, the smell of the lake still on their hands and their clothes.

We go the butcher for meat, cut up outside with a long wicked panga on a stained and crusty tree stump, which the flies buzz around in the sun. The steaks we buy had been walking down Kampala road yesterday under their own power. It's nothing like Drandrad's butcher shop on Heppingstall Lane; no ice, no artificial grass, no sawdust.

We go Kirefu's store for anything else we need – cans of Heinz baked beans, a bag of sugar, flour, a newspaper, an ice-cream bar from the big metal chest if we've been good, picking what we want from the pictures on the glass, their colors bleached out and faded and never quite matching what's inside the wrapper. If we need soap flakes for the laundry, or flip-flops, or a place to spend my pocket money, Kirefu's is the place. On a blue plastic wallet, perhaps, garish and shiny from India. Or a keen little penknife that cuts my thumb deeply – I sit in the car bleeding, afraid to tell Mummy until she sees the blood trickling down my wrist, and runs back inside to buy bandages and plasters, one more of the things they sell in the shop.

Under the tin awning covering the front of Kirefu's there is always a beggar boy, one hand shielding his wet eyes from the sun. Gaunt lips pull back pathetically from his monstrous teeth, the other hand cupped out and up.

"Tafadhali, M'zungu," he pleads, smiling pathetically, stick thin legs and big knotted knee-joints curled uselessly under him on a piece of filthy cardboard, his feet wrapped in shredded rags. His cupped hand stretches, trembling. "Asante, asante sana, memsa'b," he says softly if anyone gives him anything. Thank

46

you, thank you very much, madame. Tomorrow and the next day, he'll be here again, on his piece of cardboard, until someone comes to get him in the evening. Once again, I think M'zungu must mean white person, European, because they call me that so often, the cripples and the beggars and the Africans who don't know my name.

Mummy's car is parked on the road just outside the shop door, her Volkswagen Beetle.

"I can't drive that thing, I just can't," she'd said to Daddy, about the rumbling great Jensen sports car. "It's much too powerful for me. I just need something for running about, to the shops and back. It's far more motorcar than I need." Daddy relents – it's not hard, because it means that he gets to drive it himself instead.

"It's a good car, that Volkswagen" says Daddy. "They've got an air-cooled engine, you never have to worry about boiling over if you're out in the bush."

"Oh, and I can see myself being out in the bush quite often. I'm off in the bush all the time, aren't I? You are a silly sod." Daddy just shrugs, and winks.

Mummy loves her Beetle. It's dark blue, with a white interior dusted over with red murram that has worked its way permanently into the thousands of tiny dimples that cover the vinyl seats, and a handle on the dashboard that Mummy can grab to slow the car down when Daddy's driving too fast. There's a special secret place behind the back seat, the Very Back, where Lulu and I take turns riding, and having all to ourselves.

To the left of Kirefu's on Airport road is the post office, and just past that, the entrance to the Entebbe Golf Club. Mummy and the other M'zungu wives and children go there in the afternoons and evenings while their husbands play golf, to talk and play whist and drink gin and tonics. Airport road carries on, forking at Bugonga road, which swings downhill to the left, toward the lake. There, after the coup, is where the drunk, stern-faced

47

soldiers will wait at the roadblock for Mummy, who will always so generous with our groceries when they stop her and poke their rifles inside the car, giving them whatever they like, because she's nice like that.

Just past the fork in the road, is the Lake Victoria hotel on the corner, with its two swimming pools and high diving tower, looking out over the road behind a high wall grown over with well-tended bougainvillea. The sweeping driveway slips under a covered porte cochére where a red carpet leads in to the reception desk, past racks of brochures advertising tours to the game parks and the waterfalls, and 35mm slides displayed for sale against a glass-fronted light box.

M'zungus sit in the shade under the verandah by the pool in threadbare shorts and shirts limp with cooling sweat, a flip-flop dangling from one toe, watching the water glint invitingly in the pool while they sip tea or something stronger. The tourists, on the other hand, especially the Americans, arrive clad from head to toe in brand-spanking new khaki safari suits, bush hats pulled low over their eyes, puttees and stout walking boots, cartridge belts around their waists. Even though their rifles have to be checked in at the reception desk safe, they love to wear their holsters and cartridge belts, and look the part of the great white hunter. To those of us who live here, in our shorts and white short-sleeves and black rubber flip-flops, they look absolutely hilarious.

Airport road goes on past the Government Printing compound on the right, where Daddy works. Two dark skinned *askari*, guards, stand at an idle parade rest on either side of the entrance hut. They are Karamojong, from the north – most of the askari are, Karamojo with their huge, floppy ear loops where they've pulled out the piercings for work, and looped the jelly-roll skins up over their ears in an attempt to blend in.

Further on, the road passes the army barracks and the odd village or two, clusters of cobbled together huts and mud brick houses with thatched or corrugated roofs surrounding a central packed-earth courtyard with its inevitable chicken and perhaps a caged monkey at the center, smelling of wood smoke from cooking fires and sour *pombe*, a homemade corn-mash beer. A house, cinderblock and slightly more European, with a covered car-port and murram stains up the wall, a flame tree in bloom, a crumbling cemetery, a patch of apparently untended banana trees, a causeway edge appearing out of nowhere, painted black and white to make it stand out in the dark – there are no streetlights anywhere in Entebbe, after all.

After the last of these, the road swings downhill and to the south slightly, out towards the airport on the flat ground near the shores of the lake, with nothing but banana patches following sugarcane and pineapple fields for the last few miles before it gets there.

To right of Kirefu's, the narrow strip of tarmac becomes Kampala road, passing by the turnout on the left to go up Nakiwogo hill, to the Government House, which will one day become Amin's Military Command Center. It's busier here, more cement building, less corrugated roofs, more black and white along the causeway edge, and down the narrow dividing strip which separates the two lanes of traffic. Kampala road passes by the dirt track leading down to the sailing club, where the European wives and children swim and ski and bake on the sand and drink gin and tonics while their husbands sail and talk of tacking, and jibs, spinnakers, and booms. On the way to the sailing club is the Tip – the city dump, over a slight rise down by the lake, surrounded by dead-white trees, their branches filled with vultures and corpse-like Marabou storks, and filthy, trash-eating birds of all kinds. I can barely look at the place as we drive past it.

Down Kampala Road also is the hospital, where the Africans line up each day to get salve for river blindness and quinine for malaria, and where we go to get inoculations against tropical diseases, with boiled glass syringes and sewing needles jammed into pieces of cork, sterilized over the flame of an alcohol lamp.

Scattered everywhere are the little *dukas,* garishly painted, cubby-like one room shops selling cigarettes and bright boiled sweets and oil lamps ingeniously folded from scraps of tin cans, soldered together at the seams, and petrol pumped by hand from 55 gallon drums, thick glass bottles of lukewarm Fanta and Coke, Canada Dry and Schwopp. Between the dukas, and behind them, are open spaces with packed dirt and banana trees rotting slowly into the background, tall, spiney acacia trees, and short, broad-leaved jacarandas, a scorched place here or there where a temporary cooking fire might have been lit. And everywhere, *everywhere,* at the roadside edge, under trees, outside the dukas and the shops and the huts, the garbage - scraps of rotting paper, stacks of wooden crates, empty plastic bottles, discarded bits of plastic, rubbish, takataka.

Picture it; picture Entebbe, and you *M'zungu* – a stranger, in common everyday Swahili. But despite the differences, you are also African, and by degrees, as your skin darkens in the sun, the only thing that makes you technically white – makes me M'zungu – is the pale straw color of your hair. It isn't long before everything else, starting on the inside, feels as African as the boys with whom you play. This is now your home, and it is more of a home than England *ever* was.

Chapter 4

There was little or no television to either interrupt or become
the topic of conversation; the odd children's program like Sesame
Street from America, or Playschool and Jackanory from England,
or old episodes of *Mission: Impossible*. The only other programs
shown with any regularity were the Indian films, all singing and
kissing and dancing, car chases and fighting and then some more
dancing – a bit of everything, for everyone, all rolled up into one
disjointed, impenetrable mass. This was all the television we ever
saw, save for the news, read by a nervous-looking man speaking
Luganda or Swahili or hard-accented African English. What
bonded the M'zungus was, of course, the insular nature of our
community; unlike South Africa, we lived as invited guests
among the Africans in their own country, so instead of being
separated from the world of the Ugandan people, we were all
perpetually surrounded by the complete *otherness* of the place.
But like all colonial expatriates since Britain first set her eye on
Empire, we were all part of something that no one in England
could even imagine.

One of my teachers, Mr. Peters, comes over in the evenings to
play Chess with Daddy. Sometimes he brings Miss Llewellyn
with him, and with Mummy the four of them play a game I learn
to call *Scrabbleanmonopoly*, because Mummy always seems to be
saying it as one joined word. At home, I can call them Uncle Tony
and Auntie Kathy, but not at school.

I know what Chess is, that the rules of the game are to see
how long you can look at the funny-shaped pieces on a draughts
board before you have to move one. I don't know what
Scrabbleanmonopoly is, because it's always past my bedtime before

51

the grownups are finished drinking their gin and tonics on the verandah, smoking their cigarettes and talking.

Uncle Anthony, being a teacher, talks very posh; that is to say, any accent which sounds like it came from a place anywhere south of the broad Yorkshire I grew up with. The Yorkshire accent, with its archaic slang *Thee*s and *Thy*s, its hard, upside-down sounding vowels, the hard, working-class coarseness of it. Uncle Anthony calls me "Young man," which makes my ears burn, and I feel very grown up indeed. Unlike Mummy or Daddy, unlike anyone in my family or anyone we know, he's been to college, but they seem to like him anyway.

"What do you want to be when you grow up, young man?" he asks me.

"A frogman," I say, "With air tanks and a real rubber frogman suit, and a knife to kill sharks with." He laughs.

"Very good, very good indeed. You'd better start practicing holding your breath then, hadn't you?"

Jeliati gives Lulu and I our bath, and outside I hear Daddy laughing, hear the glass door *snick* open in its metal frame when Mummy come into the house to freshen the drinks. Underwater, practicing to be a frogman, all I hear is the sound of the blood in my own ears and the bubbles Lulu and I blow when we fart.

Daddy and Uncle Anthony sit in wicker chairs on the verandah. The chess board sits between them, with the knobbly prawns and slit-headed bishops all standing higgldy-piggldy on the red and black squares. Bruno is lying curled up near Daddy; he is the color of lions, and outweigh me by a good twenty pounds. He has a wide ridge of backwards-facing hair down the center of his back and large, cracked callouses on his elbows. Bruno was given to Daddy by a M'zungu family who left shortly before Mummy, Lulu and I arrived; he lays by Daddy's chair most of the time, but I know he's really *My* dog. When I whistle the syllables of his name, he comes at once, and he will never let anyone near us, or our house, unless he's told it's alright. Daddy wasn't kidding when he'd told me at the airport that Bruno was a big dog; he seems massive to me, half way up Daddy's thigh at the shoulder. He's pure muscle, loose-jointed as a cat, with a deep, intense bark that makes him seem bigger yet; he's scared away more than one African peddler from the door, and God knows how many kondos. Callused and scarred from an untold number of scraps and tussles with snakes, dogs, monkeys and Africans, he's good natured when it comes to the careless and often thoughtless play of Lulu and I, but stern and absolutely devoted when it comes to the job of protecting us, his family, his pack. He is still, his ears twitching against the mosquitoes, but his eyes are open and he looks from Daddy to the darkness outside without lifting his chin from his paws. I sit on the settee in the living room, wrapped in a towel, reading a comic, or pretending to, because it's much more fun listening to the grown-ups talking outside. The metal framed window behind me is open to the night, and the sound of Daddy's voice is soothing, the smell of his cigarettes painful and pleasant at the same time. In the darkness, beyond the curling smoke of a burning mosquito coil, crickets and singing frog, armies of them, waiver and pulse in a rhythmic tattoo.

Anthony Simmons, being fresh from an English University, was something of an idealist. He'd rail about the absolute *hubris* with which the British government – all European governments, for that matter – had dealt with the countries and peoples in their charge. He'd come to Africa to try to *Make a Difference*, he liked to make it known, to try and give something *Back to the People*. He believed that for over a century, Europe had grown wealthy off the exploitation of these countries; England in Uganda, Kenya, Sudan; France in Algeria and Morocco; Portugal in Mozambique; Italy, Belgium, Ethiopia, Congo; the list went on and on. He felt duty bound to set it all right, to do what he could to correct the mistakes of past generations. And so, he assumed, did all the other European expatriates who were here in Africa. The "White

Man's Burden," for him, was the task of giving back to these people that which had been taken away from them.

He was a little disappointed with Daddy. My father understood the teacher's point of view, but he by no means shared it. Such noble aspirations were a bit beyond Daddy. He believed that it wasn't possible to go back and change the past, and even if you could, it was impossible to pass judgment on the colonial attitudes of a hundred years ago based the modern standards of 1970. Daddy certainly believed that his being here would make things better for the Ugandans, and would help them better run their own country. But the fact of the matter was, he just wanted to get his family out of Sheffield and see a bit of the world. If he happened to make his fortune while doing that, so much more the better, he thought.

And see a bit of the world we did. Social life became everything; in the week, it's the golf club – but that's mainly for the grown-ups, and especially for the men. For me the golf club is nothing more than a swing set, a sand-box, a lemonade and a bag of crisps, a tiny twisted cone of salt in the bag to shake on them before eating, while Daddy plays golf and gets a bit sloshed and Mummy plays golf and tries to keep up.

On the weekends it's the sailing club, at the end of a rutted murram road, driving the car on Daddy's knee, looking for the occasional enormous six-foot monitor lizards that wander across the road under the hanging Tarzan vines, past a chain-link gate. The sailing club, the morning drive there, is what I look forward to most every weekend. The club itself is little more than a series of corrugated tin shelters in a line along the shore, and the open-fronted clubhouse bar on a small volcanic rise above the beach. Each is tin shed big enough to keep the rain and sun off a small sailing boat, as long as the centerboard is up and the mast is down. A few larger boats – small cabin cruisers, a couple of newer fiberglass ski boats, a little chugging wooden fishing vessel

– stay moored on buoys out on the water. M'zungu families start showing up just after breakfast, with picnic baskets of cold chicken, bacon-and-egg pies, lemon meringues.

A half mile off-shore is an imaginary line, the middle of the world; the Equator. When we cross it on a boat, or on skis, we never really think about it. A little buoy floats in the water, a symbolic token, noting the very middle of the world. We might cross the equator back and forth ten or twenty times on a given Saturday without even noticing.

I run splashing into the water, feel the coarseness of the beach, hear the *skritch* under my feet, the pebbly sand and an equal amount of small crushed snail shells, small as a baby's thumbnail, generations of them. The lake isn't cloudy at all, it's the color of weak tea mashed without milk, and my legs fade into the clear darkness and turn dead white, my toes pale and distant. The surface few inches is bathtub warm but below that it becomes a hard kind of cold, a good kind that I never feel anywhere else in Africa.

The water is flat as newly poured gelatin in the morning, perfect for skiing, and everyone vies to be first out on the water, first one to take a run outside the wake on its flat, mirrored surface. As the wind picks up and the day grows hot, and the ski boats start churning the surface back and forth, it grows choppy, and by late morning, no one will want to ski anymore. Small tufted whitecaps will by after lunch be playing across the surface, and the motorboats will be beached or tied to their moorings; in their places, sleek Fireballs and little Lazers will be dragged from their sheds, their masts raised, their bright white sails unfurled, and the snap of sailcloth in the breeze and the call of crews *Coming about!* will echo across the water.

Up carved steps that circle along the crumbling blood-rust lava cliff is the clubhouse, glass-fronted, open to the breeze on two sides. An icebox hums behind the bar, full of chilled crates of Fanta orange or sweet, pink Schwopp, and squat brown bottles of

Tusker beer. The daddies stand by the chalk board, discussing and arranging who will crew for which boats in the afternoon, who will sail with whom, who will race, from where to where, whether for prizes or for money, for beers or for fun. They discuss the wind, talk about engines and sails and squint out over the lake, smoking cigarettes and drinking.

Past the boat sheds stands the cinderblock building where old skis and polystyrene ballast sheets and the buckets of copper sulfate are kept, big white pails of beautiful crystal blue, blue the color of the sky at noon in the dry African summer. The color and texture of the slick blue crystals makes me want to put them into my mouth and let them dissolve under my tongue, like fizzy sherbet or sweet Blackpool rock. But when I do, they taste like blood and old spoons, like money and bent nails, and I spit them out again. Every month one of the grownups goes out on one of the boats carrying a white pail of copper sulfate and a cut-off bleach bottle to use as a scoop. We cruise slowly through the waters back and forth, scattering scoops full of copper sulfate into the water to kill the Bilharzias snails that live everywhere in the lake. There are posters everywhere warning of the dangers of Bilharzias, with drawings that show the life cycle of the disease, of the tiny little worms that live in the snails in the reedy shallows at the edges of the lake. I've followed the arrows around, from the picture of the larvae entering the man's leg as he washes in the water, to the picture of him sick and weak and blind in his bed, of him squatted down and having a poo near the water, the poo with blood in it, the little larvae hatching from eggs in the poo, being eaten by the snails. There are posters up in the school, and on the wall in the sailing club toilets, and at the hospital, next to other posters showing all the horrid diseases I could get if I'm not careful what I eat or where I walk or where I wash, or even how our laundry is dried on the line. Photographs, of people with skin swollen from hundreds of blistery pustules, something caused by a certain tiny fly biting them, or rotting strips of decaying flesh and deep weeping sores on a bulbous, still-living arm from a snake bite; or swollen, misshapen feet from an insect sting – *Warning!* the posters say; wear your shoes, wash your hands, don't drink this, don't eat that, don't poo there! Uganda is such an interesting place.

But back at the sailing club, by the time the sun sits low in the sky, when all the chicken legs have been eaten and the last piece of bacon and egg pie has turned hard and greasy, I still don't want to go home. I climb onto Daddy's lap, press my ear against his chest, feel the comforting muffled boom of his voice coming through his ribs, distant, growing further away by the minute.

I wake as the car swings off Airport road and turns down Bugonga road past the Lake Vic hotel. I'm twined with Lulu across the back seat, looking sleepily out of the rear window of the VW. The moon hangs low over the lake and it follows our car, racing next to us down Bugonga road, past the guava trees at the side of the road, past the telephone wires that bob and rise as they leap from pole to pole alongside the car. The moon stays level right up until we turn into our own driveway. I know I'm asleep as Daddy carries me from the car. I have the greatest Daddy in the world. I know, because even the moon follows him.

Sometimes it's more than just Uncle Tony and Auntie Kathy who come over to our house. Sometimes Mummy says, "All right, Jeliati is going to give you your tea early tonight, because we're going to be having a cocktail party." For tea I know it will be our favorite, something great like beans on toast or Yorkshire pudding and gravy, or cream of tomato soup, or boiled eggs and soldier fingers, all the kinds of good things I love to eat most. Mummy pulls her hair up into the tight double bun on the top of her head and wears a bright flowered dress, very short. She puts on lipstick, and I tell her how pretty she looks, and she says,

"Ooh, thank you lovie," in that way that makes me glad I complimented her. Daddy wears long trousers, and soon, when I peek through the crack in the door, I see all the people start to come in; Uncle Tommy and Uncle Stan from the sailing club, and Auntie Helen and Uncle John from the golf club, others I've never seen before, just arrived in Uganda and being introduced around, wearing new-looking safari suits and standing out like polished pennies. Sometimes, they bring pretty girls, but always M'zungu, never African. Often there's somebody in a smart blue uniform with wings on his cap, a pilot from BOAC or KLM, laid over for the evening, invited by Uncle John. Uncle John works at the airport, and knows all of the pilots.

I can hear them down the corridor, behind the closed-off hallway, past my bedroom door propped open just a crack so I don't have to sleep in the full dark; not their words, but the merry surf left over after their words wash down the hall; that, and their laughter. I can see their blurry reflected selves moving back and forth in the shine of light against the bright polished concrete of the hallway on either side of the carpet runner, and see the lights of a car fanning across my bedroom ceiling as a latecomer arrives. I hear the coarse guffaw of Uncle Jack, the sound of heels on the hallway runner as one of the ladies comes to use the toilet or when Mummy comes back to check on us.

I pretend to be asleep as the slice of light travels down the wall across my bed, but I pretend too well; even though they're all talking, and laughing, and Carly Simon and James Taylor and Johnny Cash are playing on the Hi-Fi and I can smell their cigarettes, it's suddenly morning and I'm just waking up, to the bright quiet of the damp early day.

In the living room the ashtrays are full to overflowing and smell sharp and acrid, and there are dregs of sour-tasting things at the bottom of the glasses and squat brown beer bottles on all the tables. I sample the contents of some of the fuller glasses but after the first wet sour fag-end hits my tongue, I stop trying the

Tusker bottles until I've checked them carefully against the light for soggy brown cigarettes.

There's a half-full bottle of waragi on the sideboard and I try a little tiny sip. Daddy says waragi is made from bananas, so I expect the clear liquor to taste sweet and smooth and creamy, but instead it smells like banana flavored nail-varnish remover and burns my mouth like drinking petrol. It leaves me choking, like someone dipped a string into mashed banana paste then used it to strangle me, and I hope nobody ever makes me try and drink waragi ever ever again.

The lid of the hi-fi is flipped up and the cardboard record sleeves are spread out along the top of the cabinet and leaned up against the wall next to it. A record by Simon and Garfunkel is on the turntable. There is a long cigarette burn on the top of the hi-fi that wasn't there yesterday. Someone has spilled crisps between the settee and the wall; they're a bit soggy but I eat some anyway. In the fridge there'll be leftover cheese and pineapple cubes served on toothpicks stuck into a potato covered in tinfoil, like a spiny cheese hedgehog. If I'm lucky there might be one or two of those little triangular ham and watercress sam'wiches left, with the crusts cut off, if I'm lucky. How wonderful, I think, how wonderful it all looks, and wish I could have come out of my room to be here and see it all.

Mummy and Daddy go to another party one night. It's at a lady's house, her name is Nora Headly. I've seen her at the golf club, but she doesn't have much to do with the children. She's a very old lady, tall and regal and with a stern face and short grey hair. She sits in a wing back chair and reads the English newspapers while drinking brandy, and when she plays golf, she always wears a long grey flannel skirt that looks far too hot for Africa.

"She's got a Karamujong house-boy," says Uncle Dave. Uncle Dave lives next door to us. "Very primitive people, the

Karamojo." He has a smirk on his face when he says it, like he's got a secret that he's not quite ready to share.

Jeliati gets Lulu and I our tea ready and puts us in the bath before bed, even though it's still daylight outside. Mummy and Daddy get dressed up in very nice clothes, Daddy in a white dinner jacket and bow tie, Mummy with her hair up and a long dress and a tiny little white sequined handbag.

Nora Headly's house is very big and low, up on Nakiwogo hill facing slightly south and east over the lake. Bougainvillea has taken over the high stone foundation, has grown full but is kept trimmed and tidy, like everything about her house. The paint of the front steps is red, fresh and shiny. There are a half dozen or so other couples at the house when Mummy and Daddy arrive, all of them M'zungu, all of them fairly recent arrivals. Nora makes it her job to welcome people, especially English people, to the country.

"Very much like Sheffield, this," says Daddy to Mummy, sidelong under his breath as they walk around the elegant verandah, sipping chilled gins and tonics. Mummy laughs to herself and looks fondly at Daddy, but is very uncomfortable – this is so *unlike* Sheffield as to seem like a different planet. Daddy can see the discomfort on her face, and takes her hand. "Stop worryin' love," he says. "You're just as good as them, or better."

"We don't belong here," she hisses. In Sheffield, her world was that of the hair salon where she'd worked until I was born, and Drandrad's butcher shop. Daddy's had been the grubby inky mess of a newspaper pressroom. She kept house and shopped in the little row-shops off Heppingstall Lane in Attercliffe, the same shops her mother and grandmother and Aunties and sister shopped at. He'd done a little boxing, and worked on his string of clapped-out old cars parked against the causeway edge in front of the house. Needless to say, there had never been a lot of money knocking about. The backdrop of their lives was brick, and people of Nora Headly's social station would most likely never

60

have it cross their minds to even speak to such as them back in England other than as tradesmen offering a service, let alone invite them as welcome guest into her home. Though to be fair, such class snobbery was one of the reasons that people like Nora, despite the expectation of others of her station, emigrated to a place such as this.

"So good of you to come," says Mrs. Headly, taking Mummy's hand in both of her own. "I do so like to make newcomers feel welcome." She has the bearing of the colonial matriarch, and though Mummy's upbringing has left her not particularly fond of *toffs*, aristocrats like Nora, she feels genuinely flattered.

"Oh, thank you for having us, Mrs. Headly," she says, gathering herself.

"Please, call me Nora. Everybody does." She has the dismissive casual charm of true nobility. "Now tell me, dear, tell me about yourself. Where was it you came from?"

"Sheffield," says Mummy, somewhat defensively, as though preparing herself for Nora's disappointment at such a humble industrial background. If the older woman notices, she doesn't let on.

"Ah, good, excellent. Steel, the backbone of the British Empire, eh? My late husband did a good deal of business in Leeds. I know, different place entirely. But I did enjoy traveling to the north." Chances are, Mummy knows, that she probably never ventured very close to the parts of the north where *our* family is from.

"How long have you lived in Uganda, Mrs... Nora?" says Daddy.

"Hmm? Oh, it must be twenty... almost thirty years now. Do you like it here?" Mummy has been very homesick, but Daddy answers for both of them.

"Oh, it's wonderful. I've never seen so many continuous days of sunshine in my life!" He means it, as well.

"And how are the *totos* liking it, your children? How old are they?"

"My daughter is three," says Mummy, "And we have a son who's five."

"And a half," adds Daddy. "He never lets us forget that *half*. Oh, they're loving it, especially the lad. He's already picking up a bit of Swahili from our house girl, and he seems to be settling in at the school quite well."

"How wonderful," says Mrs. Headly, sounding genuinely pleased. "Now you must forgive me, my dears," she says, "I have to go and check on our dinner. Do excuse me, won't you?" She withdraws back into the house.

"Wonder what m'Dad would have t'say about all this, then," Mummy mutters to Daddy. The lights of the house glitter and dance off cut crystal brimming with flowers, sprays of violet Jacaranda brought in from the garden less than an hour before, and honey-sweet blossoms of Frangipani floating in shallow dishes of water. The house and decor draw a delicious balance between spare colonialism and ostentatious reserve. An air not of wealth, but of financially stable austerity.

A small bell chimes. Mrs. Headly comes out onto the verandah, her hands folded primly at her waist.

"Dinner is served," she announces cheerfully, "If you'll just follow me." She leads the way to a formal but comfortable dining room, past mounted game trophies staring down into a living room cluttered with a quarter century's worth of Africana; carvings, masks, spears, zebra skin rugs and antelope skin drums, a leopard hide stretched out diagonally on one wall. "My husband, rest his soul," she says, by way of explanation, "Liked to do a bit of shooting," though her tone seems more relieved than aggrieved. When her guests are all seated, she rings the bell again and the kitchen door opens.

Standing in the doorway of the kitchen is a tall, slender young African man about twenty years old, in a clean white shirt and black trousers, carrying a soup tureen and wearing an expression of haughty indifference to the M'zungus at *his* dinner table. He is young and handsome, with hair that glistens under the lights of the dining room chandelier. He has the dark skin and strong, wide features that mark the people of the north. Mummy and Daddy have seen Karamujong before, of course. Their supposedly primitive reputation, though more likely their poor and remote education, usually mean they end up taking the lower paying jobs in town, such as *askari*, the security guards on building sites or in front of banks. But for a moment, Mummy can't believe she's seeing what she clearly knows she's seeing.

There are two remarkable features about this young Karamojong, the first being his incredibly muscular physique; his skin has an almost burnished and backlit quality, stretched taut as it is across his sculpted muscles. Veins bulge and tendons writhe like cables, just beneath the surface as he moves towards the table. The second thing that Mummy notices – the larger of the two, in more ways than one – is the fact that the front of the houseboy's trousers, from just below the waistband to just above his knees, have been tidily cut away and hemmed flush, leaving his... impressive, to say the least, male member, on uninterrupted display.

Around the table, the ladies try to muffle giggles of shock and embarrassment, and men raise their eyebrows in wide-eyed disbelief, both at the display and the dimensions. The houseboy, oblivious to the attention he is receiving, walks the long way around the table, affording everyone a good look at the private pageant occupying the space under his tureen. He stops at the service side of Mrs. Headly's chair, and offers her the soup. If she has noticed the show, she hasn't let on.

"Thank you, Paul," she says, as she serves a delicate portion of watercress soup into a fine bone china dish. The Karamujong house-boy straightens and moves down to the next guest, each serving themselves a portion while struggling to find reason to avoid comment on the servant's unusual attire and prodigious anatomy. Daddy squeezes Mummy's knee under the table, and she tries to elbow him surreptitiously, which is difficult to do in the taut but good-humored silence that follows the soup tureen – and that which lies *under* the soup tureen – around the table. Nora Headly examines her glass of wine against the light, and seems not to notice the silence as the soup course is served.

Only after Paul has gone back into the kitchen does Mrs. Headly brightly lift her hand and smile at everyone.

"Well," she says, "Shall we?" she dips the wide bowl of her spoon into the soup, tastes it, nods her approval. Dabbing unnecessarily at her cheek with her napkins, she addresses the table.

"The Karamojo are an almost stone age people," she announces, looking off into the distance and punctuating the importance of certain words with the tip of her silver spoon. She is the sort of person who knows that this is technically a violation of the stricter rules of etiquette, though no one at the table seems to mind. "They're a hunter-gatherer people. They run around in the bush up north almost completely naked all the time. They're absolutely without shame when it comes to their..." she pauses, then makes a dismissive gesture with the spoon rather than come up with an appropriately polite euphemism. "It's their natural state." She delicately sips another taste of soup. "The men are... well, let's just say they're quite rightfully proud of their marital *accoutrement*, so to speak, and take great pleasure in displaying themselves whenever the opportunity presents itself. My, I do so love watercress soup, don't you, dear?" She smiles brightly at the young woman next to her, who turns a peculiar shade of bougainvillea purple before Mrs. Headly's gaze moves on down the table. "Paul is young," she continues, "His... well, as you see, it's still an important point of pride with him; manhood is a very *public* thing with his people." She seems not the slightest bit perturbed by her naked house-boy, this elegant and refined example of English aristocracy. She rings the bell again and Paul appears, his arms at his side, his prodigious member resting comfortably against his thigh. "Paul, do be a dear and go put on your proper trousers, all right?" He hesitates a moment, a fierce look of pride on his face, but nods and turns away. "Such a wonderful house-boy," she says. "I'd be simply lost without him."

"Bloody hell," said Daddy, as they're driving home. "I've never seen anything so big." Mummy laughs. Daddy goes on, "Made me feel a bit inferior, though. One like that'd ruin a woman for any other man."

"Nora seemed happy enough."

"Well, y'can see why, can't you?"

"If you came at me with one of those, I'd chop the bloody thing off!"

"'I'd be lost without him,'" Daddy says, imitating Nora's refined accent. "Yeah, I'll bet she would." At this, Mummy starts giggling so much she can hardly breathe.

Chapter 5

Mr. Trotter is my favorite teacher. He's English, too; he wears safari shorts and oxblood walking shoes with heavy olive socks, and has a fringe of sandy hair that flops down when he talks. He tells the class about what a wonderful place England is, how it has helped so many other countries – see, on the map on the wall, all those pink countries – all of those were once owned by England. So much pink; the English must be very good indeed. He talks about how Queen Elizabeth gave Uganda back to the Ugandans on October 9th, 1962 – *now wasn't that nice of her?* – and how we're all still friends, English and Ugandan both. He talks about the history of Uganda, of our flag, red, yellow and black, top to bottom, and the crested crane standing on one leg just like they often do on the shores of the lake, fishing in the muddy shallows among the papyrus.

He talks about the exiled Kabaka-king, and about the President. I'm sure everyone must like President Obote a lot, because his picture hangs above the blackboard in every classroom at Lake Victoria school, and on the wall in every shop I visit, and in most homes as well, at least the ones that are made out of mud.

He talks about the tribes, the Baganda, the Bosoga, the Karamujong, and the languages, Luganda and English, Swahili and Bantu. He talks about the products of our nation; he writes these words on the chalkboard, in block capital letters; THE PRODUCTS OF OUR NATION so I know it must be important, the many things our country makes that the world so very much wants. Copper, and cobalt, bananas and sugar. On the big wall map of the country are little marks showing a pick and shovel for the mines, green and yellow squares for the great banana and sugar and pineapple plantations.

We learn about reading, from a book about John and Jane and their dog, Spot. We read about pirates, a cannon that dreamed it could shoot to the moon, and about a boy who could suck the whole ocean into his mouth so his friends could gather fish, and look in wonder at the pictures of all the colorful fish flopping on the dry ocean floor. We read, terrified, about how they were all washed away in the flood after they got greedy and the boy couldn't hold the sea in any longer.

Mr. Trotter talks about how numbers work, and how they can be added together, and taken away, and divided up and timesed with each other, showing us how it works with rows of chalky tick-marks on the blackboard.

"Susan, what's five into twenty?"

"Sir, four sir." *Sah, foa sah*, she answers. We copy down, then recite, our times-tables, in unison; twenty three little African voices piping together,

"... four times six is twenty-four, five times six is thirty..." All the way up to twelves, we eventually go, in a practiced cadence, like a syncopated metronome, a liturgical chant. Twelve times twelve is a hundred and forty four! I didn't know numbers even came that big.

Every day, the hand-clanked bell chimes loudly, rung on the dot of twelve o'clock by Mr. Shelley, standing on the covered concrete walkway in front of the classroom. It echoes down the covered corridor and across the sparse murram quadrangle. I sit up, see the corners of Mr. Trotter's mouth white with a little crust of salty spittle from having talked so much. We wait impatiently for his permission to put our exercise books and pencils away, before lining up by the door, again waiting permission to file out into the playground.

Every morning I walk to school and at the end of every morning I walk home again at twelve o'clock for dinner. My

Father, along with all the other fathers, comes home from work also – the businesses and stores close their shutters, and everyone goes back to their homes to eat at midday – all the teachers, the shopkeepers, the workers in town.

Our driveway dips under the spreading jacaranda behind the servant's quarters. It makes a tight little turnaround at an overgrown island of wild flowers, to the garage and the back kitchen door, all glass, square panes in a metal frame that's been painted so many times it looks rounded and plump, like skin blistered by the sun. Bruno greets me at the door, running towards me with his lopping, cat-like gait, his paws big as saucers, the sunlight catching the tawny strip of backward running fur down the center of his spine.

The house is cinderblock, single story, with a bare concrete floor polished shiny and slick, and a roof of red tile and bubbled tarry seams. Just like every other building in Entebbe not made of mud, the red murram earth has begun to creep up the walls, to claim it, staining the whitewash along the bottom the color of a laundered bloodstain.

Jeliati is in the kitchen cooking, wearing one of Mummy's cast-off housedresses, her hair up in a brown kitangi turban. She smiles at me with big white teeth and chestnut eyes, her skin dark as shoe polish. She slices potato wedges underwater in the sink, whips up batter for Yorkshire puddings. The house smells faintly of lemon-scented kerosene, sharp and not unpleasant. The legs of all the furniture and the meshed covered hutch we use as a pantry all stand in little shallow plastic dishes of it, to keep away the termites. If it wasn't for the dishes of kerosene, the termites would climb up and burrow into any free-standing wood and make the insides look like crumpled sheets of folded paper. This is the reason the houses, the M'zungu houses, are made of concrete; the termites will eat anything else. Every M'zungu house smells this way, that lemony citrus floor-polish smell is, to me, the defining smell of childhood, and of Africa.

Past the kitchen door, the dining room is separated from the living room by bookshelves. On the shelves are carved wooden giraffes and rhinoceroses and elephants with ivory tusks. Next to Daddy's Ian Fleming novels and Mommy's love stories and the big atlas and dictionary there's also a book on tropical insects, ones that can kill you and others that just simply make you poorly for the rest of your life – tsetse flies and leeches and ringworm, Bilharzias snails and mango flies that lay eggs in the collars of our shirts hung out on the line to dry.

"Make sure you run a good hot iron over the collars before folding them shirts," Mummy would tell Jeliati, "To kill the eggs." If they're not killed with a hot iron, if the eggs are left to hatch while the garment is being worn, tiny maggots will burrow into your neck and pupate, and you'll end up with a seething, writhing black boil that will eventually burst to let the newly formed adult mango flies out. The book has pages and pages of mosquitoes, too, close-up photographs and sketches of the many different types, including the malarial kind, for which we have to take Nivequin every week. Foul tasting, bitter stuff it is, mixed in with passion fruit juice to make swallowing it a bit more bearable. But all that does is make me hate passion fruit, thick and sticky, with the bitter bite hiding on the back of my tongue as the quinine medicine goes down.

On the wall of my room are three paintings I did in art class, heads and shoulders of Mummy with her golden yellow hair and a flowered dress, and Daddy with his thick black beard and a white shirt, me and Lulu, standing by our house. I stuck them up to the white concrete wall with flour and water paste, and now Mummy says they won't come off with anything less than a blowtorch.

Outside my window, near the back corner of the front garden is the hedge that separates the house from Bugonga Road, and in the middle of the hedge is the tree where the weaver birds live; their nests are hanging globes of grass, on stalks like the husks of long tawny fruit, dried and bailed and growing down from the branches. They sway and swing as the mottled yellow birds pop in and out of their dark round holes, grey speckled wings by their sides as they perch on the threshold, holding tufts of grass and sticks between their broad little beaks.

When we moved into this house, my bedroom, or what became my bedroom, had been the kitchen, sort of. Before we lived here, a Karamojong family had lived at number 22 Bugonga Road, and they didn't use the cooker and the sink and other sorts of things that were common in an English kitchen. Instead they preferred to cook over a small open hearth on the cement floor at the back of the house. Before this was my room, the ceiling had been black with soot over where the fire had sat, and in the proper kitchen, in the unused oven, cockroaches lived, in abundance. When Mummy first came into the kitchen and opened the oven door, they all fell out, a solid seething cube of cockroaches that spilled across the cement, little tiny teeny baby fingernail ones and great big ones, Madagascar hissing cockroaches, fat as a pack of cigarettes and broad as a grown man's hand. Every square inch of the cooker had a cockroach in it and when Mummy opened the door they spewed out, thousands of them, each kicking free of the pack and running in every direction.

Mummy wouldn't go back into the house again until the cooker was replaced, nor until something was done about the cockroach and gecko eggs stuck to the door jambs and window sills and the underside of all the furniture, and the black sooty ceiling in the back bedroom. The oven was carted away and a new one installed, and all the walls were painted. Not very well, though – here and there are places where cockroaches (only medium sized finger-joint ones, but roaches just the same) had been climbing up a doorframe or a wall, and the painters had simply run a brush straight over them, cocooning them in paint, permanently anchored to the living room wall. Daddy insisted on

70

leaving them as he found them, as a testimony to African efficiency; they stayed there for the nearly five years we lived in the house, as did the gecko eggs painted over on the kitchen walls.

Down a single step, out of the metal and glass door, is the concrete and breeze-block verandah, and down another step is the big green garden. Islands of color dot the grass; the spiky sisal cactus, the bright magenta bougainvillea bushes, the hibiscus hedge where I go to catch chameleons. Two tall jacaranda trees in full purple blossom anchor the far corners of the garden, another tall hedge running between them, thick and impenetrable except for on narrow place near the bottom, down towards the left. Pineapple plants grow along the hedge, their spines broad and sword-like, an extra layer of protection from any *Kondos* who try to break through the hedge in the dark. Beyond the garden are the cassava fields, the banana plantations, tended by the women from Bugonga village; beyond that, the rolling fields of elephant grass, the old scruffy murram soccer field, the cliffs, and then the lake. The lake, flat and gray-green, stretches out in crisp bright focus straight on to the horizon, reflecting clear as a liquid mirror the clouds sailing slowly overhead. This is the view, from my garden; a lake as big as a sea, framed by clouds, hedge and brilliant purple jacaranda.

Uncle Dave lives next door, with Auntie Ida and their daughter, Auntie June, who is the same age as Mummy and her new best friend.

"He's not really your Uncle," says Mummy. "But you can call him that, if you'd like." Since coming to Africa I've all of a sudden got a raft of new Uncles that aren't really Uncles, and Aunties as well.

Auntie June has a *divorce*, though nobody tells me what this means. I think of it as something on wheels which she must tow around behind herself. She also has a little girl the same age as Lulu. Rebecca and Lulu are the same height, same size. They both

71

have short red-blonde hair and in photographs, people sometimes have difficulty telling them apart. I don't though, as Lulu is usually the one holding Ellie.

Auntie Ida keeps bars of Nestlé's milk chocolate in her icebox and will often call Rebecca in to their kitchen when we're there, and give her a piece. She watches her granddaughter eat, which she does messily, smearing it on the sides of her mouth. She doesn't share, and Auntie Ida doesn't offer us any.

"This is for my *good* little girl," she coos, *may goo'd little ge-rul*, she says, all beaming Glasgow pride. I wonder if Lulu and I have been bad, and that's why we don't get any.

"There's sem'thin' wrong wi' that boy," she says to Mummy. "Ah think he's retarded." That word sounds so much different when the *R* is rolled off a Scottish tongue. I'm not offended, because I don't know what it means, but Mummy is, though. Mummy is terribly hurt. Auntie June comes over to sit with her on the verandah.

"She's only ever known Rebecca," June says apologetically, "She doesn't know what to do with boys." While they talk, I spin circles on the lawn with my arms outstretched until I fall over, stare at the sun as long as I dare, rub my eyes until red dots throb behind my lids like a field of neon roses, cover and uncover my ears with my hands and make the world go *shoosh shoosh shoosh*. I make guns out of the few blocks of Lego that I brought with the few toys I own, and hold them close to my face as I shoot imaginary German paratroopers out of the sky. I don't care if I am retarded or even care what it means. Maybe it means someone like Tucker, the American boy in my class who rides in a wheelchair, who wears braces on his legs and who can't walk or run or play, who can't even lift his own head. He sits in the back of the classroom with an African man who pushes his chair, who lifts him in and out to go to the toilet. It's odd to see a grown man in a class full of little children, legs curled under the miniature desk. Tucker wears thick glasses and makes grunty little piggy noises that the African man understands and writes down in Tucker's exercise book. I don't care if Auntie Ida thinks I *am* retarded. I would have just liked to try a piece of that cold English chocolate.

At the table, Jeliati serves our lunch – steak and chips, thick cuts of sirloin that Daddy will smother in HP, with potatoes fried brown and crisp. Me and Lu both begin to whine.

"Uuugh, not steak and chips again," I snivel, "I'm sick of steak and chips."

"Sit ob steat an' chits," says Lulu, staring at her plate. We had steak and chips yesterday. We had steak and chips the day before yesterday. Daddy loves steak and chips; Mummy and Daddy are children of the war that Mr. Hitler and the nasty Germans started, the war that Drandrad went off to help finish, and for them, the abundance of meat in Africa, choice cuts for next to nothing, is a wonderful thing. The Africans, who prefer their meat stewed, and usually preferred goat meat anyway, ended up ignoring the tenderest pieces, whole loins and filets, which Mummy buys off the Entebbe butcher for a few shillings. To have steak this good for dinner every day is, to Daddy, the best part of living in Uganda.

The best part, to me, is *Fenai*.

"Don't play under that Jakfruit tree," Mummy tells us. "One of those bloody things'll crack your skull wide open." Jakfruit – Fenai, the Africans call it – is big as man's head and so good that it's always a temptation to try and bring down one of the massive heavy fruits before they drop by themselves, off the tree in front of Jeliati and Powlino's quarters. I'll hear them when they do, a thud like a cannonball hitting the deck of a ship. Their green skin is thick and tough like the rind of a concrete melon, covered in hard pointy little nipple-bumps. Hard to open, full of sticky white sap that's equally hard to scrub off, the smelly, rotten-banana bubblegum tulips of fibrous chewy meat inside are deliciously and wonderful. Fresh, that is. Put it in the fridge or try to save

73

any and it quickly turns to a stinking, thoroughly unappetizing brown goo like congealed banana snot that even the Africans won't eat.

Jeliati and Powlino had each shown up on our doorsteps within days of our moving in, each carrying a small bundle of belongings and a carefully folded letter of recommendation from the last few families, either M'zungu or Indian, for whom they'd worked. They were each given a dutch-doored room in the murram-stained cinderblock quarters at the top of the drive, they shared a shower and a squat toilet, and had off Saturday afternoon and all day Sunday to go back to their villages and see their families. Jeliati the *aiya*, Powlino the gardener, the *shamba-boy*, despite the fact that he was a full-grown man. For their work, they earned more money each week than they might have earned in a year, scraping and scratching cassava and matoké out of the earth back home. Powlino mostly keeps to himself, smiling broadly at us while tending the garden, arranging for the big towed tractor-mower every week; but Mummy and Jeliati have an odd relationship – part employer, part friend, part teacher, part partner, part rival in the mothering of us, her children.

It's getting close to Christmas, and an Indian grocer shows up one afternoon in a dilapidated grey Citroën van. When he opens the back doors, two fat trussed turkeys flap their wings and hiss and relieve themselves all over the floorboards. He pulls them out and lays them down so Mummy can pick which one she wants for our Christmas dinner.

"Choose which bird you like, Memsa'b," he tells her cheerfully, "I will dress him and return him tomorrow." *Chuse wich bad*, he says. One turkey manages to flap away, up to the hedge, where the man catches it again. I laugh.

Look!" I say, pointing at the big smelly green and white piles in the drive. I can't take my eyes off it. "Poo!" In a week, this same flapping, pooing bird will be roasted with potatoes and sage and onion stuffing, and we'll eat it in shorts and T-shirts with the windows open to the heat of the day – so much the opposite of a cold English Christmas.

Animal poo is a never-ending source of fascination to Lulu and I. In the game parks, Mummy and Daddy *ooh* and *aah* over the vistas and the mountains and the sweeping expanses of grassy savannah. At giraffes a hundred feet tall craning up to reach the tippy top-most leaves of the thorn trees; at a million Gnu that stand chewing and swishing flies off their dusty backs; at baboons grooming each other, close enough to hit with a stone; at the black and red-brown zebras bending low at water-holes, their manes like a close-cropped broom running the length of their necks. At ant hills, really termite nests, like cathedrals of mud and bug spit, with spires taller than a man, sharp pointed and knife-edged, harder than cement. Around Entebbe, the Africans break open the nests with picks and spades to harvest the insects for food, and inside, the nests are dark, fascinating, another world, the layered mud walls no thicker than a sheet of paper, thousands of tunnels that meld and ride around each other like reams of crumpled foil surrounding the fat, gravid Queen.

But Lulu and I, in the back seat of the VW, we'd rather have contests to see who can spot the biggest and freshest or oldest, rankest pile of elephant crap in the road.

"Look!" I howl with delight. "Look at that one! It's big as my head!"

"Nem a poo head!" Lulu squeals. We love them, great steaming piles, fresh and sludgy like rotting avocados, or crusted brown and day-old, smeared open where the scavengers have been looking for a meal or predators were covering their scent – they sit along the side of the road in the bush, where the animals are free to roam and there aren't any fences. We compare, contrast, evaluate; elephant versus lion, lion versus water buffalo, water buffalo versus giraffe.

"Honestly, you two," says Mummy. "Y'don't know what it w'like, growing up in Attercliffe, around nothin' but brick. Where we grew up there was nothin' green, nothing. We didn't have any o' this where we grew up. D'y'know, the view out of my back window..." I've heard it before, about the view of a paved macadam yard, a brick wall, the back of the house on the next lane over, and everything not asphalt or cobbles being built made of iron-red brick, and the smoke from the steelworks hanging over everything. I remember it, though it doesn't seem real to me – *this* is what's real, the sky and the animals and most of all, the *poo*. Lulu and I roll our eyes at the back of her head – or I do, so Lulu does it too, just because I did it, and we smirk at each other and look out the window again.

"Look for a big smelly one," I whisper to Lulu, and we both giggle quietly, press our noses to the glass and pull poo faces, making our faces look to each other like we think poo looks to us.

The lions rolling in it to attract mates – that's what I like to see the most. We sit in the back of the Volkswagen, Lulu in the back seat with Ellie, me in the Very Back, and Daddy has Mummy drive slowly past the pride that occupies the middle of the narrow murram road. Daddy is taking pictures for the tourism bureau and for his own collection too.

The young males roll in the fresh piles of elephant dung, which is now smushed and smeared across the road, a lumpy green-brown stain as wide as the shadow of the Bug. The lions, well perfumed, walk past the Beetle with only the barest glance at us as they wander off to find females to impress. I can hear them easily, the metallic back-flush of their growling breath, since Daddy has the window all the way down and his door open. His foot is braced on the running board and he's perched his Hasselblad on the open window ledge, leaning out as he looks down into the viewfinder. Click and wind, click and wind. Mummy inches the car slowly forward.

"Slower," scolds Daddy, not looking up from the frosted glass viewing window on top of the camera. "Bloody 'ell, woman, I said *slower*." She's trying to watch the road and watch Daddy and watch the lions watching us. He's more out of the car than in, and so close he could reach out and touch some of the bigger males without putting a foot on the ground.

"Oooh, lovie, I don't like this..." Mummy is nervous and frightened, but Daddy just looks at her and rolls his eyes as though at someone spooked by distant thunder.

"What?" he says. "Shurrup, woman, they're all right. Just slow it down a bit, will you? I want t'get a few more pictures!"

The lionesses drowse in the dry grass just a few yards off to the side of the road, or watch us without raising their heads, or look off into the distance, watching the horizon. Occasionally one raises her nose into the air and closes her eyes, as though trying to place a scent; the smell of ripe English children, perhaps? She could be at the car in three bounds, before Daddy could get his leg inside, let alone get the door shut and the window rolled up. She's so close, I can see the dark circles under her eyes and the row of plump teats along her belly. One of the females looks over at the males rolling in the poo, another turns and looks at me – right at me, right into my eyes – then blinks soft, disinterested lids and turns to look the other way, off down the road.

"Look, Mummy," I say, pointing. A male has mounted a female and their bottoms drop low, his tail pressing flat against the ground, his elbows push down on her shoulders. His bum rolls and twitches and dips, and I know from what the boys at school told me that they're *doing it,* that they're *facking.* Mummy turns to me and pulls a funny face, and says "Oh, yucky, don't look," but she says it as a joke, and we don't stop watching. Daddy clicks picture after picture. When they're done, they walk away from each other like nothing ever happened.

"Not a bad life, that," says Daddy, and Mummy smacks him lightly on the arm.

On Christmas Eve, Lulu and I hang empty pillowcases over the footboard of our beds, for Father Christmas to put all of our presents in. I lay awake, listening for the bells that Daddy has heard so many times when I wasn't paying attention. Mummy is worried that we might miss having snow; all I want to know is how Father Christmas will get in, since we don't have a fireplace or chimney.

There's a Christmas tree in the living room, with big colored bulbs on it, and long fragile glass ornaments that smell like the inside of Nannan's handbag. Shiny silver tinsel hangs over the tree, and a big star on top nearly touches the ceiling. A golden garland is draped over the living room mirror, and a red one hangs around the window. The Christmas cards that came from Nannan and Drandrad, and those given to us by all my new Aunties and Uncles, are clipped to a string by tiny red and green clothespins like a dolly's laundry. The house smells of mince pies, and sage and onions, of citrus lemon kerosene, and of the night blooming flowers outside the open windows. Of all the things in the house, it's the tiny clothespins that most make me think of Christmas.

On Christmas day, after we've ripped open our presents, Daddy sets the timer on his camera and takes a picture of everybody; me sitting in my usual chair, turned around to face the camera, Mummy with her elbow on the table and her hands folded under her chin, Jeliati stands on one side of Daddy, hands at her sides, smiling: Lulu, grinning, chews on her fingers across the table from me. Daddy stands ready to carve, the table laden down with bowls of mashed potatoes and peas, plates of Yorkshire pudding, and Mummy's big fat turkey steaming and crispy and stuffed full of sagey onion breadcrumbs. Daddy smiles broadly, knife poised over a breast. It's a hot day; we're both in our usual khaki shorts and flip-flops, he and I, and all of the windows are open. Snow, and chimneys, are the last thing on my mind.

It's New Year's eve, the last day of 1970. Mummy and Daddy have a party, everyone comes over to our house, all the Uncles and Aunties. They play their music louder than usual, and cheer, and kiss each other at the door. Just before midnight Daddy comes in to wake me up, and carries me into the living room. It is nothing like the magical wonderland I'd pictured. It's full of wide-eyed grownups, smelling of beer and looking too much like dolls, with glass eyes and lipsticky smiles, all laughing too loud and trying too hard to make a fuss over me. Johnny Cash is playing on the hi-fi, *Ring of Fire,* and the smell of cigarette smoke and banana waragi breath is thick in the air and somehow appropriate to the music. I'm still sleeping, almost, hanging on to Daddy, but the lights are too bright. Everyone counts backwards from ten, shouts "Happy New Year!" and kisses each other and kisses me – "Here's to 1971!" bellows Daddy, raising his big pint beer-mug into the air. "Hip, hip," cries someone, somewhere behind me, and everyone joins him, "Hooray!" I throw out my own soft hooray, just the one. It's all I can manage before I fall back to sleep, and I doze off to the opening, drunken strains of *God Save The Queen.*

How could any of us know that in less than a month, everything we knew would change?

Chapter 6

Overnight, it happens. Literally. One day, all the shops and all the offices at the Government Printers and all the classrooms at Lake Victoria school have a framed photograph of president Milton Obote up on the wall. And the next, all those pictures are gone, and new pictures go up, of a big, round-faced soldier, a peaked cap with shimmering gold braid pulled squarely over his dark brow. He must be a great and very brave soldier, with his wide shoulder boards on a smart green uniform dripping with medals. It's the first time I've ever heard the word *Coup*. A *Coo*, they all say, a *coo*, there's been a *coo*.

It'll be my birthday in a week – I'll be six! Not five any more, not five and a half, five and three quarters, nearly, but honest to goodness Six. Next week my friends will come to my house and we'll play games and have balloons in the garden and Mummy will bake a big chocolate cake and cover it in hard sugar icing. I'll get a fountain pen and a compass and ruler set and a Husky car and a book, and a blue plastic wallet from Kirefu's. We'll play *What's The Time Mr. Wolf* and *Pass The Parcel*, and eat little butterfly buns and drink orange squash. But now all everyone is talking about is the stupid old coup.

On the morning of January 25th I'm sitting down for breakfast, a bowl of Weetabix drowned in milk and crusted over with sugar. Daddy is having his bacon and eggs and grapefruit half. Uncle Dave comes over from next door. Daddy is listening to the BBC for the news from the world, just like he does every morning.

"Morning all," he says, then to Daddy, "You might want to tune over to Radio Uganda." He looks serious and a bit worried.

"They're saying there's been some kind of shake up with the government last night. The army says it's in charge, but Obote's people are claiming everything's under control."

"I thought Obote was out of the country," says Daddy.

"He is, that's just it. No one seems to know what the hell's going on.... well, you have a listen." Daddy goes over and twiddles the wireless knob, and finds the whistley, whiney signal.

Last night there was an attempted coup, the man on the wireless says. President Obote is away in Singapore at a World Leadership Conference, he says, and in his absence a senior army officer attempted a military takeover. His attempt has apparently failed and the officer, a Colonel Amin, has been arrested.

"Well, that explains the martial music they were playing earlier, at least," says Daddy. "Any word on who's in charge?" Uncle Dave shrugs.

"Your guess is as good as mine on that one, mate. Are you going to go in to the office today?"

"I suppose we'd better, hadn't we? I mean, at least we can make a few calls and see if anyone knows what's going on." Daddy kisses Mummy and they leave the house. "Ta-ra, love," he says, winking at her.

There's an odd stillness hanging over Entebbe that morning; it was unnerving. Driving towards the Government Printing compound, the women of the various small villages around Entebbe, whose normal chore it was to carry jerry cans of water up from the lake, were nowhere to be seen. The shamba boys working in the gardens, picking the bananas and tending the cassava patches were conspicuous in their absence. No clattery bicycles overloaded with long stalks of sugarcane or unidentified burlap bundles being ridden by men on their way to the marketplace. No sound of news or pop music playing over radios from any of the *dukas*, the little one room shops – all, even Kirefu's, were still shuttered up tight.

At the Government Printing compound the big gates were closed, the workers all standing idle inside the gates, looking anxious and fidgety. Two uniformed askari manned the wooden guard hut, beneath the high wall cemented along the top with broken bottles. The askari opened the gates for Daddy's car and closed them again quickly behind Uncle Dave's. The guards gruffly told the African workers to stay inside. Why the workers might be milling inside the gate, trying to leave so early in the morning, troubled Daddy and Uncle Dave both. The workers seemed frightened, unsure what to do next.

The two M'zungu walked to Mr. Ringwell's office, the general manager. He waved a hand dismissively.

"Nothing to tell, really," he sniffed. "There was a coup attempt last night. Like children they are, the lot of 'em, squabbling about who's in charge." He stepped outside onto the wooden verandah of the building, affected a pose with arms akimbo, attempting to sculpt himself into the picture of a colonial master from another century, a man in the know, rather than an ordinary little Englishman in charge of running a simple printing company. "Amin tried to pull a fast one last night," he said to Daddy, "But he got caught out. He's been arrested, you know, and they're rounding up his troops even now."

"You've heard all this for certain?" asked Uncle Dave. "Even the BBC didn't seem to have the full story."

"Oh, I'm sure of it. I've got my sources," he said slyly, tapping the side of his nose. "Come on," he added, walking down the manicured gravel path towards the Africans at the gate. "Let's get these lazy buggers back to work."

Just as he was about to start shouting at the muttering and nervous men, there was a tremendous explosion to the west. If the workers were frightened before they were now terrified, and they all scattered, determined to get out of the compound, get past the closed gates and away by any means they could. Mr. Ringwell was knocked to the ground as one man bolted straight into him as though he wasn't even there; from the ground the M'zungu manager started to protest, but the man was already too far away. Even the askaris ran at the sound of the explosion, and the rest of the Africans charged through the gate after them, disappearing into the overgrowth across the road, and down little side paths through the banana fields. Within seconds, there was nobody near the gate but the three white men.

"Bloody hell," said Uncle Dave. "I think that came from the airport."

The only people left in the compound beside Daddy, Mr. Ringwell and Uncle Dave were the few African managers, who stood wide-eyed near the pressroom door. They seemed to be undecided as to where they would rather be.

"Staying with the M'zungus, are you?" Daddy joked. They tried to laugh but didn't do a very good job. "Where'd they all go anyway, the rest of 'em?" he asked.

"They have gone to their homes, their families. They are frightened of the army." *They'a homs, they'a fam-i-liz. They ah frytend.* These young men looked pretty *frytend* of the *ah'mi* as well.

I column of dark smoke rose above the trees to the south and west, down towards the lake; it did indeed seem to coming from the direction of the airport. In the distance came another sound, the low, slow roar of a diesel engine, and the sounds of shouting. The sound drew closer up the road and the men, M'zungu and Ugandan alike, all went over to the gates and looked out.

Several large trucks, army green, were chugging at a walking pace towards them from the direction of the airport. A large crowd of people was following the lead lorry. The crowd whooped and shouted and jeered. Some of the men in the crowd, and even the women, picked up stones and threw them at something in the back.

It was a man. And not just any man.

"Shit," said Uncle Dave quietly. "It's Obote."

"What, the President?" asked Mr. Ringwell, incredulous.

"No, his brother. Don't remember his Christian name, d'you? You know, the chap who owns that bar down the road?" Daddy nodded. He and Uncle Dave have visited the bar before, just a shack serving beer, really, with some chipped Campari ashtrays on a rough wooden counter.

The President's brother was standing in the back of the open vehicle with his hands tied to either side of the metal support frame, its canvas cover removed. The two men could have been the mirror image of one another.

"Bloody hell," said Mr. Ringwell. The figure struggled to retain his balance in the lorry's lurching bed. "They could be twins."

"I think they may be," said Daddy. "Jesus, look at the poor bastard." They were talking very quietly all of a sudden, rooted in place just outside the gate, watching the scene on the road before them in a state of shocked disbelief. The man in the truck had blood running down his face, and the crowd was booing and jeering loudly at him, and Daddy had the feeling that they were playing up for the three M'zungus watching from the side of the road. The stones they threw were clearly and eagerly aimed at the bound man. He twisted and ducked, but they came at him from all sides, and the ropes binding his wrists prevented him from getting out of the way of all of them; many of the stones had already found their mark, and now even more cracked horribly against his bleeding head, thudded against his sweating body.

As the truck drew level with the entrance to the printing compound, one of the soldiers in the back who was facing the prisoner, looked over his shoulder and saw the three M'zungus standing with the well-dressed African managers inside the gate. He stood, and with this fresh new audience to watch, made a show of raising his weapon and slamming the butt of his rifle into the bound man's face. Obote's nose and one eye disappeared into a bloody mash, his head dropping to his chest. The soldier looked

84

straight at Daddy and the other men, to make sure they'd seen what he'd done. He sat down again, staring smugly at them. He sneered, thrusting out his chin contemptuously. He was clearly proud of himself. President Obote's unconscious brother sagged limp against the ropes, and didn't flinch anymore, even when the stones smacked against his head.

"Let's go back inside," said Daddy quietly. They all stepped slowly backwards, behind the unguarded gate, suddenly aware what sad little security it offered. They walked back towards Mr. Ringwell's office without speaking.

Seated again inside the cooler shade of the raised wooden office, they tried to make sense of what they'd just seen.

"Obviously, the coup wasn't quite as unsuccessful as reports would have led us to believe," said Uncle Dave, looking over at the silent Mr. Ringwell, the undisguised sarcasm clearly ringing.

"So who's in charge?" asked Daddy again.

"Obviously, the bloody army," said Uncle Dave.

"Yes, but who's running the army?"

"Well, it's got to be Amin, doesn't it? I mean, who else could it be?" said Uncle Dave. But then he doubted himself for a moment. "But then again, if Amin tried last night and failed, and some other bugger had a go today, God knows who could be in charge. Is there a wireless around?"

Just then there was a pounding of feet along the wooden verandah outside and Mr. Suffolk, one of the other M'zungu managers, came running in.

"Any news?" asked Uncle Dave, leaping to his feet. "What was that bloody explosion all about?" Mr. Suffolk looked scared.

"The airport. I just got back. Some silly bastard in a tank popped off a round to show everyone he was serious. Some over-eager lieutenant named Malyagamu or something. Blew out a few windows, put a bloody great hole through the walls. They're saying a couple of catholic priests got killed by shrapnel." He looked at the three men for a moment. They can tell there is more.

85

"Look," he said, "I going home, and you chaps might want to do the same while you can. There're reports going around that soldiers are going house to house rooting out resistance. I've heard there's been some looting, and... and…"

"And what? Get on with it, man." Uncle Dave sounded harsher than he'd wanted to.

"And a couple of rapes." There was only a slight pause, and no further questions. Daddy and Uncle Dave leaped to their feet and sprinted to their cars, their tires spinning gravel as they headed out of the abandoned gates and onto the now-deserted road.

I'm in my bedroom reading when Daddy's car comes roaring into the driveway. I hear his footsteps coming up the steps as he rushes into the house. Mummy and Auntie Ida are sitting in the living room listening to the radio. There's been nothing on all morning except military marching songs, and the occasional announcement to stay in our homes. It's very, very boring.

"Are you all right?" I hear Daddy ask. The women sound more frightened by his bursting into the house than by anything else.

"Yes, of course we're all right." says Auntie Ida, looking puzzled and just a little irritated. *We'ir alrrreyt.* "But what's happened? We thought we heard a big boom or some such." Daddy hesitates, no knowing quite where to begin.

"There's been a bit of... trouble," he says. "Are the kids in?"

"Yes," says Mummy, just as I walk into the living room. "John Shelley sent them all 'ome, said 'e'd been advised to keep the school closed f'today by the minister of some such something or other." Daddy looks relieved. Out of the window, I see Uncle Dave, running through the gap in the hedge towards the verandah door.

"Bloody hell, woman," he says. "When I got home and you weren't there…" He doesn't finish the thought. He looks almost happy to see Auntie Ida scowling at him.

"Och," she says, "Dina fash yoursel', man."

"So what happened?" Mummy asks Daddy. He hesitates again, glances at Uncle Dave, then at me.

"Well, there's definitely been a coup of some kind. The workers were all a bit panicky this morning. Dan Suffolk told us there'd been an explosion at the airport, artillery fire or a tank or something. The workers all scattered when they heard it – the mood they were in, it wouldn't have taken much. The next thing y'know there's this convoy of military vehicles coming up the road. The army was leading the parade, and they had Obote's brother tied in the back of a truck. They'd… we watched 'em… well, they made a bloody mess of him, is what they did."

"Who did?" asks Mummy.

"The soldiers. The crowd. The stupid bastards following the lorry." He tells them, without being too graphic, about the ropes, and the stones, and the rifle butt.

"Oh, deary me," says Auntie Ida, her hand moving protectively to her throat. Mummy puts her arms around me, pulls me in close against her.

"We heard reports that the army were going from house to house, robbing and raping the women." At this, Auntie Ida begins to laugh.

"Och, no, unfortunately there's been none of that here," she says. "We should ha' been s'lucky."

On the radio, the military march that had been playing softly in the background abruptly stops, and a man's voice comes on. It is strong and deep but a little awkward, like someone not used to speaking into a microphone.

"Fellow countrymen and well-wishers of Uganda," he says, "I address you today at a very important hour in the history of our

87

nation..." *Well wishas*, he says. *Im'po'tant ow-wa*, he says, *of ah ne-shon.*

"That's Amin's voice," says Daddy. Uncle Dave nods.

"Certainly sounds like him."

"A short while ago," booms the voice from the speakers, "Men of the armed forces placed this country in my hands. I am not a politician, but a professional soldier. I am therefore a man of few words, and I shall, as a result, be brief..." *Eh man of few wad. Aye shall be brif.*

He speaks about a free civilian government, chosen by the people, supported by the military. He speaks about the mistakes of the past. He speaks about his goals for the future. Indeed, he does not sound like a politician, at least not the ones I've heard Drandrad listening to on the radio in England. When he's finished, the wireless hisses for a minute and another voice comes on, a proper news-reader voice. He announces that the forces of General Ida Amin have taken over Kampala. There's fighting in the hills, but they're in the process of suppressing the last of the resistance. Meanwhile, everyone should continue to stay indoors until further notice.

"General? Looks like he stumbled onto a promotion since yesterday," says Uncle Dave, laughing.

"Well, at least now we know who's in charge. Or who says he's in charge," says Daddy.

After a while, after no further news comes on and the radio and its *thrumping* drums and piping brass bands are turned down to be just barely audible, Auntie Ida and Uncle Dave go back to their own house. Mummy and Jeliati start making tea, frying eggs and toasting bread and cooking peas and sausages, and banana custard for afters. Daddy and Mummy read for a little bit, Lulu and I draw and play and leaf listlessly through comics. I want to go outside and run around in the garden, but Mummy says no.

As soon as Jeliati and Powlino are off duty, the doors to their quarters are shut tight, both top and bottom. There's no thin

88

smoke from their charcoal fires, no smells of goat stew and matoké, no light showing around the cracks of their doors, no sign at all that they're home.

Daddy listens to the radio, which continues to play inspirational tunes of military glory, interrupted from time to time with news. But it isn't really any different than the news they've broadcast the last time or the time before. The *ahm'd fo'ses*, says the newsreader, *ah sappressing thi risistance*. The sky darkens; the stars come out. Once in a while, at a distance, I hear a sound, *pop, pop, pop-op-op*, without really knowing what it is.

"Okay, you two, time f'bed," says Daddy. Between not going to school, not going outside and the funny music on the radio, it's been the strangest day I can ever remember.

In the night, I'm continually woken up by the sound of lorries and land-rovers passing slowly by on the road outside, sweeping the hibiscus hedges and bougainvillea bushes with bright powerful searchlights, turning my room into a peculiar kind of high-blasted daylight. As another truck moves on past, Bruno starts his slow, savage, basso *woof!* at the kitchen door, running through the house to continue barking out towards the verandah. I get up sticky eyed and shivery and pad into the living room. Daddy is already in there, holding Bruno by the collar, his face closed up against the darkened glass.

"What is it, Daddy?" I ask.

"Shoosh," he says. "Be quiet." In the moonlight streaming through the dining room window he sees me reaching for the switch. "Don't turn on that bloody light!" he hisses. I catch myself, step away from the wall, staring at the switch as though it might turn into a snake and slither away.

"What are you looking at?" I whisper. He doesn't say anything, but fans his hand in a quieting gesture. I go over to the window next to him and look. My eyes take a while to get used to the blackness of the garden, but the moon is high and the stars are bright and eventually I see what looks like a man crouching behind the hedge about fifty feet away, his eyes very wide. Suddenly the man separates, splits down the middle, and I realize there are two of them. They have on the dark green uniforms of soldiers but no berets, and both are barefoot. Even though it is night, and even though they aren't very close, I can see by the way they glance around and stay low that they are petrified with fear. Bruno has been quiet since Daddy took hold of his collar, but keeps glancing up at us while keeping the two frightened soldiers directly at the center of his attention. His ears are locked up and forwards, and every muscle in his back is quivering, ready to spring between the men and the house; all it would take would be a look, a gesture, from Daddy, and it's clear that Bruno would kill both intruders without a thought. It's also clear that until that look or gesture comes, he will not move a muscle.

"Looking at them uniforms, I think they're part of Obote's bodyguard," Daddy says softly. "That's the only reason the poor buggers would be running and hiding like that. Look!" The searchlight from the trucks on the road passes by again. I follow the long shadows cast by the trees at the top of the drive as they track across the garden. As the light comes streaming through the dining room window behind us, I see my own shadow spread out onto the verandah. The men duck as they see our shapes outlined in the living room window. Daddy turns, shielding his eyes, and walks over to the dining room window, waves. The men in the army lorry must have seen that he's a M'zungu, not a deserter, and the truck moves on. "That was a stupid thing to do," Daddy says to himself. "The buggers'd as soon shoot me as look at me." As soon as the searchlight beam passes by, the two soldiers in the garden turn and run away from the house, down through the gap in the hedge, towards the lake.

Daddy kneels down, rubbing Bruno's head and praising him for doing his job so well. "You good dog," he says, "You bloody good dog." The dog accepts the praise with a grateful stoicism.

He turns to me. "C'mon then, lad," he says, ruffling my hair with warm, doggy-smelling hands, in the exact same way as he'd just ruffled Bruno's ears. "Get back t'bed."

"Why, Daddy?" I ask.

"Why what, love?"

"Why are those men running away from the army?" Daddy pauses, thinks through his answer.

"The soldiers in the truck work for Amin," he says. "They're trying to catch all the soldiers that used to work for Obote."

"But why?" I ask. "They're all the same soldiers, aren't they?" Daddy pauses again, then answers without answering at all.

"Well, I suppose, lovie, but... come on, it's bedtime. Let's let them all figure it out for themselves, shall we?" He walks me down the hall, into my bedroom. Bruno follows, turning off into the dining room and flopping down on a cool patch of cement floor near the kitchen door, chin on paws, watching the night through the glass.

I go back to bed but I don't sleep very well, because the searchlight trucks keep driving past every half hour or so, and three or four times in the night I hear that same strange mechanical sputtering noise, clanky and fast and metallic, like pebbles poured into an oil drum, sometimes quite nearby. Just once, the noise abruptly chatters loudly from right outside the house, just up the street outside my bedroom window, as a jeep passes by searching the hedge on the other side of the road. The sound is accented by rapid flashes of soft yellow light, and I pretend to be asleep when Mummy comes in to touch my face and check that I'm all right.

The next day everything seems normal again; Daddy drives me to school on his way to work. Driving, we can't use the steep murram goat path up the hill by the old mission, and so we have to take the road, up towards the golf course, around to where it joins Circular Road, then back along to the school. On the way down Bugonga road, there is something lying in the monsoon ditch, partly obscured by weeds at the side of the road, just past our house; something that looks like a man, sleeping on his back. But he doesn't look comfortable, pitched at an odd angle, his arm across his face as though protecting himself from the sun. We pass too quickly for me to get a good look, and as we pass, I hear Daddy mutter a curse under his breath. Further up the road, almost on the golf course, there are two more men, lying still in the long grass. Both of them wear green army uniforms, one of them with a big dark stain across the back, as though he's been sweating.

"Who are they?" I ask Daddy.

"Soldiers," he says. "Obote's soldiers." He slows a little as he passes where they lie, speeding up a bit when he sees me trying to get a better look as well.

"What are they doing?" I ask, of the men lying stained and uncomfortable in the grass.

"They're having their resistance suppressed," he mutters.

"What?"

"Nothing, pet. I didn't say a thing."

Chapter 7

"It might not be such a bad thing," Uncle Anthony says to Daddy. They're playing chess, just like they normally do to pass the time in the evenings. "I mean, Obote kept the peace for the most part, but he was never exactly the most popular chap since he booted out the Kabaka. I mean, when Obote took over in '66, a lot of these people got left out in the cold. Amin's popular, he's a charismatic leader, and he's not your typical politician. He's a come up through the ranks as a common soldier. We never saw bodies at the side of the road when Obote was president, but that didn't mean political opponents didn't disappear into the night, am I right?" he says. Daddy's response is non-committal.

"Sounds like you're excusing all of this…" he waves his hand around, as though try to capture what we, the M'zungus, have all been seeing the last few days; furtive soldiers fleeing in the night, bodies in ditches, tanks, roadblocks. He doesn't finish the sentence, instead making his finger and thumb into a gun and firing into the side of his head.

"I'm not excusing anything," says the teacher. "I'm just saying that in the kind of environment that they've been living in for the last few years, there's bound to be a bit of… *unrest* until things settle down a bit. A couple of his kids are in my class, y'know," he says. "He's got about two dozen kids by three or four different wives. One of his daughters is a right terror."

However, both me know Amin is not exactly what you'd call qualified for running the country. The British, like the Romans, preferred to form new regiments using the native soldiers of the lands they'd pacified, to staff them with British officers, and then allow the native troops to be the hammer with which it ruled.

Amin had started out in the King's East African Rifles as a cook, and it was pretty widely known that he couldn't write and could barely read, and had moved up through the ranks simply by being the kind of vicious local bully-boy that British officers counted on to enforce discipline among the younger, weaker soldiers. But the fact was, the Sergeant he'd been under the British was not a self-proclaimed General. He now had twenty thousand rifles and the entire Ugandan army at his disposal, and he clearly had no compunctions at all when it came to moving aside anyone who stood in his way. Uncle Anthony summed it up;

"Shrewdness and brutality aren't exactly the hallmarks of good government. But it worked in Rome for nearly four hundred years, so why not here?"

There were other reasons that many people thought Amin might be a positive change for the country. His first major act as president, for example, was the return of the king; Amin claimed that he'd just been following Obote's orders when he'd blasted the Kabaka's palace to kingdom come in 1966. King Freddy had since died in exile; now, and with great pomp and ceremony, he brought the Kabaka's body back from England returned him to his people, where he could be interred in the great, thatched dome that was the tomb of the kings of the Baganda people.

The plane carrying the body arrived before a crowd of ecstatic Ugandans, Amin standing in full military parade dress on a reviewing stand draped with bunting and the Ugandan flag, somberly saluting the coffin as it was wheeled out the cargo doors and onto a decorated scissor-lift. An honor guard of Ugandan officers escorted the body somberly from the plane, the coffin draped in the black, yellow and orange of the Ugandan flag, to a hearse waiting at the end of a cortege of saluting soldiers.

King Freddie was entombed with his ancestors in the great thatched museum near Kampala. His genitals were pickled separately from the body, as was custom, like shriveled walnuts under glass, and displayed behind mirrors to prevent anyone from gazing directly upon them. The Baganda were beside themselves with joy at the return of their Kabaka. This despite the fact that King Freddie's jawbone could not be buried separately from the rest of his body, as was also customary; the English embalmers had had so difficult a time getting the mouth to stay closed for the flight that they'd sealed it shut with a generous dollop of Mastic before loading the body onto the plane.

Obote *never* had this kind of popular support, and it's the support of the people, said Uncle Anthony and those other optimists who saw Amin's takeover in a positive light, that makes for good government.

Amin was popular for other reasons as well. In the *Argus*, the *East African Standard*, and even the London *Daily Telegraph* brought in by BOAC and East African Airways pilots, a famous picture of Amin ran, showing him in standard, unadorned army fatigues, driving himself around Entebbe in an open topped jeep, a single armed soldier sitting helmeted in the back seat. He actually passed Daddy several times on the Kampala Road, headed to his palace on Nakiwogo hill. Amin even waved. This was almost unheard of for a world leader, especially the military dictator of an African country, and a far contrast to how Obote had always chosen to travel.

I'd seen Obote's car myself many times. A long, black, bulletproof limousine with armed police escorts front and rear, and police motorbikes *bruuumming* on ahead and *vruuuming* up behind. Obote went everywhere in that bloody limousine. Driving down the Kampala Road, all the M'zungus and everyone else on the road had to stay alert for the first sign of motorcycles approaching from either direction, so they could get the hell out of the way. The armed riders would force any car off the road, at any speed, if they failed to yield voluntarily.

But Amin drove himself almost everywhere, almost all the time. Jim Hollbrook, a friend of Daddy's, was one of the engineers brought in to maintain the landing approach gear at the airport. He was out at the tower late one night, checking the equipment when a great big African soldier, black as the night he drove out of, pulled up in a jeep and asked what Jim was doing on his airfield. *His* airfield, no less. It was Amin, of course, by himself, not a bodyguard or motorbike in sight. Jim introduced himself, told Amin that he was doing an inspection. Amin started asking questions, about how the landing and aircraft approach systems worked and about all the rest of the airfield operations. Evidently, Amin couldn't sleep and had gone for a drive. He'd seen the lights on while he was passing by and took it upon himself to do a spot inspection of the facilities. Eventually Amin thanked Jim for his time and drove off, back into the night.

Even HRH the Queen of England gave her tentative approval of the changeover, along with both the Americans and the Israelis. England didn't have much choice *but* to support the new regime, having invested so much in the country already. And the Israelis were a given, since half of the army and all of the Air Force pilots been trained by them. Israeli contactors had designed and built Entebbe Airport, and most of the military aircraft and the army's equipment was maintained by them. No government ever wants to give up such a potentially good customer. Tanzanian president Julius Nyerere wasn't very pleased about Amin's take-over, though. Nyerere had long been a supporter of Obote. Both he and Jomo Kenyatta of Kenya offered asylum to Obote until he could raise an army and get his chair back; Obote ended up in Tanzania, across Lake Victoria from Entebbe, where he waited with an ever-growing number of soldiers loyal to him, those who'd been lucky enough to slip across the lake or the border and dodge the searchlight trucks and the rifles.

About the killings, most M'zungus reckoned at least some of it was to be expected. There always had been a lot of tribal animosity. It had gone on for generations, long before a single European got here, and we supposed it would be going on long after we'd left. Once things settled down a bit, prevailing wisdom said, once the Obote loyalists realized that it was going to be a while before he came back, things will get a lot quieter, you'll see.

Others weren't so sure. The mob Daddy and Uncle Dave saw on the road torturing Obote's brother, just for having the wrong *name*, seemed to be a portend of worse things to come. Obote was a pretty common surname in the south. Stories circulated that anyone named Obote, even people not related, had started turning up missing. Officers, usually from tribes loyal to Obote's ruling party, were every day being denounced and turned over to the soldiers under their command for a bit of sport, before being taken out to the lake. *Sport*, in this case, is offered in the unkindest and most cruel sense of the word.

Things, we all assume, will begin to settle down here in a few days.

The first real sign that things are now different is the photographs on the wall in the shops and in the classrooms. Where the pictures of Obote had hung before the coup, there now hung the face of Idi Amin, smiling big and benevolently. From above the register at Kirefu's, from above the blackboard behind Mr. Trotter, on the back wall of the bar at the golf club next to the large portrait of the Queen, above the portraits of the past presidents of the club going back to before The War, Idi Amin Dada smiled down on us all.

The second sign, noticeable only by its absence, is the absolute disappearance of anything related to Obote; his picture, his name, *everything*. Amin himself at one time had often glibly shown support for his former leader by inspecting his troops wearing a T-shirt emblazoned with a large portrait of Obote, front and back, as a sign of his loyalty. But now, even the Apolo hotel in Kampala – the hotel sharing Obote's first name – has been renamed, literally overnight; it's now the Main Hotel; *Main*, strangely, rather than the Amin Hotel. Nobody is sure for a while if this isn't in fact a very large typographical mistake, and what the consequences might be for the person responsible if it is.

All other references to Obote in whatever context have disappeared completely. People – Africans – don't talk about him anymore, his name is never spoken aloud, never even mentioned. It's not just as if he'd never been president. Except for the occasional muttering by the M'zungus, it is as if he had never *been*.

The third sign of change, the third sign is the bodies. I can't help but overhear, nosy as I am, the rumors circulating among the M'zungus, that army trucks full of recently arrested prisoners from the jail – some, Obote's government officials but mostly, discredited soldiers – were being brought down to the lake, marched into the surf, and sprayed over with gunfire. Such stories are of course preposterous and easy to doubt, at first, just like the rumors of soldiers going house to house to rob and rape. Surely such things don't happen in a civilized country like Uganda? But it doesn't take too many days to find out that it's true – I'd already heard the machine gun fire that first evening, and not even known it.

I begin to hear that same staccato clanking of automatic weapons more often in the night, and I begin to associate that sound with the men I'd seen on that second morning after the coup, laying uncomfortably in the monsoon ditches at the side of the road. Just once or twice, at first, I might wake up and hear the *nyur-nyurh-nyhhurh* of a big army lorry passing the house in the late wee hours of the night, the headlights tracking up the cupboard doors, across the ceiling, the wedge of light arcing above my head as the big trucks trundle past. Off in the distance, across the banana fields, down where the murram road swings parallel to the lake, I might, if I were awake, hear a *pop* in the distance, soft, like a cat's paw patting the lid of a biscuit tin. The crickets would suddenly stop as they do if any sudden change comes over the night, their abrupt silence spooky and deafening. Three or four more soft tapping metallic pops, sometimes maybe twenty or thirty, a pause, another burst, then silence, until the truck comes back the other way. Sometimes I hear it all, if the wind is low and the night is still.

The sun will rise, I will go to school, and nobody will talk about the noises, not even children I know who live in Bugonga village, close in amongst the matoké plants and banana trees, close down by the edge of the lake. All week this has been going on, a truck, the gunfire, the truck returning the other way.

Then it's the weekend, and Mummy takes us to the swimming pool for our Saturday swim. As we pass the grey-brown sand at the lake's shore, as we approach the racks where the fishermen of Bugonga village dry their catch, I see someone lying in the short spiky grass that grows up through the sand. A man, lying face down and very still, with no shirt and no shoes and wet trousers, and black, glistening skin, with odd white patches his back, on his side, above one eye.

"Don't look," says Mummy, but I look anyway. "It's all right, you don't have to look."

"But I *want* to look," I tell her. She doesn't seem to understand just how *fascinating* the sight is. We drive on past, up the rise to where the road ends, and I'm still looking back down towards the prone figure, one arm just barely touching the water, half buried and sunken into the wet sand. The car turns left, out onto the promontory where the swimming pool sits overlooking the lake, and soon the man in the grass is out of sight. "Mummy, who was that?" I ask. But Mummy doesn't answer.

Daddy drives us all down there the next day with his camera on his lap, and there are even more of them. I see the bodies lying in a row, all barefoot, most shirtless. There are a dozen or more today, lying high on the beach where the fishing nets would normally be spread out to dry. Each man has a ragged white patch on the side of his head, and each at least one or two more on his back, or chest, or belly. Daddy stops and *snicks* off a picture, rolling the film through the camera with one hand while he shades the lens with the other, looking up from the hooded viewfinder just long enough to step around the figure closest to him, cranking the little winding handle, shooting off another one.

On Monday after school, Mummy and Auntie June drive down to the lake while Daddy is at work. Lulu, Rebecca and I sit quietly in the back of the car, and for once, I try not to make noise or draw attention to myself, because I know that the quieter I am, the better chance I have of Mummy forgetting I'm there. Mummy wants to stay in the car and have a look from there. Aunty June wants to go closer, so they walk out onto the sand. The bodies lie partly submerged, just a few feet from the verge of the murram road. Across from where we're parked are the rickety wooden drying racks hung with row after row of stinking desiccated Tilapia and perch and whatever else that had been pulled up in the fisherman's nets. The smelly fish market, Lulu calls it, even though it isn't a market at all, just rows of free-standing frames cobbled from tree limbs, across the road from the narrow strip of muddy beach. The stench of fish is so thick here I can usually smell it on my clothes long after we've driven past. That smell overpowers everything else on this road; even the bodies, their black skin broken out in patchy blotches the color of perch bellies, can't compete with it. If there's a smell to them, I don't notice it.

"Stay here, you three," Auntie June says brightly to me and Lulu and Rebecca. "Y'mummy and I will be right back." Lulu and Rebecca are playing with cutout dollies, folding the tabs of the little paper dresses over their little pasteboard shoulders, and completely absorbed in their game. I climb forward into the driver's seat, kneel up, rest my elbows on the window ledge and look at the row of dead men on the beach.

"Are you sure this is such a good idea, June?" says Mummy.

"Don't be silly. There's only us. And I don't think *they'll* mind," she says, pointing towards the bodies with a lacquered nail. She unstraps her sandals and walks out onto the beach. "Have you ever seen a dead body before?" I hear her say.

"At my Nannan's funeral. Not like this."

"What do you suppose happened?"

"What does it look like?" It seems obvious to me, from the ragged little puncture wounds on the arms and backs, that the men have been shot. What I want to know is *how* something like this can happen, how bodies can just come to be left lying around as though nobody wants them.

One man's arm waves back and forth as the short waves break, the water washing his white bleached wounds just a little too late for it to do him any good. It would be easy to believe that they might be playing, perhaps, men bathing and clowning and lying in the surf as me and my friends sometimes do for fun, relaxing and letting the water tug and tow, pretending we're shipwreck survivors or pieces of driftwood or crocodiles. But then a short, hard wave rolls up, straight into the face on one of the bodies, and it doesn't flinch as I do when that happens to me, it doesn't sit up and blow water from its nose and blink its eyes at the sight of the lost desert island on which it has pitched up. It doesn't come to its senses after its long ordeal at sea, as we do in our games. Instead, their chests are still, their bellies large, their skin shiny-black like a greased rubber inner tube splashed with whitewash and all plumped up with water. They never flinch when the waves come in, and it is that one fact that makes it clear to me what *dead* really means.

"Oh, God," says Mummy, noticing something even more shocking. "Look at that." She points at one of the bodies, a thick-set man with skin a shade lighter than that of the others. "All his fingers are missing! Oh, Jesus. We shouldn't be here, Junie, we should go." I of course immediately sit up for a better look. I've never seen a man with no fingers before, not even a dead one.

101

"Alright, we'll go in a minute then," Auntie June says. But she doesn't move. After a pause, Mummy asks,

"D'you think they'll... I don't know, arrest anyone for doing this? I mean, murder's still a crime, right?"

"I don't know. The way the newscasters are putting it, these chaps are the ones who've been arrested. They are the criminals. This is *their* idea of justice, I suppose. The army, I mean."

"Please, June, let's get back in the car. I don't like being out here at all."

"Look, love, this has got nothing to do with us! We're M'zungus, we're English! This is their business, not ours." From my perch in the back of the VW, I'm not sure she sounds convinced herself. I may be young but even *I* know that seeing dead people – *machine gunned* dead people – lying on a beach in the middle of the day isn't what would commonly fall under anyone's description of normal. Auntie June goes on. "Admittedly, this is a little... stranger than what we're used to, but..." We all hear it together, hear a familiar *nyur-nyurh-nyhhurh* coming up the road behind us. A big lorry rounds the corner from Bugonga Road, and for a moment, I think it might be an army truck bringing another load of prisoners. *I wonder if they'll let us watch,* I think to myself.

"Oh, shit," I hear Mummy say, which is thrilling; it's always so much fun to hear grownups slip up and swear in front of us. Dead bodies and swear-words; I can hardly wait to see what happens next.

As the lorry approaches they back away from the bodies towards the car, and I watch as it pulls around us and drives up a short way ahead of where we're parked. Two men get out of the cab, both of them dressed in Entebbe City Council overalls and wellington boots. For the most part, they ignore the two M'zungu women; they have a job to do and like most council workers everywhere, they plan to simply get on with it. They tie rags around their faces, pull folded tarpaulins out of the back of the lorry, and slowly, begin rolling up the bodies in canvas. They pour something onto them from dented silver jerry cans – even from where I'm sitting this far away, even over the cloying fish-pong, I can smell the sharp metallic bite of what's in the cans.

"Disinfectant," says Mummy. "Smells like the hospital."

The council men heave the bundles into the back of the lorry like rolls of carpet. Their job done, they stop, shake out cigarettes from a pack, and are now watching the two M'zungu *memsahib* standing by their car at the edge of the beach. They don't speak, they don't ask questions. They just stand, staring at the women.

"Come on," says Auntie June. I wonder if she feels like I do, suddenly aware of how utterly out of place we must be, two unescorted young M'zungu women in short summer dresses standing on the edge of the road, three young children sitting in a car, all of us watching workers dispose of bullet-ridden bodies at a secluded lakeside beach. Mummy nods, turns away, and they walk quickly back towards us.

In the rear view mirror, I watch the council workers still standing there, smoking and watching the Volkswagen, until we're out of sight.

"Did you see the look on his face?" says Mummy.

"The council chap? What about it?"

"He just looked so... blank, like he was loading sacks of coal or something. Like it was just a job. Could you have done something like that?"

"Just forget about it, Joanie. It's got nothing to do with us." There is silence for a while, then Mummy speaks.

"Where d'you think they're taking them?" she asks. Auntie June shrugs.

"Probably off somewhere for burial, I expect. What else would they do with them? Look, I told you, just forget about it. It's their business, nothing to do with us." Mummy nods, but from the look on her face, I don't think she can forget about it.

103

Neither can I. I can't forget the bodies, nor can I forget the blank, disinterested look on the faces of the men loading them.

While it was a novelty in those first few days, it doesn't take more than a week or two for life to become normal again – not just for me, but for all of us. The definition of *normal* simply changed. It became normal, now, for all the M'zungus, adult and children alike, to look for corpses. To me, it is no different than looking for chameleons in the hibiscus hedge, or elephant poo at the side of the road. Most often I see them – the bodies – at that same spot, less than a mile from our house, on the short step of a beach by the lakeshore by the road leading to the Entebbe swimming pool. I see them there most often because that's most often where we pass closest to the lake But there are other spots; out in the game parks, where the leopards and hyenas make seeing them uncommon, at least whole ones. Or in the quiet little back-waters of the many little bays around the lake, where they bob in the current, a scurf of leaf litter and greasy detergent foam surrounding a glistening black island of skin.

It becomes part of our normal routine; on the way to the pool, Mummy pulls over to the side of the road and Daddy gets out his Hasselblad and clicks off picture after picture of the men swaying in the small surf at the water's edge. Usually they're military men – I know this because of their trousers, green army issue. They wear no shoes, no shirts. Sometime they're in plain black slacks instead of uniforms. Then, they could be just about anybody – a junior minister who had once said something that President Amin didn't like, perhaps, or a tailor or shoemaker who happened to have the wrong surname, or have been denounced by an angry customer as an Obote sympathizer, or whose pretty wife had caught the eye of a recently-promoted officer. Whoever they'd been, by the time we see them, they're all just quiet dead men, washing themselves in the surf.

Every few days, the council workers come in their lorry, cover their mouths and noses, and douse the bodies with industrial disinfectant from five-gallon cans. They roll the bodies in tarps or canvas ground cloths, load them onto the back of the truck, and then they're gone.

We never know from one day to the next when there will be another collection of corpses for Daddy to photograph. One day, we'll drive down the road and there will be rows of boats pulled up on the beach, low wooden dugouts with tiny outboard motors bolted precariously to their stern. Families of shining dark people, smiling with such white teeth, will wave at us, the amusing M'zungu family as we pass, the littlest children chasing along behind the car whooping and laughing with delight. The people of Bugonga village seem so busy and happy as they unload and carefully fold the long nets, untangling fish as they work, washing them and slitting them open with impossibly big pangas for so small a fish, gutting them with the sweep of a finger and hooking them on sticks to line up on the racks for drying. Then the next day the beach, the drying, stinking fish, the distant cluttered huts of Bugonga village, will all be silent, the men out on their boats, the women working in town as house-girls or aiyas. The tall tawny grass pulses with the *skrit* and *skree* of grasshoppers, and there will be a man, or two, or five, or what used to be men, part-way buried in the sand of the beach, arms waving slowly at the sky. And tomorrow they'll be gone again, doused in disinfectant and heaved into the back of a council lorry, but it never once occurred to me to ask: *why?*

Members of Obote's elite, his supporters, those rewarded with rank and prestige for supporting his actions in '66, and loyal party members, mostly from the Acholi and Langi tribes, they all went first. Amin found them, knew who they were, had been keeping secret lists of names, and had waited *years* for the right time to move. When his chance came, these enemies were loaded

105

three or four or thirty at a time into the back of a three-ton army lorry, driven to some dark beach or game park where there would be no one around to see, and shot. *Sprayed* might better describe what was done, as accuracy or efficiency were not exactly necessary or even desirable. Often, they were tortured a little first, for the entertainment of the troops who'd once served under them; beaten, burned, raped, castrated; fingers and toes amputated, they were stripped of everything but ragged trousers, walked knee-deep into the surf, and shot, *pop, pop, pop-op-op*.

"But they've been killing each other for years," say the M'zungus. "The Baganda have had blood feuds with the Acholi since God was a lad, the Hutu and Tutsi down on the border have been at it for centuries, with pangas and spears when they haven't got guns. What the bloody hell are *we* supposed to do about it? It's not our problem." That's what the grownups say when they talk grownup talk, at the sailing club when the boats are all moored at their buoys and pulled up into their sheds, and they're sitting at the bar to drink beer and smoke cigarettes and play liar dice.

"Besides, Jesus, what can we do? Who's to stop the soldiers from coming up to *our* front door and marching *us* out next. Who'd ever know? Keep our mouths shut, I say. A pair of shoes by the side of the road, your name listed in The Observer as missing, whereabouts unknown... They're already talking about a curfew, to keep us from seeing what goes on out there every night." This, the shoes, became a common symbol for the army and Amin's takeover. A person would be walking in the wrong place at the wrong time, give the wrong answer to the wrong soldier, have the wrong last name or be from the wrong tribe or clan... the following day all that would be left was their shoes, left at the side of the road, removed upon arrest. They'd be bound, stuffed in the boot of a black Mercedes, and their shoes left at the roadside as a warning. An unoccupied pair of shoes meant another person would never be seen alive again.

106

"Amin's renamed Government House his Military Command Center; that should tell you *his* thinking in all of this. And what about his State Research Bureau? SRB headquarters is across the street from the Israeli embassy, and the Israelis have already lodged a formal complaint. They can't work for the sound of screaming and gunfire coming from the basement at all hours of the day and night!" That's what they say at the golf club, when the sun has set and the gay lights are all on in the bar, and me and the rest of the children come in from swinging on the swings to eat a bag of crisps and drink a lemonade.

Curfew. In my mind I see a roadblock of the type they're fond of here, a white wooden pole pivoted near a guardhouse, an oil barrel filled with stones or cement as a counterweight. Jagged steel caltrops welded from angle-iron sit like giant jacks barring the shoulder, and soldiers walking around with their guns out, making people wait while the guards look serious and very cross.

"We're all right, though. They invited us, after all. They shalln't muck about with *us*, we're *British*."

No one seems to have noticed that they *already* muck us about. At the top of Bugonga Road, where it comes together with Airport Road and joins to become Kampala Road, there's a permanent roadblock set up. There are roadblocks like this all over the place. Coming and going, the soldiers always stop our cars – those belonging to the M'zungus, and Indians, or anyone who has a car, for that matter – and always take a look inside to see if there's anything worth having.

"What do you have for me today?" they'll ask, resting their arms on the rifles slung across their chests. *Wat dooyoo hiv foa mi?* They always walk away with something; a jar of jam, a bar of soap, a few 'spare' shillings. There's always *something* in the car they'll ask for, and something they take as well anyway.

"It's getting a bit silly," Mummy says to Daddy at the dinner table. "It's getting to the point where I have to buy an extra packet of biscuits or a spare bag of sugar every time I'm at

Kirefu's, because every time they stop me on the way home, one of the soldiers will have a look in my shopping bag and say, 'I like this'. I mean, what choice to I have but to offer it to them?" *Ay lyk thees*, the soldiers say, and what the soldiers like, the soldiers take. Daddy starts laughing.

"Oh, so what? What difference does it make if we have to buy a couple of extra packets of biscuits every week? They're paying me a bloody fortune, love. We can afford biscuits for the whole bloody army, if it makes life easier! The poor buggers don't get paid shit anyway. This is how they make their living. Amin pays them in whiskey and transistor radios, for Christ's sake. Stop worrying. They're not going to hurt you!" But sometimes, when Mummy is getting a ten shilling note out of her bag, or reaching over the seat to get them the bottle of cooking oil they've pointed to, they smile tightly at me with cold eyes. They smile like boys do when someone is about to get smacked across the fingers with a stick-sword; they grip their rifles with both hands as they wait, and as we drive away, they point them at the car, laughing, their fingers on the trigger. Though this isn't unusual - their fingers are *always* on the trigger.

We drive up to Jinja one Sunday, on a family outing, a "Sunday Run," Daddy calls it.

"Jinja is where they make all our electricity," Daddy tells me. "I thought we'd go up to see how they do it." At Jinja is a huge concrete dam, built near the spot where Speke first discovered the Nile flowing out of Lake Victoria. Standing on the lookout area, the lake placid and quiet behind me, I see the water from the falls-side of the dam, blasting like thunder through several huge outlets. "The water spins giant propellers inside the dam and makes electricity," Daddy says. I think of the toy windmills I was given at the seaside as a child, paper pinwheels on sticks, spinning in the North Sea wind, and assume he must be teasing me. "See?" He points to the tall steel towers marching off into the distance, at the wires leading down into a large building at the far end of the dam. "That's the power station."

"Nu-uh. Where does the water go after that?" I ask.

"Uh-huh," he says, "Honest. This used to be called Ripon Falls. There used to be a great big waterfall here, until they built this dam. See that down there? He points to the ribbon of water far below us. "That's the Nile. You've heard of the River Nile, haven't you?" Of course I have. Everybody knows about the River Nile, about how it runs all the way up through Egypt, and how the Pharaohs all hunt crocodiles in it and Moses parted it when him and Jesus led the Israelis out of bondage because it started raining frogs for forty days and forty nights. I nod.

"They taught us about it in bible stories at school." I look back and forth, amazed at the contrast between the lake, calm and huge as a sea on one side, and on the other, the great spuming outflow blasting out of the middle of the concrete dam face, churning below like cream in a mixing bowl.

Walking over to the dam's lake side, I see down below, out of sight from the lookout point, a long floating island of detritus and garbage running the whole length of the dam face. In amongst the trash and wads of discarded clothing are several long, brown rubbery objects. The more I look the more of them I notice, floating all along the face of the dam, bobbing and moving, some bumping others under the surface as the pressure of the water being drawn into the intakes deep beneath the surface stirs the seemingly calm lake. I suddenly recognize what they are, and how many of them there are. They're men, or the bodies of men, no shoes and no shirts, most of them wearing just the tattered remnants of trousers, and some of them with patches of that dead, fish-belly white visible on their skins. What had looked at first glance like a long raft of spilled laundry and inner tubes are in fact bodies, more than I've seen before in the lake at any one time, almost too many to count.

109

They bob around one another like driftwood in the currents and eddies below, thick enough to walk across the face of the dam if I'd have wanted. Here and there, long sleek shapes move among them, which I realize is part of what is helping to stir them around, rolling some over, bumping others out of the way.

"What are those?" I ask Daddy, pointing at one of the moving shapes. He stares for a moment, then understands.

"Crocodiles, pet," he says, "They're crocodiles." I stare, fascinated. I like crocodiles because they give Tarzan something to wrestle, and there are plenty of them down there. Certainly, there are enough to make any Pharaoh happy. They're big and fat, basking on the far bank, cruising through the shallows, moving into the mass of corpses before rolling suddenly under the surface with sudden splash, leaving a momentary open space in the water where a body had once been. Mummy comes over to where we're standing. She jerks her head towards a group of soldiers who have driven up at the far end of the dam.

"Come on," she hisses quietly, giving Daddy an irritated shake of her head before sweeping up Lulu and I like goslings and walking back towards the Volkswagen. "Before those buggers notice us." Even now, the soldiers are starting to pay attention to us, nudging one another, pointing. They haven't moved yet, but with Ugandan soldiers it's best not to wait around to find out if they're going to take an interest.

"But I want to watch the crocodiles," I protest. For the briefest second, I think that Mummy might slap me.

Chapter 8

You'd never have known it – it wouldn't have seemed possible to me – but apparently, just weeks after the coup, it turns out there are spies amongst us! Real live spies, just like in Daddy's Ian Fleming books, with the pictures of guns and flick-knives and black lacey knickers on the covers.

It's the Israelis, we're told on the news; they're all spies, all of them. The engineers who designed and built the airport, the military advisors who train the army and air force. And not just them but their families too, on holiday, roasting slick with suntan cream around the pool at the Lake Victoria Hotel. The Israeli businessmen off spending their money on safari in the game parks, and the odd few who come as the guest of a member to race at the sailing club or play at the golf club. Even the little Jewish boys from Lake Victoria school with their special packets of Kosher milk, they *must* be spies, because President Amin said so.

The Israelis, Amin reasoned, built his airport; they built his air force, they know its weaknesses, and the weaknesses of his army. But the main reason he decided they're all spies has to do with weapons. An army needs weapons; not just guns and bullets, but tanks and planes and mines and great big pieces of field artillery. An army needs *all* of these things, if it expects to be taken seriously. Amin is a soldier, he wants a strong army, and he needs weapons to make it strong. The government of Israel, however, has decided that it doesn't think it's a good idea anymore to sell their weapons or send military engineers and advisors to Uganda, especially not with President Amin getting so chummy to his new friend Mr. Gadhafi, who they don't much like, and who doesn't much like them.

So perhaps he found out they were all spies from Mr. Gadhafi. The President had gone to Libya to see Mr. Gadhafi after his Russian MiGs started crashing and all of his tanks started breaking, after Russia told him they didn't think it was a good idea to sell him any replacements, since it was Mr. Obote who'd bought them for him in the first place. Mr. Gadhafi told him that the tanks and planes were old and used and not very good to begin with, which was the reason that the Russians had even sold them to President Obote.

Perhaps it was because President Amin had just now remembered that he was, in fact, a Muslim, or at least his Granddad had been a Muslim, and he decided that he thought he ought to try and be a Muslim too, just like Mr. Gadhafi. Perhaps they were all spies because Mr. Gadhafi told him that if President Amin didn't send all the Israelis home, he wouldn't help Uganda get new planes, and tanks, and guns, to replace all his old broken ones. Most especially, perhaps the President decided they're spies because Israel's very good friend, Queen Elizabeth of England, finally came out and said that She didn't like the way President Amin's State Research Bureau keep shooting people and leaving them lying so untidily around the lake.

But regardless, one day the President comes on the wireless and on the television, and says that if anyone has a passport from Israel, they have two weeks to leave the country or they'll either be put in prison as criminals or shot dead as spies.

Daddy has some friends that he met when he first arrived in Entebbe, Israeli men who are trainers for the Ugandan army. They're the ones who teach the Ugandan soldiers how to drive the tanks and fly the Fouga Magister jets and the V-tailed Russian MiG 15 and MiG 17 fighters, and how to shoot their rifles without hitting themselves in the foot, which, being fond of waragi, they tend to do a lot.

Uncle Ari is a big man, with a chest like a barrel of bricks and a long thick mustache, who waves his arms in wide expansive gestures when he talks. He has an thick accent, different from the other accents I hear, the African and the English and the Scottish and the Indian.

He'd been a tank commander in the war. Not *The* War, the one that Drandrad won, the one against Mr. Hitler and the Germans, but another war which didn't have a real name but was very short, because it was over in just six days, not six years like Drandrad's war. I think, it can't have been a very exciting war, only lasting for six days, but Uncle Ari talks about it all the time. Sometimes he cries, a big loud man who cries when he talks about his friends who died in the war, and then laughs again between tears, and tells stories about the Arab soldiers who took their shoes off and left them in piles so that they could run away just that little bit faster.

Uncle Ari has some friends who are in the Israeli Air Force, who come over to the house in crisp blue uniforms for drinks. They're here to teach the Ugandan Air Force to fly the MiG 17 fighters that the Russians had so very kindly sold to President Obote and which now belong to President Amin. They talk, and all laugh about the time they put on an air show at the airport; President Obote had ordered his proud Ugandan Air Force pilots – all three of them – to perform a fly-by in formation. The Ugandan pilots were very frightened of flying too close to each other, say the Israeli pilots; they wouldn't come within a half mile of each other's wing tips, which doesn't look very impressive if you're on the ground watching an air show. So in order to perform the fly-by that President Obote had ordered, the Israeli pilots had to blacken their faces and walk out to the waiting jet fighters well away from all the people who had come to watch. Pretending to be the Ugandan Air Force pilots, they mounted their aircraft a good distance away from the crowd, and as they flew by in formation, the commentator assured the audience that

113

these brave Ugandan pilots controlled the skies, and would keep them all safe from harm.

I go with Daddy to the airport to watch the real Air Force practice and train. There's a big place in the grass alongside the runway where the red dirt is blackened and charred, a low spot filled in with fresher, darker earth. Daddy asks Uncle Ari what had happened. Uncle Ari laughs his big laugh and says,

"A few months before you arrived here, one of the Ugandan pilots was practicing aerobatics and came in low across the runway. The stupid bastard did a barrel roll and then went to ascend. But he forgot that he was upside down, and when he pulled back on the stick..." Uncle Ari takes his hand, palm up, dives his fingers towards the ground; he makes a rumbling wet *boom*, his thick arms rolling up explosively into the air. "They called in an investigator who told them what had happened, that the pilot must have forgotten that when inverted, the plane's controls would be inverted also; that up was down, down was up, yes? But when the official Air Force report was released, the Argus and the other newspapers said it was sabotage – that someone had inverted the controls. Sabotage! Ha!" He laughs loudly, and Daddy has to laugh too. It doesn't sound like sabotage to me. I just sounds stupid. But that was before President Amin discovered that all the Israelis were spies.

The Israelis, the families and children in school and the workers and soldiers who had been training the army, all pack up what they can carry in their suitcases. All the M'zungus cry when we say good-bye, and Uncle Ari hugs Mummy and shakes Daddy's hand, and all the Israelis let the other M'zungus buy what they can't fit on the aeroplane with them – their furniture, their hi-fi sets, their boats, their cars.

And that was that. Two weeks after the President's announcement, there is no more Uncle Ari, and no more need for Kosher milk after assembly.

From then on I don't see any Israelis at the Lake Victoria Hotel, shiny and baking brown around the pool. After that though, I do see a lot more Arab men, in long white robes and dishtowels with plaited ropes on their heads like they just got finished playing shepherds in the Christmas play. They sit in the shade, not in the sun like the Israelis, their dishtowels pulled across their faces. They move them out of the way to drink their beer. They drink lots and lots of beer, and all the grown-up M'zungus find this very funny, because apparently their god doesn't think beer is very nice stuff and can make you go to hell if you drink it. I don't think beer is very nice either, but not so much that I'd make them go to hell for it. Waragi on the other hand is a whole other story.

The Libyan men aren't friendly like the Israeli families were; they don't have plump wives or children my age to play with, and they have hard, mean eyes, even when they smile, and teeth like white daggers in their dark brown faces. They smell like spices and sweat, like they haven't had a bath or even a good long swim for a very long time. I don't go near them very much; Mummy doesn't even have to tell me not to.

Apart from that, after the coup... well, life just *went on*. One might think that such violent upheaval changes the world in some way, or at least the way we look at it. But in truth, it doesn't. Life just *goes on*. The sun comes up each morning; there is work to do, for Mummy, for Daddy, for Jeliati. School, work, day, night; the ones whose time it is to die will end up one morning on the beach, but for everyone else... life in Africa just keeps on happening, all around us.

Chapter 9

In Uganda there is no twilight, not as you'd notice. Entebbe sits within a half mile of the geographic dividing line that is the equator, and each evening, bright day becomes black, black night in minutes, every day, at the same time, without fail, year round. The paltry, earth-bound lights of Entebbe – a few feeble street lamps, a village fire, the lights of the M'zungu houses and others wired with electricity, the smoky bent tin oil-lamp glow of the huts that are not – the lights of Entebbe aren't enough to drown out the stars, and the night sky is a solid blaze of them. So many, so bright, so close together, that picking out an individual cluster becomes a challenge. The fizzy tapered sherbet of stars at the northern horizon broadens and thickens into the rich white band of the Milky Way, then thins and dims, just a little, to where they end in a clean black stripe at the dark horizon of the lake, and in a ragged fringe at the hedges on either side of the garden.

Every morning at the same time each day, black, black night becomes sudden bright day, almost before you notice it, the air wonderfully cool for just a little while. The sun is already hot by seven, the light clear and sharp as though focused through a lens and decanted through crystal. The daytime smells are different from the night-blooming smells after sunset – wood smoke and frangipani, as the sun laps the moisture from the air. The crisp live smell of grasses dance with and soften the warm rust smells of the dirt. The day-smells differ from those of the night in both direction and intensity – sweet drifting night breezes are harder to place, because I can never see just where they're coming from, or see what growing thing it is that's in bloom.

116

I wake up early, the sun just coming up but the air already thick with light reflecting off the clear underside of the sky. It's Sunday, we'll be going to the sailing club today, or for a drive to the Botanical Gardens, or to the big concrete circle that marks the equator, on the road running west, out past the airport. Or to a game park – one of Daddy's Sunday runs, but we can't go until Mummy and Daddy get up. On Sunday, they like to have a lie in. Their bedcovers rustle behind their closed door. Daddy breaths hard and sometimes Mummy moans or calls out to God in her sleep. It is Sunday, after all.

Lulu and I are in the living room. We've pulled all the pillows and blankets and sheets off both our beds;

"Put that cushion over here," I tell her, "And tuck the roof in behind the settee." She does whatever I tell her to do, because I'm her brother and her champion.

She's only two years younger than me, but Mummy and Daddy still occasionally have to ask me what she's saying. I always know exactly what it is she's asking for, a mouthful of misshapen sounds that became a biscuit or a strawberry or a cup of tea with milk and sugar when they ask me, *What did she say, love?* She still calls me Nem, out of habit. The warren of sheets and pillowcases, and the upturned armchair in the corner, have now become our castle. Mummy and Daddy will be delighted – what clever children, they will say, how wonderful that we never thought to make the living room this much fun; we should keep it like this always! That's what they'll say, I'm sure of it.

We run down the hallway to their door, and I knock. I hear rustling, a phlegmy cough from Daddy.

"When are you getting up?" I ask.

"Soon, lovie," says Mummy.

"When's soon?" Grownups have words for everything, that say nothing, none of which I understand. They say "Next Weekend" when what they really mean is "Not tomorrow and not tomorrow and not tomorrow but the next day."

"When's *soon*?" I ask again. "How soon's *soon*?"

"Go away," says Daddy softly, and I hear Mummy say, not to us but to him,

"Davie!" and she giggles, like she does when pretending to scold him after he's said something funny that she thinks she shouldn't laugh at but does and wishes she'd said herself. "Go outside and play," she calls to us.

"We'll be up in a minute. Get Jeliati t'make y'some breakfast," Daddy says, but it's Sunday, Jeliati's day off. Lulu and I both sigh and mooch back past our castle towards the kitchen.

There is no movement outside the house. It's still cool outside the kitchen door, in the shade of the house against the garage wall. There's a certain delicious crispness that will only last only until the sun warms everything enough to get a breeze going, bringing with it the heat, which will radiate off everything. Both the top and bottom half of Jeliati's door are still closed. She may be sleeping, but more likely she left before sunrise to walk into Entebbe, to catch the bus back to her village for the day. Bruno looks up at me from where he lays next to his water dish on the steps, but he doesn't get up either.

The fat Fenai hang in the tree on their thick pale green stalks and I think about getting sticks and trying to knock one down, but remember the trouble I'll get into if I do. I halfheartedly throw a stick anyway, just in case one fat pod happened to be ready to fall and the breeze from a passing branch might give it the extra push it needed, but it doesn't.

We make tea for Mummy and Daddy. I lay some Arrowroot biscuits on a plate and eat one, and give one to Lulu. She holds it in both hands and nibbles it.

"I na mouse," she says seriously, gnawing. "Lut amee, Nem, I na mouse," smiling up at me. Neither of us have ever seen a mouse, not for real. Only in storybooks. I've seen puff adders and Gabon vipers and foot-long red-bellied cockamander lizards; I've seen geckos that can run up walls, and Nile crocodiles grinning invitingly under muddy water. I've watched tiny pointy-horned dik-diks and sleek-coated otters, and I've stroked the slime on a baby hippopotamus's back. From hand to hand I've passed chameleons that changed from bright green to pale orange to as dark as Daddy's beard, and fed groundnuts to Colobus monkeys shrieking black and white in the trees. I've walked up on gazelles that spooked and leaped sideways straight over parked cars from a standing start. I've seen an elephant sit on the bonnet of a Fiat and squash it flat to the ground. I've seen Nile perch break the surface in the lake while I was skiing, great fish big enough to swallow me whole. And I've seen dead men, bloating in the sun, waterlogged on the beach, melting into the bush, more of them than I can remember. But I've never seen a mouse.

"Mummy, we've made tea for you," I call through the door. "D'you want us to bring it in?"

"Ooh, thank you lovie," she says sweetly. "How wonderful! Just leave it outside, Mummy'll come and get it in just a minute." Daddy is breathing hard in the background and the sheets rustle as we go back to build some more rooms on to the castle.

There is no spring in Uganda, nor autumn, not as you'd notice, and certainly nothing resembling winter; just a perpetual, if changeable, summer. On occasion, bright day one morning may instead be grey solid clouds to the horizon, and then The Rains come, *The Rains* plural, capitalized, a season unto themselves, soaking, drenching, torrential rains that will fill the monsoon ditches; the Rains are what the monsoon ditches are there for. Through them, murram-red rivers will spill down the sides of the road, run off the edges of the driveways, flow around the perimeter of the gardens in a never ending race back to the lake. Most days I can see so far out onto the lake that I can follow the curvature of the earth, but on those occasions that it rains during the day, the water comes in sheets so thick I can't even see down to the hedge.

There are actually two seasons, the Wet and the Dry, that change and trade places throughout the year. Christmas is dry, Easter wet, but the rains then are usually polite enough to wait until after dark before they come. Then, within an hour of the sun's rising the next morning, you'd never have known a drop had fallen. While school is out for the long summer holiday, it is dry, but by Guy Fawke's day in November, the sound of water rushing off the eaves will be what lulls me to sleep, and not the grasshoppers and crickets and singing frogs. In the dry we wear plimsolls to school and flip-flops the rest of the time. In the Wet, we wear flip-flops all the time, because plimsolls will simply rot off your feet. The dry is hot, as is the wet, but the wet is steamy, close and organic, and the garden floods as the ditches dug around the perimeter the house channel all the water away.

There is no spring, nor an autumn, and seasons are named for the rains or the lack of them, and for other things; on the horizon, a black cloud like the smoke of burning tires rises up off the water and hangs low over the surface of it. It spreads, moving closer.

I stand watching the cloud, and Daddy comes outside. "Come back in the house, Sunshine." Daddy says calmly, "Come on, quickly now. Close the windows. Bruno! Come on boy, inside." The dog trots in off the verandah, his clicking nails muffled by the woven palm rug in front of the settee. Daddy's face is concerned, though not frightened, and I do as he tells me when he says to go and get some old towels from the linen cupboard, and some blankets. "Lay them around the bottom of the doors... yes, like that, push them into the cracks." The cloud is closer now, thick and low to the water. Mummy looks out at it, chewing her lip. Daddy puts his arms around her. "'S'all right," he says, smiling at her, "They won't get in."

"What is it?" I ask.

"Lake flies," he says. I look up at him, relieved.

"Flies? Is that all?" I look over at the fruit bowl, see the slow moving halo of fruit flies that perpetually hang over it. "Why do I have to come inside?" He just looks at me and smiles.

"You'll see in just a minute."

Every so often, when the temperature of the lake is just right, and the moon is just so, the lake flies hatch in the mud at the bottom, out in the deep water. They float to the surface, vast rafts of them, and rise off the water, mating and laying eggs, millions of eggs, millions of millions of eggs, which sink slowly down and settle into the mud, ready for next time. Then the cloud of flies, millions of flies, millions of millions of tiny black specks buzzing and circling, rise like a curtain of smoke and move with the wind to die. If the winds blow towards the Entebbe peninsula, everyone goes indoors.

That's all they do, the flies; they die. They don't bite, or sting, or eat, or ruin, or despoil, or carry off small English children. They just die, but by the thousands, by the millions, by the hundred millions, in thick, choking clouds, making drifts against doorjambs and windowsills, against the concrete foundation, in the space where the reddish watery stains begins creeping up the bottoms of the exterior walls, against the tires of the Jensen, on the roof of the Volkswagen, around the roots of the frangipani tree.

Outside, no matter what the time of day, the air is a glittering midnight with lake flies, fresh waves like billowing black cinders moving past the house to die in the street, next door at Uncle Dave's house, to die in sooty drifts and fertilize the soil of the banana patches and cassava fields. That's all they do, is drift, and die. But there are so many of them; stray dogs, children, unprepared adults caught out in the open, anyone caught outside could smother, could choke, could find it impossible to breath, and would die too. Tomorrow, Mummy will sweep up the dead flies with a dustpan and brush, small and black and brittle, *scritting* along the cement floor in front of the stiff wooden broom,

121

crisp like little burned cornflake crumbs rubbed together in my hand.

Sun, rain and occasionally, flies – these are the things that mark the only real seasons of Africa. Who happens to be running the country, or who happens to be standing in front of a bullet on a given day, these things are really secondary. The flies will come, and the rains, no matter who's in charge.

Chapter 10

I walk through the banana trees with my friends from Bugonga village, the air hot and thick and sour. The trunks *thwock* hollow and fleshy when we smack them with sticks, and peel away in long sticky strips that lie rotting around their punky stalks. We swing our sticks at a low hanging leaves and at the moldering corrugated stumps, like rolls of wet cardboard planted in the dirt.

The village smells of wood smoke and of starchy white matoké steaming between layers of banana leaves over the charcoal braziers, and of goat-meat stews swimming with foamy yellow grease. There's a pleasantly warm and sour smell of people working. Women move around slowly, with big wobbly bottoms wrapped up in busy yellow and black kitangi dresses; with rolled headscarves over their hair they carry jerry cans of water, full, and bundles of wood bigger than themselves balanced on their heads, without using their hands.

The distinctive smell of pombe drifts out of the huts, yeasty and sour, and men sit in doorways sipping the thick maize beer from china mugs like it was tea. The walls of the houses, huts really, are plastered mud over wattled sticks, with grass and palm frond roofs, or tin and tarpaper if the owner is a little better off.

Chickens *pockpock* around, and cockerels call out now and again, *aar-ga-gaaar*! Women sweep the hard-packed dirt floors of their huts with short hand-brooms made from the tawny grass that grows everywhere the banana trees do not. Some of the men work at jobs in Entebbe, as shamba boys, some as porters or waiters at the Lake Victoria Hotel, or loading and unloading

123

luggage out at the airport. Some, like the men who work for Daddy at Government Printing, wear a dress shirt and tie to work every day, taking it off every afternoon when they return home to their hut, hanging the shirt and trousers carefully before putting on shorts, a kitangi robe, an old T-shirt.

But most of these men work on the lake, setting nets back and forth to catch the schools of tilapia and perch, *putt-putting* along ahead of a tiny wired-together outboard motor. They sing as they work, repetitive chanting songs that are echoed from hut to hut, boat to boat, and work is done in time to the chant; the sweeping, the sewing, the drawing of nets, the pounding of tall wooden pestles being thumped into tall hollow mortars, mashing hulled groundnuts or millet into a speckled buttery paste, to be eaten with matoké and stew. The singing is how all the real work gets done; the lifting or moving, hauling boats to the water or nets up the beach, the loading and unloading, the pushing, the pulling – all are accompanied by the sound of African voices in unison.

Beyond the village is the rolling dun grass, the color of lions and hand-brooms, running downhill to the soccer field. We stamp our feet as we walk the paths through the grass, to scare the well-hidden snakes before we get to them. We see them darting across the path, grass snakes and puff adders, as anxious to avoid us as we are to avoid them.

"Are there snakes in Uganda?" Mummy had asked, when Daddy first told her we'd be coming here. He didn't know, so later he looked it up in Drandrad's encyclopedia.

"Hmm," he said quietly to Drandrad. "It says here that the area around Lake Victoria contains the highest concentration of poisonous snakes in the world."

"Whatever y'do, don't tell my daughter that," Drandrad told him. "You'd never get 'er out o'Sheffield!"

My friends and I race one another down across the soccer field, past the swampy papyrus shallows to the water's edge. It's not really a beach here even though that's what we call it, just a wide and mucky grey-brown shore more dirt than sand. There are muddy flats, and a slough grown thick with the sharp-sided triangular spears of papyrus, flair-headed like skinny green cranes. I keep away from the water, here – this isn't the sailing club, there is no copper sulfate in the water here, and I know the shallows and the spiky lake grass are where the snails live. I don't want to get Bilharzias and have blood in my poo like the man does in all the posters.

We chop down papyrus stalks and use them as long skinny whips or foils, and try to raise welts on each other's legs. If this were another day, we might run up and down the waterfront playing tiggy, or cowboys and Indians, or throw stones in the water. If this were a different day, we might stand on the shore and pull out our willies and see who could send their arcing yellow stream of wee the farthest out into the lake, and laugh until we fell down, thinking of the fish and snails all swimming around in our piddle. If we'd come down to the beach on any other day we'd make swords and rifles from sticks and branches, divide up into Germans and English and fight the Second World War all over again. We'd build forts in the trees and throw stones at trenches of imaginary Germans or Tanzanians, or simply at each other. We'd make up rules as we went along to make sure we didn't get hurt, about how long you have to be dead when someone shoots you, no fair pretending they missed when they didn't, no hitting when the other one isn't ready, and no hitting fingers on purpose. Still, despite the rules, someone would eventually get a horrid gleeful look in their eyes and throw too big a stone, or smack someone across the hand with their sword. Then there'd be tears, and the game would stop because everyone is afraid that someone will tell, and if someone tells, the grownups will all know we've been down here, by the water's edge, and want to know what *else* we'd been up to. We'd think about the cigarettes we'd stolen from our Father's last pack, or the fires we'd tried to start, and none of us wanted any of *that* coming to light

But we stop in our tracks as we arrive on the beach, because were this another day, there wouldn't be a fat man washed up high on the beach, dead in green army trousers and no shoes and no shirt. With skin like greasy blue-black parchment stretched tight and shiny across his belly, and one arm thrown up and away, like a sleeping sunbather. Head flopped over to the side, cheek smooshed flat against the muddy sand. Leaves and dried grass, tangled in the tight knotty little curls of hair on his bare chest. Eyes open, just a little bit, and dry, like a football that's had most of the air let out of it, eyes less alive even than those of the fish laid out on the tiled slabs down in Entebbe market.

There's a white patch coming up the side of his neck, speckly pink a little where it meets the black skin of the throat. There's another white patch on his side, coming up from under the waistband of the trousers, just above a ragged round hole near the pocket.

Someone steps behind me, shoves me closer. I lurch, step backwards and away and raise my stick as a threat, but he grins and so I grin back.

"Touch it," somebody says. *Tash eat.*

"You touch it."

"No, you." That's how close we are to the dead man.

"We must do eenie-meenie." Of course. *Inny Minny. Wi mast.* It's how all things are fairly decided, with eenie-meenie or one potato two potato, democracy as seen through the eyes of children. One potato two potato when one of us wants to be the one chosen — there are two chances and the odds are better. Eenie-meenie is what we use when we *don't* want to be picked – just one chance, and then you're out and in the clear.

A circle is formed, everyone places a hand into the middle of it. With reverence, the nonsense rhyme begins;

"*Eenie meenie maka raka ray rye dominaka chika pocka lollypoppa rum tum push*. You're out." The relieved boy steps back, puts his hands behind himself as if to ensure that they don't get counted again. He watches from outside the circle as the rhyme goes around again.

"...You're out," and another one steps back. The circle closes a little, the tension mounts. Another boy steps back. Another. Then it's down to two. "...Rum tum push." And we have a winner. And a loser.

"You first. Touch it." *Yu fast.*

"No. I don't want to do it." But he knows he must; he played eenie-meenie and he agreed. He lost eenie-meenie and those are the rules. He has no choice in the matter.

The boy steps forward cautiously, as close as he dares, leans the rest of the way and pokes the plump belly with his stick. I stand ready to run if ghosts come out or if lake worms spill from the bullet holes, if the head falls off or if the corpse sits up and starts screaming, but it doesn't.

"Not with a stick. With your finger." *Weeth yo'a fin-ga.* The boy hesitates, but then reaches out, slowly touches the corpse with the tippymost tip of his outstretched finger, pulling back his hand quickly.

"Who is it?" asks a little one. An older boy speaks up, just a little bit of contempt in his voice.

"He is a bad man. They must take the bad men out in the helicopter, and shoot them. They must be punished." *Thi heli copta. Thei' mast'i be panish'd.* "Look, he is a soldier, he wears soldier trousers. He is Obote's man." *Solja trowsas.* Just like the two men hiding in our garden on the first night after the coup.

I haven't heard anyone mention Obote's name in a long time. The dead man's skin is very dark, the face long – it does look like the pictures I've seen of president Obote in a way, but not really very much – at least not enough to get shot for.

127

The olive drab trousers are unhemmed and faded, not yet threadbare but getting there. Not that the dead man is troubled any longer by the mercurial vagaries of fashion.

"It's your turn," the boy says to me. *Yo'wa taan.* "You have not touched it yet." I look over at him – he is challenging me, the way African boys challenge each other, with his head up and his chin thrust out, his body turned a little, aggressive. He points towards the body with his bottom lip; this alone is a dare in itself. What's strange is that I can tell by the way the challenge is being offered that I'm also being accepted as one of them. He doesn't see a M'zungu. He sees another African boy.

"Easy peasy," I say. *Izzy pizzy.* "It's just a dead man." *Jast eh did mhan.* I push my finger against the dead man's stomach, harder than I intended to, and it is cold like a piece of raw steak, chubby and yielding like a Christmas turkey stuffed full of sagey bread and onions, waiting to go into the oven. When I pull my finger back, the skin stays bent in for a moment, straightening back out very slowly. There's something plastic and thoroughly unalive about it, like a link of plump overstuffed chipolata sausage hung on a hook in the window of Drandrad's shop. I look at the older boy, and he nods approval. I move a little to stand next to him, waiting for someone else to be called to the task, or to have the courage to try it on their own.

"Now you," he says, pointing at another boy with a stick. "Now you." In turn they do, each reaching out to poke an arm or a shoulder. No one touches the head. In a way it surprises me a little that the body never moves or breathes or blinks; the eyelids stay half open over dry, cloudy eyeballs the whole time we're poking him.

"Touch the cock," says my new friend to the boy nearest the body, but he is joking now. This is something we can all laugh at, and it gives us a reason to find something else to do. "You touch the cock!" a little one yells, *no you, no you, no you touch the cock!*

128

"We should go," says a boy. "Before someone comes to take him away."

"Away to where?" I ask. *Ahwe to weya*? The boy shrugs. The older one, who first dared me, answers.

"To the tip, of course." *Thi teep. Off cos*. "To the tip, where all the rubbish is taken." *Ol thi rabbish*. There's only one tip, one rubbish dump, the one out at the end of the road leading out to the sailing club.

"Nu-uh," I say, "They've got to bury them, or they can't go to heaven. My Mummy told, me, they've got to be buried. They can't take them to the *tip*." The boy looks like he might smack me for contradicting him, but he doesn't; I touched the dead man, and that means I'm not afraid.

"It's true. My father's brother, he works for the council. He takes them there all the time." *Fa-thas brotha. Waaks foa' thi council*. I can hardly argue with that.

"But what happens to them there?" I ask. *Wat happens theya*? The boy laughs.

"What do you think?" He spreads his arms like wings and does a reasonably good impersonation of the ugly smoker's caw made by the marabou storks, his face taking on a malevolent sneer, his chin tucked down into a wattle like the fat liver-spotted goiters hanging under those ugly birds' beaks. I imagine the hooked barb at the beak's tip snagging this dead man's flesh and peeling the meat back in wide tasty strips. The boy turns his attention to a younger boy, and begins to chase him, still flapping and cawing like a stork, and the boy shrieks like a girl and runs away.

The dead man on the beach is suddenly very boring, not interesting at all – there are wars to fight and mangos to splatter and cassava seeds to smack like cricket balls, and banana trees to *thwok* with sticks, and fields of tall tawny grass to build trip-snares to try and catch elephants in. Besides, bodies are washing up so often now that another dead man sunk down a little into

129

the smelly sand is hardly enough to hold our interest. This one isn't even missing any fingers or toes.

I come home hot and tired, red dirt on my knees, green stains on my shorts from the cassava seeds and papyrus stalks.

"Y'tea's nearly ready," says Mummy, smiling. "Y're a right state, you are, y'look like a sack o'potatoes tied up with string. Go and wash your hands and face." I go down the hall, into the bathroom, pull up the stool on which I stand to reach the sink. I turn on the water, let it run over my sun-darkened hands. When I glance up to the mirror I am startled to see a little white boy looking back at me. My heart thuds in my chest for a moment, and I look around quickly to see who he is, where he came from. Only then do I realize, he's me. I pull my hair back, examine my scalp, my arms, those bits of my skin most often covered by clothes. I rub my hands together under the running water, cup water to my face, rub it vigorously into my hair; I grab a flannel, rub it well the bar of Lifebuoy soap, and try to wipe off all the *white*. But it's no good. When I'm with my friends, I don't see myself, I see them, I see Africans, dark and handsome, hair uniform, curly, tight against their heads. I hear them speak, and I hear my own voice speaking the same as them, no different from them, and from the place behind my own eyes, I am one of them; my skin is dark chocolate brown, my palms pink, my eyes dark. But alone in the bathroom, face raw from rubbing, despite how African I feel, when I look in the mirror it's still a M'zungu I see looking back at me.

Chapter 11

"We're going home," Daddy announces, "On leave. We're goin' to g't'Mombasa and then down through Africa, t'make an 'oliday of it. We'll take a ship from South Africa, all the way back to England. What d'you think about *that*?" Mummy is so happy she's practically sobbing. *Home*, I think? But we already *are* home, 22 Bugonga road, our house, where we live. *This* is my home.

"Are we coming back?" What I really mean is, *I don't want to leave*.

"Drandrad will be waiting for you," says Daddy. "Don't you want to see y'Drandrad?" He's got me there – I remember Drandrad's face only from photographs, but he's still a presence in my life, an ideal, a force; in many ways, Drandrad is the only part of England that I've ever really cared about.

I'm seven. Seven! Will he even remember me? I was little and English when we left and now I'm big, a M'zungu, almost an African. Will he even know who I am?

"It'll be a lovely long rest for y'Daddy," Mummy says, and I can't help but agree with her. Daddy plays golf every night after work and sometimes twice on Saturdays, then skis and sails all day Sunday. I'm not surprised he needs a rest.

Aunty June drives us to the Kampala railway station, and we eat samosas on the platform while we wait for the train, samosas bought from a man carrying them around for sale out of a greasy cardboard box, still crisp and hot, spicy enough to burn our mouths. From Kampala station, we ride the train east past the hills of the city and, chug slowly out through great rolling plains of tawny elephant grass, broken by the occasional village, the occasional patch of maize or groundnuts or cassava. We cross the

131

border just after night-fall. On the Uganda side, sour-faced Ugandan soldiers come aboard to check our passports. After we'd first arrived in Uganda, I'd decided that since Lulu and I had traveled on Mummy's passport, our pictures should be in there too. So with my best ink pen, I'd drawn a picture of myself and my sister in the space under Mummy's photograph, so there'd be no confusion as to who we were. The officer checking documents is very angry at this, slapping the passport, telling us that this is a criminal offense. Mummy is very sorry; but when the officer opens Daddy's passport, I catch a glimpse of him slipping something out from between the pages, putting it into his pocket. Suddenly he's not cross anymore; the officer hand back Mummy's passport, and the soldiers move on down the train, which soon moves off again toward the Kenyan side of the border.

The Kenyan soldiers on the other hand, are polite, and better dressed; they think the picture of me and Lulu is quite amusing. It isn't until they've left that I realize it's the first time I've ever seen a soldier without a rifle in his hands.

In our carriage, Lulu and I brush our teeth in the tiny little bathroom tucked into the corner of our carriage; when we come out, the seats are folder into beds, the backrests rolled down into bunks. Daddy draws the heavy blue curtains across the window, and we drop off to sleep to the *clackety-clumk* of the swaying train wheels, eating up the miles towards to coast.

The following morning I wake to find our train riding the edge of a sheer drop, straight down a rock face that ends far below on a pale grassy plain that stretches to the horizon. The absurd *bigness* of it all stuns me. This is the escarpment that looks over the Great Rift Valley, the giant lengthwise tear down the wide belly of the continent, and I'm seeing Africa as it was for centuries, before we got here, before Stanley or Burton or Livingstone, before Speke, before M'zungus, before *anybody*. We spend the day staring, mostly, at the distant horizon, at the immense herds of antelope and wildebeest and zebras, at villages a day's drive from anywhere, at the clouds on the horizon that will soon be the coast.

The sea at Mombasa is nothing like I could have ever imagined. It is flat, calm, a dazzling brilliant cyan than falls between the cracks of any color I've ever seen before. It's a color that God might have stumbled across, the day He invented copper sulfate and mangos. Mombasa itself is a town of brightly painted shutters and narrow alleys, and white dazzling sand, shimmering like powdered soap flakes

We stay in Malindi, in bungalows run by a M'zungu man who has lived on the beach and worn flip-flops for so long that he can no longer get his feet into regular shoes. He has a son, my age, whose hair has turned green from the salt water of the ocean and the pool chlorine he swims in every day. The owner has a daughter, too, about sixteen, and in the quiet of one early morning I see her standing in a doorway, brushing her hair, my first look at a fully naked woman. I decide then that when I die, Heaven will look a lot like Malindi.

All down through Africa, at Malawi, Rhodesia, in Durban, I smile politely when the stewardesses hand Lulu and I the packets; wings, enameled tin wings, and identity cards for us to fill out. Special as I know they are, and happy as I am to get them, wonder if I should tell her we already have some, or if I'll get into trouble for having more than one set.

Johannesburg is the biggest city I've ever seen, the buildings taller, the streets wider, and at night from our hotel window I see more lights than I ever knew existed. We go walking, seeing the sights, and are quietly scolded and *tsked* at by a group of Africans when we sit on a bench to rest. An African man points to a sign painted on a wall over the bench – *Nee Blankes*, the sign says. Their language is harsh and unpleasant, M'zungus as well as Africans. None of them talk to us or smile or say *Jambo toto, Jambo Meb'sab, Jambo Bwana*. I find myself looking for the novelty of

133

another African like myself, since almost everyone else I see is white, except for laborers and taxi drivers and maids, waiting at takataka bus stops, standing in groups by the back doors of buildings. None of them seem very happy. Later in the hotel, Daddy asks a clerk what *Nee Blankes* means. The man laughs.

"*Kafirs* don't like it when we use their facilities. Whites, like us lot. Nee Blankes, no whites. Those are special areas just for blacks. They have their own bus stops, toilets, shops, everything. It's better that way." *Fisilitiz. Jest foa bliks. Bitter thit waey.* I don't understand this place at all. I can't comprehend why the Africans like me wouldn't even want to share a bench with us.

In Durban we board the ship that will take us to England, the *H.M.S. Tintagel Castle*. The ship's horn sounds, and we all start moving towards the railings. We're given narrow rolls of gay multicolored paper streamers and little bags of bright tissue confetti. Everyone begins to cheer and laugh, and throw the strings of paper spool out from the stacked decks to the people waiting on the dock below, and before long there are thousands of thin paper strings connecting the ship to the shore. Dots of pastel tissue flutter down like a slow reluctant snow storm. The steel deck shudders, and as the ship moves away from the dock, the curtain of paper anchor-ropes break and slip away like nothing, wafting like a slow anemone feeding in a reef.

At first, moving around Cape Horn and up the western coast of Africa, the weather is bright, warm, normal. We swim in the saltwater pool, watch in grim fascination as passengers and crew are doused in shaving cream and dunked into the water from a trick barber's chair when we cross the equator. We stop along the way, buy souvenirs in Lisbon and the Canary Islands; Daddy buys a new invention called a Cassette Tape Recorder, and we laugh at how silly it makes our voices sound, and play the soundtrack to Disney's *The Jungle Book* over and over again.

Throughout the journey, I think often of Drandrad. Will he remember me? Will his memory be as hazy as mine? In my mind,

Drandrad is no longer a face, but a sensation; Polo mints and cigarettes, the prickle of his narrow movie-star mustache, the mustiness of his trilby hat when it rained. What does he remember of me, I wonder?

As we move north the weather gets progressively colder, the sky more steely, and now I stand on the deck in a woolen coat with wooden toggle buttons, and balls of cotton wool in my ears because of the icy wind, watching the ships of Southampton dock slowly slip by as we're towed towards our berth. I don't remember ever feeling this cold before, not even when I've taken my deepest deep breath and dived down into the dark water to the mud on the bottom of the lake.

Southampton is a grim, industrial place, all shipyards and warehouses under a sky like wrinkled grey linen, with enormous rusting cranes looming out along the dock-front. Old wooden sailing ships with reefed sails, flying flags like jubilee bunting in their rigging, are tied up near squat oily barges with pug noses bound up in an elaborate bandage of woven rope. The air is sharp with rust and diesel and cold, and tastes like the blade of a nail file run down the edge of my tongue.

I know Drandrad the second I spot him, wearing a thick brown jacket and a hound's-tooth flat cap the color of stewed peas. He looks exactly the same, except for the walking stick in his hand, and the plaster cast on one leg. Mummy's sister is holding up a baby, Nannan stands smiling sternly in a heavy woolen coat, waving. They're standing in a clearing amongst shipping palates and gantry cranes, shouting and waving up to us as the ship is tied up to its berth.

"'Ello, love," they're yelling, "'Ello pet." Drandrad is blowing kisses up by the fistful, and Mummy is squeezing my hand so tight I can't feel my fingers.

We pile into a van they've rented to pick us up in, and the grownups talk and talk, everyone at once, everyone smiling. Their words are thick with the taste of Sheffield – solid chunky vowels that thud hard against my ears, letters that roll and grate across their tongues like a whole other language. I'd thought Mummy's accent sounded thick in among the many varied accents in Uganda, but I notice for the first time how much different, how much harsher, they sound than Mummy and Daddy do now, even though we're all from the same place.

"Ey, don't you sound posh," Every one exclaims. "Look at y'! Yer all brown as berries!" and it's true, we are – their skin is pale white, like steamed fish without the parsley sauce, and compared to them I finally – *finally!* – look like an African.

Drandrad holds me tight against his chest, hugs me and kisses me, every whiff of him completely familiar, as though I'd never left.

"Don't worry about the stick," he says earnestly, concerned that I might be after what I said to him when we left two years before. "I've only broken me leg. I'm not goin' to gentle Jesus, not jus' yet." He laughs, and smells of Benson and Hedges and peppermint and wet wool, a solid wholesome smell that I could cut into cubes like gelatin, and put into homemade soup.

They want to know, in hushed voices, if the rumors they've been hearing about on the news are true, about the killings, about the bodies. Daddy nods.

"Yeah, it's true, I'm afraid. I'll tell you later," nodding towards me and Lulu, as though I didn't already know.

"So what're y'going to do? Are y'goin' back there?"

"Oh, of course. We love it. All that political stuff, that's all tribal, between *them* lot, the Africans. It's got nothin' to do with us. We're there at the request of *their* government, so they'll 'ardly 'ave a go at us, will they?"

"S'what's it like?" says Nannan.

"Oh, it's beautiful. The sun shines all the time, every day. It's a very colorful place..."

"No, I mean bein' back 'ome."

And this is typical of the whole rest of our visit. All they seem to want to do is talk about life in Sheffield. Of all the pictures they could ask us to paint for them, of weaver birds and jacaranda trees and cockamander lizards bulging out their crimson throats, of the brightness of the sunshine and the stillness of the lake and the screeching of the grasshoppers in the lion-grass, of the corpses bobbing ashore all riddled with white-patchy bullet holes, all they want to hear about is what we think of the new roundabout on such-and-such a road, of the new high-rise estate going in up the street from Drandrad's house, of this or that English politician forced to resign in disgrace.

They've moved since we left, from Attercliffe and the rows of two-up, two-down brick terraced houses with the outside loo and no bathroom, to a house with hot running water and a front garden and a view of the distant steelworks to the northeast from the upstairs window. The loo is still outside, though, off the bare brick hallway just outside the kitchen door. There's no heat, but at least it's covered so I don't have to go out in the rain whenever I want a tiddle.

From the leaded panes of the upstairs bedroom windows, I can see the smokestacks of the steelworks; through the smoke, the hazy hills in the distance where the collieries sit out at the edge of the moors, and the tall buildings that make up the heart of Sheffield. It's ugly and grey and depressing in the daytime, but at night, the lights of the city make it look like fairyland.

Nannan takes me to see Drandrad at the shop. As we walk through the door, I remember the smells, of the sawdust, fresh and clean on the floor, and the cold metallic tang of blood in the air. In the window are steaks and roasts laid out on vivid artificial grass, and polished steel trays of crushed ice. Drandrad wears a white apron smeared pink at the thighs, and a wooden block with his knives in it on a chain around his waist. His hands are enormous; I watch him concentrating as his huge hands work a knife over a long whetstone, listening to the metal sing.

"Finest knives in the world," he says. "That's Sheffield steel, that is." He holds up the blade, checking it in the light.

He's proud of his knives, and of Sheffield, where they come from, and of me.

"My grandson, this," he says, beaming, to everybody who comes in. Some of his customers have been buying from this shop since Drandrad was an apprentice, since before Mummy was born. "This is my eldest daughter's lad, 'ome for a visit, from Africa."

"Tha lass? By 'eck, Jack, 'e's s'dark 'e could pass for a wog 'is sen!" The language they speak is stranger to me than any of those in Africa, a kind of English that borrows words from the past, that carves up words and spits them out, hard. *Thees* and *Thas* for you and your, *sen* for self, *owt* instead of anything, *nowt* instead of nothing. Drandrad tries to explain it to me.

"They're saying *aught*, and *naught*," he says, when I ask him what they mean. "And if you hear someone say, *Thaa't*, it's really a contraction of Thou Art, like, *you are*. It's a bit of a backwards and old-fashioned way of speakin', I know," he says, "But this is Sheffield when all's said and done." It's all very confusing to me. Swahili makes far more sense. And to make things worse, the customers lean down to me, and talk slowly as if I might be slow or stupid or somehow have forgotten how to speak English at all. "Oooh, I knew y'Mummy when she w'your age, love," they say. "I'll bet y'glad t'be back in England, aren't y'duck?" Some of them have never in their life left the city of Sheffield. Rotherham, a half-hour bus ride away, may as well be Paris or Moscow or Rome. A trip to the seaside, to Blackpool, to Cleathorpes, might be the furthest that the most adventurous of them has ever traveled. I smile politely and wonder why they think England is so great.

There are children that live on Drandrad's street, three in the house next door, two around the corner, another few up the lanes and down the hill towards the park. They talk funny; I know it's

English, it must be, since this is England, but they use those *thee* and *thy* words, which they sneer out of their noses as though they don't like the smell of them, the words spoken in a blurred, rapid monotone. I try to make friends, I try to tell them about Africa, about where I'm from, where I live, about the sunshine on the bougainvillea bushes and the view of the lake from up in the Jacaranda tree at the bottom of the garden. About the mousebirds playing on the branches of the sleeping hibiscus, and the taste of fenai, freshly bashed open on the ground, and of paper cones full of crispy warm ants, and about oil lamps ingeniously folded from scraps of tin cans, soldered together at the seams. But they don't care, and in fact seem quite disgusted by the whole idea. Instead, they like to watch a television program about a Chinaman who fights cowboys in slow motion, and eat fried chips and fried tomatoes and fried bread. They like to dig in the muck of their tiny back gardens with a big heavy garden fork, for worms to fish with in the filthy stagnant pond in the sad little park up the road, where there's nothing but carp and pike and empty pop bottles. They eat sour purple rhubarb dipped in sugar, and have roast beef and Yorkshire pudding for Sunday dinner, and smash empty Tizer bottles on the tarmac of the playground because they're bored. Their school is brick and iron, brick walls and iron gates and iron railings surrounding an asphalt playground painted with faded hopscotch boxes. Except for the nasty little pond in the park up the road, there is nothing green save the occasional patch of lawn, each one no bigger than my verandah.

"This is the house you were born in, Sunshine," Daddy says, pointing at a two-story wall of brick with a dark slate roof. A row of identical wooden doors and wood framed windows, all painted varying shades of green, are notched into the wall exactly ten feet apart, one door for each house, one window each upstairs and another one down. He points to a door. "Number 9, this one was ours," then at the next door over, "And that one was Nannan and Drandrad's." The brick facade of the houses dead-ends at a high brick wall at the end of the street, and faces a mirror-matching row across a lane, just wide enough for two narrow motorcars to carefully pass, as long as no one is parked on either side. On the other side of the wall is a steel-works; I can see the rows of high windows and the corrugated metal of its roof.

The doors to these houses all open directly onto the causeway, a single worn and well-scrubbed stone step leading up to each. Grotty children call to one another and stand staring at us, snot faced and mouths yawning slack and open. Even the poorest beggar-boy in Entebbe seems more cheerful than these children.

"What d'y'want then, luv?" says a woman sourly to Mummy, as though we might be handing out religious pamphlets or selling something expensive and unnecessary. She's leaning against the door frame in a flowery housecoat and apron, old carpet slippers, her hair in curlers, her eyes wrinkled against the smoke of her cigarette. "Oh, 'ello pet, I di'n't recognize y'! Come for a visit, 'ave y'?" Mummy greets the woman by her surname, there's a brief exchange of pleasantries.

"Ow d'y'like it then, over in Dronfield?" the woman asks. Dronfield is less than ten miles away, where we moved the year before we went to Africa. We haven't lived there in two years. Mummy lived on this street, in this house, from the day she was born until the day she got married. Shortly after that, she and Daddy moved in together next door when the house came up for rent. Everyone on the street remembers her as Jack the Butcher's daughter, and former neighbors come out of their houses to ask where she's been, how she's doing, being polite, being nosy. When she tells them, they look baffled, unsure what to say next. Dronfield is hard enough for them to grasp. But Africa? They don't understand. It's just too big. Not just the place, necessarily, but the whole *idea* of living there, the idea of living *anywhere* but here. It's too far away, too far removed from the reality of their lives, *life* being Sheffield, the shops and markets of Attercliffe and the steel works, and whatever kind of a life it is that people who stay in a place like this choose to make, or to settle for.

So instead, they stop listening. They don't ask questions, about what's it like, what we do there, what are the shops like, the people, the weather. Instead, they're more interested in telling her about the *real* world, as they understand it, about Mrs. so-and-so, who emigrated to Australia with her son, and Mr. such-and-such, who died in his sleep last winter and wasn't found for three days. Mrs. Woman from the corner shop, who's in hospital because of her liver, and Mr. Man from number 17 who left his wife and ran off to Yarmouth with a barmaid. No one on this narrow street can conceive of living much further away than the next lane over. Even Rotherham, closer than Jeliati and Powlino walk to go home on a Sunday, is half a day's journey away by tram, at least in their minds. They have difficulty relating to a relative of Jack's having moved as far as Dronfield. But all the way to Africa?

"Oh, I could never live there, luv!" they say to Mummy. "Oh, no no *no*. I like England, it's me 'ome. It's... *cumf'table*." Somehow, it sounds like they're phrasing this statement as a question to themselves, one to which they're not sure of the answer.

I don't know what to say. Being here now I remember this house, I remember living here, but I don't remember it or the street being so *small*, so crowded up against everyone else.

"Bloody 'ell," says Mummy to Daddy, as we walk away down Hoban Street, towards the waiting car. "Nothin's changed. It's all exactly the same as it was the day we left! God, it's exactly the same as it was when I were a kid!" Something in her tone tells me that this isn't necessarily a good thing.

She's started talking more and more like the rest of these odd Yorkshire people. The longer we're here, the thicker her accent seems to get. She catches herself from time to time.

"God, listen to me," she says. "I sound bloody awful."

There's a pile of bricks at the open end of the street, across Heppingstall Lane, rubble and masonry clumped here and there with weeds. We're facing the end of another row of houses, identical to those on Hoban Street, but clipped off clean, in cross-section, as though the block has been cut in half with a bread-knife. I can still see the faded, rotten wallpaper on what had been the inside wall of the two rooms upstairs, the two rooms downstairs, a differing diagonal line of wallpaper running up what had been the staircase. The clustered rubble pile continues for a couple of hundred feet, before the truncated row houses pick back up again. This wall, too, still has the track showing, of where an inside staircase used to be.

"What happened, Daddy?"

"Don't you remember, sunshine? It looked like this when we lived here. The Germans bombed the steelworks during the war. That street got bombed out, ooh, about a year after Y'mum w'born, about 1943. They weren't going to rebuild in case Jerry bombed again, so the council just bulldozed what was left into a pile and left it there." He points, and a stir of memory flickers. "You used to wait with y'Mummy on that corner every day for Drandrad to get home from work, right there across the street. And look at that," he says. He points to a low wall running in front of a house across the road. I've notice this before, and had been puzzling over it; there are rusted nubs of metal, like bitten-off sticks of brown licorice, poking up through the bricks every foot or so. I've seen it everywhere we've gone, all around town – low walls in front of schools and houses and public parks, with these rusted stumps sticking up.

"Used to be iron fences," says Mummy. "Mosterit were cut down f'scrap durin' t'war," She says, and tells me how, thirty years before, council workers with cutting torches had come around the streets and parks in all of England's major cities, and all such non-essential metal had been taken away for the war effort. Miles of Victorian wrought-iron fence were carted away in this fashion, supposedly to be made into tanks and Spitfires and Flying Fortresses to fight the Germans. And like the bombed out houses at the end of the street, after the war, none of it was ever replaced. Now, the fence-stumps, the rubble piles – still here in 1972 – these reminders of The War are so fresh, a person might think it had happened just last month, or last year at the most. There's just so much of World War Two left lying around. Bombed out piles of broken brick, heaped up tall and overgrown with nettles, fill the occasional block all over Sheffield. And the ongoing reminder of The War doesn't end there; every toy shop in England is stocked with model Spitfires and Hurricanes. Every tobacconist's has a magazine rack of comics for boys of all ages, stories told in luridly drawn pictures, of brave RAF pilots battling the Luftwaffe over the channel, of brave commando officers and their trusty Gurkha batmen operating behind enemy lines in the forests of the Ardennes and the deserts of North Africa. Of brave English POWs and their tireless efforts to escape from Castle Colditz or Stalag 21. The War is like a scab that no one can let heal because picking at it hurts, but also feels so *good*. The way people talk, I start to picture The War as being a strange kind of party, and having happened behind a great big wall, with a great big gate, and a great big sign over it all. *The War*, the sign says, in letters fifty feet tall, overshadowing everything, visible for miles.

Driving back to Drandrad's, we pass the high brick walls that enclose the steelyards, and drive through narrow brick arches under sooty black lichen-stained railway bridges, archways barely wide enough for a car, through which slim Sheffield buses have to wait in turns to pass. Black and grey smoke pours out from the brick column chimneys, and narrow branching cobblestone lanes lead off to the rows of terraced brick houses like the one we just left. These streets are an optical illusion, identical, in rows of perfect reflected brick perspective ending at the brick wall at the end of each brick lane.

I've never seen so much brick in my life, and so little that's green.

The looks that I get from all these people, these immobile, root-bound English people, when they learn that I live in Africa, is one of pure bafflement. They couldn't be more puzzled if they found out we were visitors from Mars or from the sun's winking brown arsehole. Which is what Africa may as well be, I hear one cruel boy say.

"*Africa*? What the bloody 'ell would anyone want t'g'there for? D'ya've to wear bones through y'nose? D'you live in a mud 'ut, and eat giraffe bollocks?"

"They're just trying to be funny," says Mummy. "Don't be upset."

I try to like it in England, for Mummy's sake and because this is where Drandrad lives, but I can't. Everyone talks different here. In Uganda, there are some different accents, Irish and Scottish, Danish and Indian, but they all blend a little, the posh and the common, with the hard bits of Swahili and Luganda that sneak into everyone's vocabulary; they all knock the rough corners off each other and after a while, make everyone sound a little more alike. Here, they run words together, use harsh, course slang that I don't understand, and the old-fashionedy words like *thee* and *thy*. And everybody, everybody, *everybody* is white. Whiter than the blistered puddings of a sunburn, whiter than the skin around a bullet hole, whiter than I've ever seen white people, whiter than I ever remember being myself, whiter than it looks healthy to be.

We're supposed to be home – that's what Mummy always calls it, and all her old friends;

"Ah y'glad t'be *'ome*, luv?" they ask, wrapping their lips into pouty circles around the word, and she nods and says how lovely it is to see everybody. But I can tell that more and more she's starting to feel the same way I do. In Africa, she missed England, was homesick for the familiarity of it, was clearly out of place in the egalitarian, post-colonial classlessness. But after being back in

Sheffield... this city is so dirty, and smells of the soiled sooty brick under railway bridges, and of the smoke of the steelworks and collieries out at the edge of the moors, and of oily coal fires in the rain. So little is green or colorful, just the occasional piece of a park whose grass is only decorative, everywhere posted KEEP OFF, or the patch of tended flowers in a window-box, or a glimpse of tightly tended rose bushes behind a garden wall. There is green in the fields, outside the city, where the cows graze and the tractors chug among the turnips and sugar beets, but the countryside is so far removed from the city of Sheffield that it may as well *be* Uganda for all we get to see of it. On some streets the only green thing for a mile in any direction might be the thicket of nettles growing atop and among a pile of bombed-out red brick rubble. And, Nannan tells me, what little green there is will be dead and hidden under a foot of snow come January. Drandrad jokes,

"The greenest thing 'round 'ere is the muck on't' top o't'pond," and he's right, practically. Nothing is green, everything is small, tight, compact; tiny houses and narrow streets and small-minded people, and everything that is not paved with asphalt, is covered in brick.

I don't like it here. I don't like how cold it is, despite the fact that it's supposed to be summer, and how the other children laugh when I try to teach them Swahili; they laugh and tell me it sounds like *uggabugga*, like a pig talking Chinese

"What did I just say?" they ask, yabbering a mouthful of clickety monkey gibber-noise. "Did I just say something in African? What about this?" and another stream of nonsense spews out of their stupid English mouths.

"You didn't say anything," I tell them, "I can't just make things up and have it be African." The big boys throw stones at me for telling them they can't speak African. They are vicious, cold, cruel.

"G'back t'Africa then, y'bloody *wog*. Thaa't a bloody *nignog*, thee!" They spit these words at us, as though Africa itself tastes ugly to them. They laugh and jeer and jabber ongo-bongo to each other as they run away, their shoulders rounded inside dirty anoraks, their hands in pockets against the cold.

I don't like this sky that won't let the sun out, the perpetual dirty rag color of the clouds, the grey sooty haze that makes the distant moors look like a pencil picture drawn on toilet paper and rubbed with an unwashed thumb. I don't like the great blocks of brick flats and always having to wear shoes and socks and trousers and a coat.

I want to go home. I may be *from* here, or so they keep telling me, and I love Nannan and Drandrad and want to be with them and will miss them so much my heart aches, but here in this cold, miserable, sad little country, I've never felt more like a M'zungu – a stranger – in my life.

Chapter 12

After a month of England, Daddy decides he's rested enough, and is ready to go home. And home, for all of us, is now Africa. Even Mummy, who had missed England so much, now that she's seen it again and remembered first-hand what it's really like, can't wait to get back to our *real* home.

Daddy leaves first, just like he did last time. He's heard stories – letters from friends, from Uncle Dave and Uncle Anthony, and read the articles that appears from time to time in the Observer and the Daily Mirror. Unsubstantiated stories, about things that may have taken place, a worsening of the violence, rumors of more killings at Mbarara and unconfirmed reports of missing persons washing up dead in the lake.

"Unconfirmed, my arse," says Daddy out loud, reading the newspaper.

"What's 'atroticies'?" I ask, trying to sound out the bigger words I read, or hear while listening to the wireless with Drandrad, not realizing that I already know what atrocities are. I've already seen them. Daddy tells me that he's going home first to make sure everything is all right before we all join him too.

The tears at leaving Drandrad are still the same, but there's also relief at leaving this horrid wet place, and at least I'm used to the flying by now. The stale smell of cigarettes in all the seats, the boiled sweet they give us to suck on before takeoff to help pop our ears, the overly perfumed soap in the tiny toilet cubicles, the little slot for discarding used razor blades; they're all familiar, yet still new enough to be interesting.

147

It's dark when we land at Entebbe, not like the first time, when we arrived in the early part of the afternoon when it was hot, and could see the lake out of the window. There are few people in the airport, and Daddy rushes up and hugs Mummy tightly, scoops me and Lulu into his embrace. He drives us home in the dark, the air cool and thick with the smell of flowers, mysterious sweet colors in my nose. I remembered their always having been there, but I'd forgotten to notice until now, until we got back, until we got *home*. And though I've seen it a hundred times before, I'm startled all over again by the brilliant luminous star-chart of a sky, the pitch blackness over the elephant grass, and the soothing perception of silence which becomes suddenly deafening when the crickets stop the pulsing chant that lulls me into forgetting they're out there. I drop off to sleep in the car, stirring only once to see Mummy looking over her shoulder at us and smiling. The chill misery of England is a lifetime away, now that we're home again.

I dream that Daddy lifts me out of the back seat and carries me draped over his shoulder to bed. I've brought an English comic in my little suitcase, and I dream that he reads me a story from it, about a man who can breathe underwater and talk to fishes and whales. He's a special man who's part fish, and my last thought before I drop, a thousand feet into the bottomless waters of real sleep, is whether the men in the lake can breathe underwater too.

A week later I come home from school to find a cardboard envelope on my bed. It's addressed to me personally and is thick, not one of the tissue-thin single sheet blue aerogrammes that Drandrad uses when he writes.

"What's this?" I ask Mummy, walking in to the kitchen. She shrugs and smiles.

"I don't know, lovie. But it came in today's post. It's got your name on it, so why don't you open it and find out?" The stamp is

English, Queen Elizabeth in left portrait profile, looking regal and really quite beautiful. There's a crest on the top left of the envelope – British Overseas Airline Corporation, and a London address. I slit the package open with my finger and inside is a small plastic bag containing... a pair of enameled tin wings with a pin on the back, and an identity card to fill in and carry around, so that everyone will know who I am and that, surprise surprise, I'm a member of the sodding Junior Jet Club. I walk down the hall and sit on the edge of my bed, looking at the letter that also came in the envelope.

Dear Sir, it says. *We'd like to thank you for flying with us, (blah blah blah...) Wear your wings proudly, (blah blah) it says, And we hope you'll fly with us again very (blah blah) soon.* I'm suspicious now, and a little bit cross. It occurs to me for the first time that the airlines might not be as selective as I'd first though, about just who they dole these wings out to. I've still got my first pair – I was wearing them on the lapel of my blazer, in fact, from the time we arrived at Gatwick to the time we got off the plane in Entebbe. *Fat lot of good that did me,* I think. One would think that someone such as myself, wearing his wings, might draw the attention of a mere stewardess. But apparently not. I gave away the all wings the different airlines had handed us on our way down through Africa, in Blantyre and Salisbury and Johannesburg, in Durban and Lusaka and Dar-es-Salaam, given them to the wretched little children in Sheffield in a bleak distant hope of buying friendship. Maybe I should have kept them; maybe the ones I'm wearing are out of date. Or maybe... maybe they're just cheap tin wings they hand out to children to keep them happy, to keep them quiet. *Buggers,* I say to myself quietly, using the baddest swear word I can think of. They *all* get them, every boy and girl who gets onto one of their stupid aeroplanes. I'm angry now, and get a wonderful thrill of badness, like a bowstring being snapped against my chest, as I tear the identity card into ship's confetti, and bend the metal wings back and forth until the enameled front peels away and the crest snaps like chilled toffee in my hands. *Bugger them bloody bloody buggers*, I say to the broken wings. Now *that'll* show them.

"Good morning Teachers. Good morning, everyone." When the term starts again, I'm in the Upper School, and we have our own assemblies, but not every morning like the little ones, the children, the *totos*, across the playing field in the Lower School. They're down at the far end of the playing field, still playing on swings and seesaws like babies.

There also aren't as many girls now as there were before. The girls are too valuable to their families, to work the cassava fields or to hire out as aiyas, or marry off for dowries of cattle and goats and maize. Come to think of it, there are a lot fewer people in general, at least M'zungu people. All the Israelis are gone, of course, and there are many African boys, some friends, some not, who don't move up schools with me over the summer. Nobody talks about where they might have gone..

"Girls must go to work with their mothers in the village," says one of the boys. "They should not go to school." The staccato rhythm of his speech is comfortingly familiar; *Gells mast*, he says, *Whaak weeth they'a maathaz*. There are two M'zungu girls in the Upper School, perhaps a dozen African and Indian ones; but mostly it is boys, mostly they are black, and mostly, I think of myself as one of them. More and more I find myself wishing I were more like them, the way their rich dark skin sweats freely, their shirts always patchy with moisture. Even when I run full-tilt playing tiggy in the courtyard between the classrooms, I am barely able to summon a speckling of moisture across my brow. I envy the rivulets of water running down their cheeks from their temples. I wish I didn't stand out quite so much, with my fair, sand-blond hair, my pale hazel eyes. True, my skin is dark enough from the sun that I can pretend, at least in the dark, that

I'm African; unless I think about it, unless I'm with other M'zungus, In my mind I am just another Ugandan boy.

There's to be a parent's day – all the Mummies and Daddies will come to the school in the afternoon, we'll be let out early, and there'll be three-legged races and egg and spoon races and sack races, and prizes and games and food.

"Please ask your parents to read this paper," the teacher says, "Please ask them to sign this sheet, please tell them to come." The school gets a jolly good sprucing up; these are the words Mr. Shelley uses, with enthusiasm, while the school shamba boys sweep off the corridors with their brooms, and wash all the windows and cut the grass with a big tractor towing a wide, wheeled mower behind it – *A jolly good sprucing up.*

There's a reason for all this attention, of course; since his children attend the school, Amin himself will be coming. Bunting the color of our flag is hung from trees and the edges of the concrete overhang that keep the rain off the classroom corridors. On the playing field, ropes strung between wooden stakes driven into the ground mark off lanes for the running events, and two teachers volunteer to hold a white ribbon between them as a finishing line.

There's a wooden platform set up facing over the lawn towards the lake, with chairs on it, a microphone, more orange, red and black bunting. A Ugandan flag is draped over a lectern set in front of rows of folding metal chairs. It all looks very gay indeed, and in the ridiculously incongruous normalcy of Uganda, it's not only the President himself who attends, but half his ministers and general staff. Amin sits in the middle of the platform on a heavy velvet chair in his grand army uniform, dark blue with red collar-boards and epaulettes, a massive, dark-black man, his shoulders and chest dripping with braided cords and medals for bravery. He wears a big peaked cap and a huge smile on his plump, wide face, and has more teeth than anyone should be allowed to have, like rows of gleaming ivory dominoes. Next to him is a boy in a miniature version of the same uniform. The boy looks tiny next to the President, and ever so small, and it takes me a few minute to realize that it's Alastair Amin, the boy who first asked me about how many cocks my father had, who questioned my father's virility for only having two children. He does not look happy, sitting on the reviewing stand, with the row of army officers sit behind him like the teachers behind Mr. Trotter at assembly. Next to him, Amin points from time to time with white gloved hands, laughing and clapping as parents and children hop along in the sack races, and relay back and forth passing their eggs from spoon to spoon to spoon.

Around the President, stern-faced soldiers guard the platform, their rifles held across their chests, their metal helmets strapped tight under their chins despite the heat. But they're not nearly as scary as the SRB men; they're easy to spot, in very modern-cut leisure suits with flared trousers, colorful ties and gold-rimmed sunglasses, their suit-coats bulging out over their holstered pistols. They stand at the back of the platform, in the shadows, watching everyone, even the soldiers. *Especially* the soldiers.

The officers' wives stand uncomfortably next to them, wearing a mixture of kitangi and European-style fashions in polyester fabrics thick as bedspreads; some wear expensive leather pumps, while others, more traditionally, are barefoot.

Mummy gets entered into a running race with some of the other ladies. They're all very fat, these other women, and very African, with big bottoms almost wider that the roped off lanes they're supposed to race down, and wrapped with bright kitangi fabric, their hair tied up in matching turbans. When Mr. Trotter yells "Ready set Go!" I just can't understand why Mummy is so obviously trying to run the slowest. The other ladies jiggle and jostle and elbow past each other, huffing and puffing and giggling, an ocean of batik-patterned, kitangi-clad arses flapping and wobbling in the sun. Mummy almost has to keep stopping and running in place in order not to be the first to cross the line.

"Why isn't Mummy trying?" I say to Daddy, frowning and frustrated, as I try to cheer her on. It's obvious she could win if she wanted to. Daddy smiles.

"Because those are President Amin's wives," he says.

"What, *all* of them?" I ask. There are six of them including Mummy, a lone M'zungu in a sea of big jowly African women, each trying to win this stupid little race, not more than fifty yards long. Daddy nods towards them.

"He's got a few more as well, y'know." He points up at the viewing platform, at the other ladies around the President, some young, some older, fat and thin, dark black from the north, lighter shades of brown from the east. Suddenly, seeing Alastair stiff and awkward next to his Father's ridiculous joviality, his claim of having twelve brothers and sixteen sisters just seems terribly sad.

At the swimming pool, the last of the summer university students visiting from England and Denmark and Canada gather loudly. They lie on towels together in one shady corner, on the inland side of the pool against the fence. On the lake side of the pool are the mummies laid out in deck chairs on the grass, their tummies glistening oily in the sun and their bikini straps pulled off their shoulders. Me and the other children sit paddling our feet and drinking red-pink prickly Schwopp and bright tingly Pepsi and sick-sweet orange Fanta from thick glass bottles, splashing noisily in the water at the shallow end.

The university students have a fright mask, an ugly hairy gorilla face which they wear to scare us. The features are a gorilla in a grotesque caricature of an old African man, and if me or my friends go too close to them they'll put it on and chase us away, laughing, shrieking *oogabooga*! It does no good for the mummies to scold them – the college students just snicker and giggle and pretend the mummies aren't there.

"Look!" one of them shouts, "Bloody hell, look at this, you chaps!" He's standing on the other side of the fence in the forbidden out-of-bounds, looking down off the tall chipped cliff into the surging water a hundred feet below. One or two of the other students go over to the fence, climb over it or stand peering through. I hear rude words, exclamations of shock and surprise – all the children sense the excitement building, like a tickle in the tummy. The air in the group of students is thick with it – the girls with their slim waists and big boosies spilling out of little tiny bikinis come over with their boyfriends, they run away shrieking, they come back with their friends. One or two of the daddies have gone over to where the crowd has gathered and stand peering off the edge of the cliff, pointing. The mummies go to have a look at whatever it is that's causing all the fuss, and walk back tutting, shaking their heads.

"What is it, Mummy. What are they looking at?" Mummy is nonchalant.

"Nothing lovie, just another body. Don't look. Just stay here with me." But I don't listen. Me and my friends run over to the fence and look down. Far below in the surf, a corpse is washing in towards the beach in the onshore afternoon breeze. Even though I'm high up on the cliff I can see him, shirtless, floating on his back with his arms spread out. He rides high in the water with a fat belly all distended and shiny.

Along the cliff, working their way down a lateral path on the rock face to the left, I can see a group of students carefully following the edge of the promontory back in to where it meets the beach. Everyone is watching now, talking about the body, talking about the silly buggers clambering down to see it, talking about whether someone could dive off the cliff into the surf without getting smashed to bits on the rocks below.

"If you timed it just right," says one of the daddies, looking as though he might be giving it serious consideration.

"Don't be so bloody stupid! Silly bugger," say the mummies crossly to the daddies, glancing over at us kids, as though we might have been considering doing just that and were only waiting for someone to voice the idea. The daddies smirk sheepishly, and make mock pantomime diving gestures to each other when they think their wives aren't looking.

The body comes in to shore remarkably fast on the current; within a quarter hour it has moved from a few hundred yards out in the open water to pitch, face down, on the beach in front of the students waiting on the sand. They find sticks of driftwood and begin poking at the corpse, poking at the swollen belly distending out to the sides, and at the wet woolly head. Mummy can't look anymore. One of the bigger of the young men actually rolls the body onto its back and the ones on the other side of it dance out of the way, laughing and cursing.

"Come on, lovie, come away," she says, putting her arm around me. "Come on, you lot," she says to the other children, "Come and have a swim. Come and play. Leave them. It's none of our business. Just leave them." They *tut* their disapproval at the older kids gathered outside the fence, all smirking ignorance, watching the fun down on the beach. I'm reluctant to leave the show as more of the university students reach the bottom and go walking across the wet sand to the corpse, carrying sticks and stones and cameras. The fright mask is ignored now, a peeled-off face tossed on the grass. I wish I had the courage to go over and pick it up, to look at it and try it on. It's *far* more interesting. I've never seen a fright mask before, but I can go poke a dead African practically any time I'd like.

But not everyone who disappears from their village or from the army barracks ends up floating as crocodile food in the lake. Some of them – including perhaps the two that first night in our garden – made it past the searchlight patrols of soldiers loyal to Amin, and the SBR checkpoints. These, the lucky ones, traveled south and west, skirting around the lake, moving at night, slipping unseen through the bush past the Jeeps sent out to look for them, and the roadblocks set up to stop them. Some on foot, some hiding in the backs of lorries, others on fishing boats. Some alone, some with the help of a sympathetic stranger, they slid southwards on moonless nights, towards Tanzania.

President Nyerere of Tanzania never did much like President Amin of Uganda; Mr. Nyerere was a friend of Mr. Obote, and even invited Mr. Obote to come live in his country once it became clear he wasn't president anymore.

The soldiers leaving Uganda find each other while they're in Tanzania, and find that there are other people like them, who'd just as soon President Amin not be president anymore either. This makes President Amin very cross, and, it's rumored, a little bit frightened as well. It says in the Argus and the East African Standard that President Nyerere has pledged the might of the Tanzanian Air Force to help topple the Amin regime. President Amin doesn't like that at all, and tells the Argus that they're not allowed to say such things anymore. Those are big words, words like *pledged* and *topple* and *regime*, but I'm a clever bugger and I look them up in the dictionary Daddy keeps in the bookcase next to his chair. Topple means to push over. Pledge means to promise. President Amin isn't very happy with promises like this at all, and neither is his regime.

So he sends his soldiers to the swimming pool, up on its strategic promontory overlooking the lake on three sides, overlooking the airport to the west and Entebbe bay to the northeast, and conveniently facing Tanzania, less than a hundred miles across the water to the south. The soldiers come one afternoon when we're swimming. We all look up as we hear the lorries coming, *nyuh-nyuh-nyurh,* up the hill, and everyone comes over to see what's happening. Lorries mean soldiers, and soldiers mean trouble.

While the soldiers jump down and begin unloading rolls of concertina wire and barricades, an officer in a peaked cap gets out and starts shouting at us all.

"This facility is now off limits to civilians! You are trespassing on military property! You have five minutes to leave!" The soldiers in the lorry are unloading boxes from the back, oblivious to the stunned M'zungus sunning themselves on the grass. Everyone begins packing up their towels and lawn chairs. It's a weekday, there are only women and totos here this afternoon. Nobody dares argue with the soldiers, even if we are British.

"They've put barbed wire all along the top of the fence," says Daddy, later that week. "They've dug trenches inside the wire facin' inland towards the road, and built a guard 'ouse. They've drained all the water, and piled sandbags around the edge of the pool. There's a sodding howitzer in the deep end! What the hell are they playing at?"

After the pool is shut down, there's no reason to go out there and see it anymore; with all the soldiers coming and going, there's even less reason, and so no more reason to drive past the beach fronting Bugonga fishing village and count corpses on the sand. But Daddy drives past it to take a look, as though he's taking the long way out to the airport, and tells everyone at the golf club what he saw.

"There were a couple of soldiers sitting on the edge of the pool, swinging their legs like they were paddling their feet, passing a bottle of waragi." I'm sad, even though I can always go swimming in the lake, or in the big pool at the Lake Vic hotel. But I suppose it must be the right thing to do, if the President is really so worried about Tanzania invading us across the lake.

"Tanzanian Air Force?" sneers Daddy. "What, three Cessna 150s and a bloody paper glider? D'you know, when they test fired that gun, it wasn't properly anchored down and the recoil knocked it backwards. Shattered all the tiles along one wall, and

157

put a bloody great crack in the concrete. Typical. Bloody sodding typical."

I don't see the bodies as often now, because we don't drive that way very often at all. It's easy to see though that they're still there, a lot of them. So many that crocodiles come back to Entebbe bay.

The bay had been free from crocodiles for almost 75 years, since the town grew up and the game stopped coming down to drink, and more boats started fishing the water. So much human activity, and noise and hunting for meat just drove them away, out to the Sese islands offshore or further west and east along the less populated banks of the lake. Before the bodies started pitching up with such regularity and in such abundance, one might see a few crocodiles up some far-off reed-choked inlet or stream, or someplace well away from people, miles out in the country past the airport or in the other direction, past Kampala. But for the most part the big broad Nile crocodiles hadn't been seen in Entebbe bay itself for donkey's years.

But one night a helicopter might hover over the bay, out over the deep water, out of sight and earshot, and an Acholi officer or two would be ordered to stand in the doorway, shoeless and shirtless, and then might fall, punctured and powder-burned, into the black water below. In the calm after the helicopter's passing, the wind might shift, and the bodies bob and toss and swell as they move toward the land, or sink into the lake. Many, if not most, find themselves rolled up on the pebbly shores of one of the nearer islands, uninhabited little nipples of land poking up from the water, hundreds of them, a mile, ten miles out from shore.

The islands have served, since the people of Buganda first ventured onto the lake, as stopovers and weathering spots for the fishermen. Their descendants still cruise these waters looking for perch and tilapia, with their improbable little dugouts and an extra can of petrol for a tiny outboard Yamaha. By the middle of 1972 the islands are thick with crocodiles, fat and slow and well-fed, with mean piggy yellow-green eyes and smirking grins; and why shouldn't they come, being fed so freely and so often? After a time, it didn't seem quite so surprising if a body were to wash up on a beach with an arm missing at the shoulder, or only half a leg, a ragged, pasty-wet stump where the limb had once been. And even then somehow these things become, after a time, not a shock but commonplace, everyday, and most of all, perfectly, perfectly *normal*.

Chapter 13

Commonplace, everyday... *normal*. Everyone gets used to things being a certain way, like the fact that the Indians own all the shops. This is just an accepted fact, and has been that way as long as anyone alive can remember. Indians first came over with the British – as army chai-wallas, officers' batmen, domestic servants to colonial businessmen, though most came with the railroad, as coolies laboring westward from the coast. They'd come when Victoria was still Queen, they'd stayed, and more importantly, they'd prospered, owning almost all the stores of any size. A few Africans own little dukas, one room cubbyhole shops that open straight onto the street, and which stock an odd mix of homegrown products; black-market cigarettes, sandals made from old bias-ply tires, petrol of questionable quality and pedigree, chewing gum, shoelaces, cheap mass-produced plastic kitchenware and the like. A duka might sell cigarettes on day, then offer haircuts and barber service the next, and ironically, most of the things they sell are often bought from importer businesses owned by the Indians. But most *real* shops, shops with actual counters and windows and stockrooms, stores that specialize in a given product or skill – a tailor, a baker, a bicycle shop, electronics, cameras, packaged groceries – are usually owned by someone named Singh, or Khan, or Patel, a good, wholesome shopkeeper's name.

Asians own most all of the bigger stores in Entebbe and Kampala, especially Kampala, those selling everything from jewelry to clothing to car parts, and some – mostly Sikhs – own the more prosperous businesses, the import and export firms, the mines, the plantations, the factories. They also own the bigger

160

houses, too, in the shaded hills around Kampala. This is normal. This is everyday.

If Mr. Patel – any one, take your pick – doesn't have what someone wants, what any M'zungu or African wants, it's a good bet they'll have a brother or Uncle or cousin with a shop in the next town closer to the border with Kenya, the next stop up the railway lines. It's a sure bet they'll be able get whatever it is that's needed, within reason, in a few days, a couple of weeks at the most. Their stores – shoe shops, clothes shops, furniture shops, every kind of shop – stay open until whatever time the customer wants, and extended families share the burden of running the business. They don't live large; perhaps a tidy but secluded house in Entebbe or on one of the hills overlooking Kampala. They dress as we do, their children go to the same school as me, the only thing different is where they socialize.

I can count at least a half dozen Patels and Singhs among my friends. True, their Mummies and Daddies drive them to school in Mercedes Benzes, but that's the only thing about the Asians that says anything of money or wealth. They've been here, their families, some of them since their grandparents and great-grandparents came over with the British army, or as laborers on the railway that was laid sleeper by sleeper all the way from Mombasa on the Kenyan coast. Most if not all are Uganda citizens, and many that aren't have married citizens, and have citizens as children. From a half-century of mixed marriages, many are so dark-skinned one can only tell they're Indian by their names. They're commonplace. Everyday. Normal.

There's a man, Mr. Madhvani, whose first name; Jayant, I mishear as *Giant*. He's a very rich man, so he could be called anything he liked, if he liked, and I'm confused that for a man named Giant he isn't very big. But Mr. Madhvani owns a lot of things; *big* things, like copper mines and factories and breweries and sugar plantations. Cement from one of Mr. Madhvani's factories was used in the big hydroelectric dam at Jinja; another of his plants made the soap we all washed our clothes in. He made the cinder blocks that built most of the houses in Entebbe, including, most likely, our own. He has, needless to say, more than one Mercedes Benz.

He also gives a lot of his money away. Money that he donated helped pay for our school, for the books that we read in the school library, for salaries of the teachers we greet every morning. That American television program? *Sesame Street*, the one with the puppets and the silly men who can never get their shirts buttoned up properly? It was Mr. Madhvani who bought that series to show on Ugandan television, so that the totos would have something to watch and help them learn how to read.

Shortly before we left to go back to visit England (I won't say back home, because this, Africa, is my home,) Mr. Madhvani died. People all over Uganda were very sad, because he was a very popular man, and had very popular money. The Argus prints lots and lots of stories about him; all the terrific things he'd done in his life, all the good things he'd done for the country, all the money he made and businesses he owned and just how much of the nation's economy was based on things he and the other Asians controlled. Everybody was sad.

But President Amin was not so sad. When the story came out, President Amin, for the first time, got a good look at something he didn't like. He'd been in charge for two years but things hadn't changed all that much. Certainly, there were a lot fewer of Mr. Obote's untrustworthy Langi and Acholi to worry about, and a lot more of the Amin's Kekwa and Lugbara tribesmen running the army. The aeroplane-loads of radios and scotch whiskey that he arranged to have flown in from England every month as payment for his soldiers certainly made the soldiers happier. But as for the average Ugandan... well, had he wanted any more than to sit in the shade of his hut, eat matoké and drink pombe, he probably wouldn't have been able to had he not earned his wage working for an Indian-owned company. The average Ugandan bought the shoes he wore in an Indian-owned shop, cooked his food in oil from the Indian grocer, fueled the motor of his fishing boat with petrol bought from an Indian petrol station. The engine itself had most likely been bought from an Indian importer. And all of it, most likely, was shipped in from the coast on trucks owned by Mr. Madhvani, or someone just like him; in other words, someone Indian.

Despite Amin's brilliant ideas for improving the lot of the average Ugandan, such as shooting his opponents, and buying tanks from Libya, and crowning himself King of Scotland (all of which he had by now done,) nothing had changed very much since the President had seized power. Except perhaps the army. This got bigger by the day, since we all apparently needed immediate protection from the terrible threat of Tanzania, standing permanently ready against us to the south. But the army needs to be paid, and to pay the army the President needs money, and to get money... well, the Indians have it all, obviously.

It's September. September, 1972, when President Amin comes on the wireless to make an important announcement.

"The economy," he says, his deep voice crackling and popping though the dusty fabric of the hi-fi speakers, "Must be placed back into the hands of the Ugandans." In order to do this, the President has decided that anyone who is Indian and not a citizen of Uganda will have to leave. Uganda, he says, is to be a "Black man's country."

Of course, any Indians who are Ugandan citizens, they can stay. They will be given the chance to start over again, this time contributing to the Ugandan economy instead of taking, taking, taking, with their greedy stores open all hours, their selfish eagerness to find the products that people wanted, their unfair advantage in having built factories from the ground up, their greedy, thoughtless, heartless, tireless hard work and effort. No, instead, they would each be allowed, whatever their occupation – shopkeeper, factory owner, lawyer, accountant, doctor – the chance to farm a whole acre of land up in the north, near Sudan, where it's nice and dry and hardly any rain falls, not even during the wet.

Of course, nobody takes His Excellency the President seriously. The British government will say something, right? The President will surely come to see that this isn't a very good idea, right? But the next day the official order went out, that all Indians must report to the sports arena in Kampala. So they do. All of them. All sixty thousand of them, from all over the country.

In the arena, papers are checked by armed soldiers, and the crowd is separated into two groups, Uganda citizens on this side, and non-citizens over there. When President Amin arrives; SBR men in their polyester leisure suits and gold sunglasses fan out around the area, watching the crowd, and over the public address system, Amin personally tells the citizens,

"You will be given title papers to your land, and a stake number, and you have a month in which to leave your present homes and take up residence. Everybody else, you who are not citizens of Uganda, you have thirty days to leave the country."

The next time Uncle Anthony comes to play chess with Daddy, he's much quieter than usual. They don't talk nearly as much as they normally do; it's really quite boring for me, trying to keep on pretending to read the spy book I've grabbed off Daddy's book shelf. I try to laugh at certain bits, like Daddy does, and chew the corners of my pretend mustache, like Daddy does, but it doesn't make the book any easier for me to understand. Finally, Uncle Anthony starts talking, and I look up from my place, relieved.

"You know, I heard something from one of the other teachers who was up at the stadium. There was a doctor in the crowd that day; he'd come from Kampala Hospital not because he wanted to but because he had to, had been ordered to, just like all the other Indians.

"This doctor approached the president and told him, 'But sir, I am a heart surgeon. I have patients who need me, who will die if I am not there to care for them. There is no one else.'" Daddy grimaces.

"Ouch. That probably wasn't the smartest thing to do," he says. Uncle Anthony nods.

"Quite."

"So what happened?"

"Well, you know Amin, what d'you think happened. He got furious, went into one of his bellowing rages. Turned on this chap, and screams at him, 'You are no longer a doctor,' he shouts. 'You are a farmer. You have four weeks, leave or stay, or you will be arrested just like everyone else.'" Uncle Anthony, I'm surprised to hear, imitates the Ugandan accent perfectly. *You aah eh fhamma*, he says. It surprises me, because that's so unlike him. "It's funny, what becomes normal, when you let it," he says. "I don't know, I came here to make a difference. But Jesus…"

"What?"

"Well, Christ, do they all have to be so fucking *ignorant*?" Daddy sounds almost soothing.

"Who, the Asians, or the Africans?" Uncle Anthony laughs, a frustrated laugh that snorts out of his nose.

"Them too. I'm talking about the government. Our government! They've done nothing, not a bloody thing to stop this. I truly thought I was going to make a difference here. Now, I'm starting to wonder why I even bothered."

By presidential decree, the Indians, those leaving – since very few are staying – use the time they've been given to gather together everything they own. Every stitch of clothing, every stick of furniture, the great and small accomplishments and accumulations of their own lives and that of their parents and grandparents, the future inheritance of their children and grandchildren. That which they can't carry, they must find some

165

way of turning it into something transportable; into something they can take with them when they leave.

Uncle Chris calls Daddy.

"Any interest in a car?" He asks. "Asian chap I work with has a nice Capri for sale. Only six months old, in terrific nick. Reckons he ought to get rid of it now while he still can. He says there's no way for him to take it with him, because he thinks the border guards will just confiscate it and sent him off on foot, it he's lucky."

"They'd probably just shoot him," says Daddy. "Thanks, but I've already got two cars, I don't think I need another one." Daddy thinks that the whole affair with the Indians is getting a bit silly. Everyone – Indian, M'zungu, African, those with any sense at least – expect someone, someone like England, let's say, to step in, to speak up, to stop this disgrace. But Parliament, on behalf of Her Majesty Queen Elizabeth II, says only that they agree it is unfortunate and that will therefore accept any Asians into England who wish to come. But stop it? Not a chance.

Every day, on Airport Road between the golf course and the Lake Vic hotel, I see more and more Mercedes going to the airport. There's the usual roadblock set up on Airport Road, just where Bugonga Road turns off to the left. The soldiers – most of them drunk, bottles of waragi and Tusker sitting open in their jeep – pull all the Indians over to the side of the road, make them get out of the car, make them undress. The soldiers take everything of value; watches, jewelry, even the dowry bracelets the women wear, quite a lot of them if the women are from a more wealthy family; these dowry bracelets are the only things of value most of the women truly own. The soldiers are ordered to do this in order to stop the looting of Uganda's treasures by the greedy, hoarding Indians, trying to depart with the wealth of their, the soldiers', nation.

"It's that bloody stupid jeweler's fault," says Daddy. "He got out in the first few days and then boasted to the reporters at the airport in England about how he'd got past Ugandan customs by smuggled out thousands in gold, melting it down into false insoles for his shoes and thin sheets sewn inside his clothes." The President, after seeing this in the English newspapers, decrees that the Indians can take nothing of value with them. Nothing.

Normal, everyday, commonplace.

The Indians that manage to miss the roadblocks still have to go through customs at the airport, customs being another squad of soldiers, most of them drunk. At the roadblock, they lose their gold, their jewelry, their watches. At the airport, they lose everything else, save maybe the clothes on their back, once those clothes have been thoroughly searched for hidden valuables.

The week before the final date, a week prior to the final day the thieving Indians are rightfully thrown out of the country they had so callously looted with their businesses and factories and television programs and philanthropic foundations, Daddy goes up to Kampala, to buy a gold bracelet as an early Christmas present for Mummy. The jewelry shops, owned of course by Indians, are all quiet; there's no gold for sale anywhere, he's told. It's simply too valuable, the one hard commodity that there's a least a chance of smuggling out. And everywhere he or any other M'zungus go, they're asked the same question;

"English pounds? You can sell us some English pounds? We need hard currency, pounds sterling. Please, you can sell some to me?"

"They're offering any M'zungu who'll listen thousands in Uganda shillings for bank drafts they can redeem in England," Uncle Anthony says. "It's just absolutely outrageous. Not even for cash – just a check, or even a promissory note, as long as it's drawn against an English bank. Pure bloody exploitation, that's what it is!"

"So what's the alternative," says Daddy, "For the Indians, I mean?"

"You're missing the point the point! Taking money from these people is like... like *robbery*." says Uncle Anthony.

"Bullshit! See, that's *exactly* the point," says Daddy. "You and I both know that whatever the Indians aren't able to take out with them will drop straight into Amin's back pocket, if not directly, then in a roundabout way. Talk about robbery! Sooner us than *that* bugger, I say. The Asians're *thanking* us for doing this, Tony. We're doing them a bloody favor!" Uncle Anthony doesn't say anything.

"Don't do it, Davie," says Mummy.

"Don't be silly," he tells her. "No one is ever going to know, and just think what we can do with all that money! Look, I'll be careful, I promise."

"I don't care how careful you are. Amin was on the radio just yesterday. You know what could happen, if you get caught. I mean, do you know who you're going to be dealing with? How do you know you can trust them?"

"Lovie, they're Indians. They're getting thrown out of the country. This is in their interest as well, y'know? Besides, how can we possibly get caught, eh? We're English, They'll not mess with us." Mummy is quiet.

"Who's going with you?"

"Pete Whitfield, Chris Eglington... c'mon, stop worrying, love. Think about it, if we don't do this, all that money's going to go to Amin! I mean, we're doing them a favor, and it certainly isn't hurting us." He takes Mummy by the shoulders, kisses her forehead. I see her pull back from him.

"Just you be carefully," she says again, too loud, as he walks out the kitchen door.

For his part, Daddy knows the risks in helping. The official exchange rate used to be fifteen Uganda shillings to one English pound. But demand drives the marketplace, and Pounds Sterling are now selling for upwards of 80 shillings per, outside the official exchange offices and banks, away from paper trails and currency exchange limitations and the ever-open hands under the table of the officials making the transaction.

The president knows that this currency black market exists, and knows that the Indians are trying desperately to smuggle out the wealth that, in his twisted mind, they have so wrongfully plundered from the Ugandan people. He is very angry at their greed, what with their profligate shops and eager businesses and productive factories and the regular lucrative employment they've so callously provided Ugandans for nearly three quarters of a century.

The penalty for someone caught exchanging currency with Indians is really quite simple. After leaving your shoes at the side of the road, after quite literally beating the shit out of you, the soldiers will throw you in a very unpleasant jail cell until they can get around to shooting you. This might take a while, because they're very busy at the moment shooting Acholi and Langi and anyone else they don't particularly like. The State Research Bureau boys will probably play with you a bit first; sodomy is a given, with the option of amputation, burning, and electrocution. Flaying with fishhooks is popular also, especially the tender skin around the eyes; if you're lucky, they might just put your head in a steel pipe and beat it with an axle-shaft until you can't think straight from the vibration and the noise. All of these things tend to serve as a powerful dissuasion for anyone thinking of disobeying one of Amin's edicts. If nothing else, the President can always be counted on to cut right to the heart of a problem.

So Daddy and Uncle Peter and Uncle Chris are very careful when they arrange to meet a certain Indian man at a certain bar well off the Kampala High Street. In order to blend in, they order a couple of drinks while they wait. The bar is crowded, the man is late, so they have some more drinks. By this time it's getting late; obviously, the fellow isn't coming. They decide they've had enough, and go outside to get into their car and drive home.

"Pssst!" The sound comes from the bushes. "Psst! Do not look! I think I was followed!" The voice has a thick Indian accent. "Go up the road a mile, there is another bar on the left. I will meet you there!" There is such a sense of comic urgency, an air of Ian Fleming to the whole thing, that Daddy and his partly drunk friends can't help but chuckle. But they drive to the bar where they've be told to go, and repeat their cunning plan for blending in.

After another hour of blending, an Indian man with frightened eyes catches their attention from the far end of the room. He glances around before giving a quick flick of his head.

"Here we go," says Uncle Chris. "Looks like that's our chap." They follow, after a few minutes, outside. Down a darkened street smelling of sour wood smoke and rusted tin, through an alley lined with rotting cardboard shanties and old newspapers and the too-sweet smell of decay, up a dirt-paved road that follows a rutted grassy hill towards the back of an old Soviet-style block of concrete flats.

"In here," says the nervous young Indian, "Upstairs."

On the second floor are three very big Indian men, waiting.

"Lift up your arms," they say. They look very serious as they proceed to pat down Daddy and his friends.

"What are they looking for?" asks Uncle Peter. "Guns? Not bloody likely." He's an engineer, helps keep the electricity working. Uncle Chris is an air traffic controller. Daddy teaches Africans how to run printing presses. They've never in any of their lives been patted down for weapons by anyone, particularly not surly Indian men with whom they are about to transact black market currency dealings for which they could all be shot. That, and the fact that the three of them are pretty much plastered, makes the whole thing seem like a very silly game. But yet somehow, normal. Commonplace. Everyday.

"It's all right, they have nothing on them," one Indian says to the others. "Go through there," he says, pointing.

170

They go through the door. Inside the flat is a family; an old man, a younger man and his wife, an adolescent boy, five or six small totos. Compared to the seriousness of the young men guarding the door, the scene in the room couldn't be more different. The family is frightened, nervous, worried. And with good reason; all that they have built and earned and worked for, is about to be taken away from them. The country in which they were all born, where their *grandfathers* were born, doesn't want them anymore. A month ago they had wealth and prestige, they owned shops, factories, plantations, estates; tonight they have only hope, in the honest intentions of three young Englishmen.

"We are trusting you," says the old man, the patriarch, the spokesman. "We are trusting you with everything." When he says *everything*, he means it. His eyes plead for their understanding, and their honesty.

The younger man brings in suitcases, and when the catches pop loudly in the quiet room, all three Englishmen jump. He opens the first case, and no one seems at all surprised to see that the suitcases are full of money. Uganda shillings, bundled together in blocks of 100 shilling notes, crammed full to bursting.

The old grandfather begins lifting out great slabs of currency, literal bricks of money, hundreds of thousands of shillings, setting stacks in front of Daddy, and Uncle Chris, and Uncle Peter. In exchange, Daddy hands the old man a single slip of paper, as do the other two. Three checks, bank drafts drawn upon Barkley's, Middleland, Bank of England, redeemable – assuming, of course, that there is an account there for each to be redeemed against, and assuming, of course, that there is anything in those accounts – for perhaps a couple of thousand pounds.

Their factories and business are already forfeit, and all they have is this, the cash they've managed to hide, bundles of paper that are literally worth *nothing* to the Indians, since they can't use it, can't spend it, and can't take it with them. For every single Indian in Uganda, a lifetime's accomplishment, two or three

171

generation's worth of work, is now worthless if not distilled down to a narrow slip of paper like these held in the old man's hand, and which the Indian is grateful to receive.

"Thank you," says the old man. The way he says it, it sounds like a prayer. "We don't know what we would have done without your help."

"Where are you going to go?" asks Daddy, truly concerned.

"To England," says the grandfather. "I have a cousin in Bradford." The man laughs, ruefully. "He owns a launderette, and lives in the flat above it. We will stay with him until we can get on our feet. Or until we can come home." Clearly, it's the latter option he's hoping for.

Daddy and his friends leave the block of flats with their pockets loaded, bundles of money down the front of their trousers, carrying plastic carrier bags filled to the top and bulging sharp-edged with bricks of paper currency.

"Jesus Christ," they say, laughing nervously. "Bloody hell." They walk back to where they've parked their car grinning in terror, their hearts pound with excitement, weighed down with cold and quite hard cash.

"You want a lift to see that chap about that motorcar?" says Uncle Chris. Daddy shrugs, nods.

"How much does he want for it?" Uncle Chris quotes a number, and Daddy laughs. Two days ago, it would have seemed like a lot of money. Now, Daddy has nearly that much in one of his trouser pockets alone. One of the shopping bag in the boot could have bought another dozen new cars, and he'd still have had change. Normal. Commonplace. Everyday.

They take Uncle Peter's car, and they're all three still shaking when they finish the transaction and pull up in front of the bar where they'd first started their evening, to pick up Uncle Chris's. Daddy admires his new automobile, the clean lines, the smell of the upholstery.

"I need a bloody drink," says Uncle Peter. "I almost ran myself off the bloody road I was shaking so bloody much." The others laugh. They put their carrier bags in the car boot and go into the bar. There they toast their good fortune, each other, the President – always a good idea in public, to toast the President.

"Shit. Look at all this bloody money," says Daddy when they come out. "God, if we get caught with this..." he doesn't finish the sentence. Uncle Peter has two children and a wife, Uncle Chris does too. Uncle Chris's son, Christopher, is my best friend; he's always likes to be Cheetah, when we play Tarzan. They all think of their wives, waiting in constrained panic at home for their men to come back, worrying about the potential roadblocks the army might have set up on the Kampala Road. Wringing their hands over their husbands, loaded with illegal cash, and more likely than not, smashed out of their tiny minds on that last celebratory round of drinks. Which, of course, they are. Or of them not coming home at all; simply vanishing, like Robert Siedle and Nick Stroh, the two reporters who'd come to Uganda to investigate the rumors of killings on the army bases, the rumors of bodies on the beaches. No one had seen either of the two Americans for ages. Everyday. Normal. Commonplace.

"Look," says Daddy, "I reckon the best place to hide it would be under the dashboard. It's the least likely place the buggers'll look." The others nod in agreement, and so that's what they do, in the car park behind the bar; Uncle Peter keeps a lookout while Daddy and Uncle Chris take the bundled 100 shilling notes, and stuff bricks of money into every available space under the dashboards of each of their cars. When they are full, they start putting the money under the seats.

When they've finished, when every possible crevice has money stuffed into it, when the vents and steering column are full, they still each have at least a full shopping bag of money left over. They stand, looking at the cash, trying to figure out where to put the rest of it.

"If we get nicked," says Uncle Chris, "The first place they'll look is in the boot. But I doubt they'll search the interior too hard. What if we lay the rest of it flat under the carpets? It'll be dark, they'll never notice. Right?" They pull back the floor mats, and begin laying the money into the foot-well, in courses and rows like paper paving stones. But there's still so much of it; when they're finished and the carpets are pulled back into place, even as soused as they are they know that it won't fool anyone for long. The floorboards are lumpy and uneven now, with obvious bulging knots from the unevenness of the bricks of money. But it will have to do.

"Driving will be a bit tricky," says Daddy, after getting in the car to try it out. "The entire floor of the car's now about 4 inches closer to the bloody steering wheel! I can barely get my legs under." Both Uncle Chris and Uncle Peter have to pull some of the bundles back out and stuff them down the front of their trousers, just so the brake pedal and clutch will work without hitting bottom.

As usual for a moonless night, it is pitch black on the Kampala road, no lights at all except for the headlights of three cars being driven too fast in a tight convoy by three terrified, euphoric, drunken M'zungus. The embankment on either side of the road rolls down and away off into the perfect darkness of the bush, into the banana patches and cassava plantations and empty thorny fields. Daddy tries not to think about the money he's literally sitting on, but it is hard, his knees crowded up under the steering wheel as he drives through the night.

Suddenly something flashes into the circle of his headlamps – a soldier, who had come running up onto the road from his hiding place along the embankment, is standing in the middle of the road waving his rifle in the air. Daddy brakes hard, goes into a skid, misses the soldier by inches, and slides to a stop well past him. Uncle Chris's wheels lock up also, and his car slews over on the other side of the road trying to avoid the Capri.

"Oh fuck," says Daddy. Up ahead, more soldiers are running up onto the road to form a cordon; handheld torches are being turned on, and a truck is just visible, blocking the road just at the extend of the beam of his headlights. This is their pattern, he knows; one man is left to waiting in the dark to flag down the motorists, to move into the road before the car has a chance to slip off down a murram side road or to turn around. The then escorts the car and driver to the roadblock, up ahead, where it will have been set up, out of view from approaching headlamps.

The roadblocks were routine but unpredictable, looking for deserters from the army, Acholis or others trying to blend in and avoid a one-way ride to the offices of the SRB and a free trip to the lake. Or, looking for taxi drivers operating illegally overloaded vehicles, which would usually earn the driver a quick bullet in the back of the head, his empty shoes left unceremoniously by the side of the road, his body never seen again, his taxi confiscated by the senior officer on the scene. This, by decree of the President, again, demonstrating Amin's progressive ideas for effective and efficient justice.

M'zungus passing thorough such roadblocks would invariably be tapped for a contribution to the soldier's waragi fund, the ten shilling note that every M'zungu always kept inside the folded red cover of their Uganda driver's license. But for the most part, outside the towns, M'zungus are left alone. It was their own kind that the soldiers were most interested in, though these last few days they'd also been busy looking for Indians trying to smuggle valuables out of the country.

Mostly the soldiers were simply looking for a little pocket money to augment their meager salaries, which were usually paid in beer, waragi and shoddy Taiwanese radios airlifted in from England, and with which they were expected to barter on their own.

The soldiers at this roadblock begin shouting at the three M'zungus.

"Kuja hapa! Get out! Pacipaci!" Daddy and the two other men step out of their cars, leaving the engines running and the lights on. An officer in a sweat-stained peaked cap and pistol holster strides up. His eyes blaze with fury and fear, his adrenaline pumping from the screeching tires that had come bursting out of the night. Perhaps he wasn't expecting M'zungus; perhaps he'd recognized the green Capri, distinctive as it was, as having belonged to the Indian man from whom Daddy had just bought it.

The men under his command, some no older than fifteen or sixteen, waver unevenly on their feet as they try to keep their mismatched collection of Belgian FN automatic rifles and rusty bolt-action Lee-Enfields leveled on Daddy and his friends. It's a dark night; the only light comes from the stars and a thin sliver of moon midway up the sky, from the torches that the officer and some of the soldiers carry, and from the headlights of the army truck and the idling cars parked skew-whiff along the highway.

"Unaisha wapi?" *Where are you all going*? he asks, but given his tone of voice, what they hear is a derisive sneer; *Where the bloody hell do you think* you're *off to*? He wears the bars of a captain, but the way the army's ranks are being purged and promotions handed out like goodie-bag prizes, yesterday he could have been a buck private who just happened to be from the right village. Daddy hands the man his license, which is really just a convenient wrapper for the ten shilling note, and Uncle Chris and Uncle Peter do the same. Every M'zungu knows as a matter of habit to keep one folded and ready inside any official paperwork that might need to be inspected periodically by a government official.

"Me and my mates, we went up to town for a drink. We were just on our way home, back to Entebbe," says Daddy, trying to bluff with a little bluster, "Before *this* silly bugger jump out at us." He points at the young soldier who blinks wide-eyed as the others turn to look at him. The licenses are handed back after only

176

a cursory glance. Daddy knows his will be empty without even checking it, though the removal of the money was done so quickly and surreptitiously that in the dim light he didn't even see the flash of its leaving.

"Why are you driving this way?" *Thees weii*, the officer demands. "Why are you driving so fast and dangerously?" *Fest anda denjarusly.*

"Were we?" says Uncle Peter, innocently. "Gosh, I didn't think we were going all that fast at all. I thought we were only doing about forty-five, perhaps fifty at most." *Aul thet Faaaaast*, he says, drawing out his vowels in an overly exaggerated public-school manner.

"Give me the keys for the car!" shouts the captain. "This one!" *Theesi wan*. He points at the Capri. Daddy hesitates.

"Now look here," says Uncle Peter.

"Give to me the keys right now!" The officer shouts again. Daddy shrugs.

"It's still running," He says. The officer doesn't respond. Daddy points. "The keys are in it," he says slowly, in a tone meant to indicate that this should be obvious. The officer walks directly to the car.

"Oh, shit," says Uncle Peter, quietly.

"Oh, bollocks," says Uncle Chris.

"Oh, fuck," says Daddy to himself. He and the others stay where they are, under cover of several soldiers still training their wandering rifles in the general direction of their chests. One of the soldiers keeps glancing perplexedly at the squared-off oblong shape down the front of Uncle Peter's trousers, so he shifts himself slightly more into Uncle Chris's shadow.

The officer opens the car's passenger door, jabbers rapidly in a dialect Daddy doesn't recognize to two enlisted men. They immediately raise their rifles to firing position, point them into the car while sighting down their barrels, peering intently at the radio and the speedometer as though they might have secret messages written on them. Even in the weak light thrown off by the dome lamp inside the car, it's obvious that *something* is amiss. But rather than looking around inside the passenger compartment, the captain reaches in the window to shut off the ignition, then takes the keys and goes around to the boot, opens it up. The silence of the car's engine being shut off is sudden and jarring.

The lid goes up and the officer begins poking through the empty shopping bags Daddy tossed back there, like he's looking for groceries, just like the soldiers do to all of their wives at the roadblock in Entebbe. The boot, it seems, is where he's convinced any contraband might be; it apparently hasn't occurred to him to examine the lumps under the floor-mats.

At this Uncle Chris can't help himself. Here they are, standing drunk and alone on the Kampala Road at three o'clock in the morning, the only M'zungus for twenty miles in any direction. They're being held at gun-point by a squad of teenage soldiers in ragtag uniforms, who have been issued live ammunition for weapons they barely know how to operate beyond the basic knowledge of pulling the trigger to make it go *bang*! Their vehicles, vehicles containing hundreds of thousands of shillings worth of illegally traded currency, are being searched. Not for the money hidden in them, but for sugar, and biscuits, and powdered milk. They are alone with men capable of shooting them in the back of the head with impunity and leaving their corpses swelling at the side of the road. By men who'd think nothing of taking their money, taking their cars, making widows of their wives, leaving their children wondering for the rest of their lives, *what happened to my Daddy?* Men who are, even now, looking for cooking oil and candy on the back seats of their cars. It's all so ridiculous, and he just can't help himself; he starts to giggle. Daddy too, he tries to hold it back but can't, Uncle Peter, all of them, giggling becoming full-on laughter, guffawing and gasping for breath like idiots at the side of the road while the soldiers, despite their rifles, look scared. Every time they look up at the baffled soldiers and try to compose themselves, they see the officer poking through the empty shopping bags in the boot, still hunting for the flour sacks and chocolate bars that are not there. They simply can't do it, and fall apart laughing again.

The soldiers whose rifles are so diligently aimed at the dashboard of the car turn at the sound of open laughter, and their commander lifts his head away from the boot as well. He looks furious at them for howling like lunatics while under his arrest, standing in the pool of yellow light cast by Uncle Chris's headlamps, trying hard not to laugh but laughing even harder for the trying.

"Kuja hapa!" he snaps at the soldiers guarding the passenger compartment. They seem almost relieved, as though they'd been expecting something armed and snarling to come leaping out of the upholstery. The officer strides over to Daddy and the others. "What is so funny?" the officer wants to know. *Waat isoh fanny*? The M'zungus just laugh harder. This is something the officer simply hasn't been trained to deal with. "Why are you laughing?" he cries. "Tell me why you are laughing!" *Tael mi!*

"Oh, no reason," says Uncle Peter, off the cuff. "Just told these chaps a joke that the President shared with me the other night. He's told it to you, perhaps?" The other two M'zungus begin to laugh even harder now, at the absurd improbability of Uncle Peter having dinner with His Excellency, The President. Daddy looks at Uncle Peter.

"That reminds me," he says. "I actually did meet him the other day." Uncle Peter laughs, as though this is still part of the joke. Daddy goes on, "No, I'm serious. He came into Government Printing, doing one of his inspection tours like he does out at the airport. I was in the darkroom, I figured I'd just keep out of his way 'til he'd gone. But one of my lads came and got me, said he wanted to meet me. So I come outside, and there he is. Shit, he's a big bugger, isn't he?" President Amin is nothing if not imposing;

179

six feet four, three hundred pounds, easily. "He reaches out, smiles that big bloody grin of his, and says to me, 'I am very good friends with your Queen. We had tea together!' I kid you not, God's honest truth." Uncle Chris starts laughing again, gestures between Daddy and Uncle Peter, looking at the officer.

"Well, there you are, then. *Our* Queen is a good friend of the President! Will there be anything else, general?"

The officer is visibly shaken. He's obviously not used to having his authority dismissed so flippantly, especially not by M'zungus. But the *President*... now he looks worried. This could be bad for him. Very bad.

He must have decided he'd had enough. Amin has issued no orders to detain M'zungus, only Asians and Acholi. He has thirty shillings for his troubles. Perhaps because it's late. Perhaps he's tired, perhaps there's a half bottle of waragi waiting in the truck back up the road.

"You go now!" he barks. Daddy is stunned, stops laughing for a second.

"Y'what?"

"Leave!" shouts the officer. "Nenda! Noyte nenda, haraka, all of you, quickly!" He waves his hand impatiently down the road, as though *they* had been wasting *his* time all along. The young soldiers take their commander at his word, and with their rifles begin pushing and shoving the M'zungus in the direction of their cars. The captain *tsks* contemptuously through his teeth as they pass, as only a Ugandan can.

"All right, all right," says Uncle Peter, "No need to shove." He turns to the officer. "Good night, old chap," he says politely, as he puts his car into gear. "Do be careful out here. *God* knows what could be hiding out here in the bush." The officer sneers, and the young soldier who first jumped out into the road breaks into a toothy, nervous smile, glancing around in the darkness at the side of the road. Daddy can't help but burst out laughing all over again.

The next morning I wake up to find a green car in our driveway, a very shiny green two-door with sparkling white seats.

"Who's car is that?" I ask Jeliati, when I walk into the kitchen.

"It is your Daddy's," she says. "It came home with him, last night." *Yo-wa Da-dees. Kem hom weeth heem.* "Did you not hear him laughing?" *Deed you notte heeya?* She giggles, hiding her teeth as she always does when she laughs, embarrassed.

By the time their time is up, by the time the last departing Indian has boarded the last hurriedly scheduled emergency flight out of the country, there is a pile of confiscated merchandise outside the airport terminal at least two hundred yards long, a hundred yards wide, twenty feet tall. It sits in a neat, orderly, squared-off heap; televisions, adding machines, typewriters, oscilloscopes, furniture, radios, alarm clocks, suitcases, clothes; the personal effects of sixty thousand people, heaped together in a pile, everything of value that was worth keeping but was too big to be stuffed into the pockets of an army uniform. The Indians have left, gone back to India or to England or to wherever they've found to begin again. Their belongings now belong, ostensibly, to the people of Uganda, though good luck to anyone who tried to take anything off of the tidy heap which the soldiers, over the next few weeks, regularly come in trucks to pick through, taking what they want or what they think looks merely interesting. Who can speak up? No one. It's Normal. Commonplace. Everyday.

Chapter 14

With the Asians gone, there's nothing to buy. There's nothing to buy, because there's no one to sell it. Yes, the President did form the Reallocation Committee, to fairly redistribute the assets of the thieving Indians amongst the Ugandan people, so there are some shops that reopen. And until the stock is all gone – sold, or simply carted off the new owner's village, bartered for paraffin and sugar and cigarettes – there are things to buy. But it doesn't last long.

We stopped taking Nivequin against malaria, because we simply couldn't get it anymore. Besides, it was rare that any other M'zungus took it either, except for those new to the country who'd brought a fresh supply with them, and were still uncertain about the realities of living in Africa. For the rest of us, the drug became impossible to find. Also, when bodies start washing up riddled with bullet holes, you tend to stop worrying about silly little mosquitoes. When there are far more dangerous things about that can hurt you, a few mosquitoes and the risk of a little malaria just made us shrug our shoulders.

Before the Asians left, Kampala's High Street was lined with shops that sold just about anything anyone could want, just like in any big city anywhere in the world. Tailor's shops, bakeries, electronics shops, furniture shops, shoe shops, camera shops, clothes shops, the finest fashions for men and women, from Europe and India both. And jewelers, lots and lots of jewelers.

Some of the departing Asians, believing that there would be some sort of change in the policy, some sort of outcry from the fellowship of nations watching that which was being done to them by President Amin, left their shops secured but otherwise as they were. They drew down the metal lattice curtains, chained and padlocked the doors, but other than that, everything inside was left ready to reopen for business upon their prompt return, within a few weeks, a couple of months at the most.

In the days before the Asians' final departure, all the M'zungus – and the Africans too, those that live and worked in the city – scramble to buy up what they can, what they'll need for the next few weeks, for the month or two at the most that the Indians are expected to be gone. Flour, televisions, powdered milk; sugar, salt, tape recorders; canned goods, shoes, laundry flakes, radios; whatever there is to be had, it has to be bought now because there won't be any more for a while.

A common, everyday thing to which nobody ever really paid much attention before becomes painfully obvious; any shop that sells anything worth having is, or more properly *was*, owned by an Indian family. Certainly, a few Africans had set up retail business of their own, out of simple rolling hand-carts or one room dukas selling soft drinks and cigarettes and sweets. One or two enterprising African souls had even ventured into the realm of a clothing shop or had set themselves up as a cobbler or tailor. But almost everything else? Well, once their time was up, the Indians securely padlocked their doors, chained their gates, barred their windows with iron, bolted their shops behind strong steel hasps, then did what they had no other choice *but* to do, which was to leave the country.

For a few days all the M'zungus and the more cosmopolitan Africans buy up what they can from the African markets, what they'll need after everyone runs out of what they've already bought from the Indians. But another common, everyday truth soon makes itself known; where did the African markets buy the things *they* sold? From the Indians, of course, from men like Giant Madhvani, who owned the companies that imported the televisions, and the bolts of cloth for the tailors, and the sugar and the soap-flakes and the light bulbs, and owned the shops that maintained the sewing machines and fixed the cars, and imported the tires that went on them. Madhvani and others like him operated the lorries that trucked merchandise from the airport to the capitol, and across the border from Kenya. They owned the warehouses where the soft drinks and sacks of flour were stored, and the factories where the sugarcane was processed. The Indians even imported the nails for the cobblers and thread for the tailors, and the flux and solder that they depended upon to make their little tin oil lamps, ingeniously folded from scraps of tin cans, soldered together at the seams, that the majority of Ugandans without electricity depend upon for light.

And so within a week, the stores that are not chained shut are empty, with shelves looted bare save for a shop-worn box of mothballs and a few desiccated cockroach hulls.

That's when the President puts together the Re-allocation Committee, to give back to the people of Uganda what he says was rightfully theirs to begin with. It's a big spectacle, and the Daddy goes to watch, early one morning on Kampala High Street. The President wants photographs for the Argus, and that means Daddy is the photographer. The President wants everyone to know just how fair a man he is, that everyone who wants to, can have a chance to get back some of what the Indians had stolen from them.

"Malyagamba was running the show," says Daddy, telling everyone about it later. I notice the grownups get curious looks of contempt on their faces at the mention of the name. "The Major had about a dozen soldiers sitting at a folding table in front of that big furniture shop on the High Street." I know the shop, I've been in there before lots of times, and sat on the big soft leather settee they have in the window. "Malyagamba gets on a megaphone and announces that they're taking applications for this shop, and a crowd of Africans comes forward to the table. You can imagine what they look like," he says, and I can. Everyone can. There'd be few with well-washed black trousers,

184

clean white shirts, perhaps a tie, perhaps a jacket; others in ragged shorts, many with at least one tear on their shirt, whether mended or not. Some, but not all, wearing actual shoes, some in flip flops, many barefoot or wearing sandal made from old tire treads. "They had to sign their names, but some couldn't write, so the soldiers wrote down their names for them. The names all got dropped in a jerry can. Who knows if it was prearranged, but suddenly Malyagamba dips his hand into the can, then stands up and announces, 'This store has been given to Mr. Endongo.' Then this Endongo chap comes out of the crowd whooping and shouting and dancing, waving his arms, up to the door of his new shop. Another soldier was there with an acetylene torch. He cut the chains and padlocks off the door and hands Mr. Endongo a broom to sweep the dust out of his new business." Somebody shakes their head, Daddy takes a drink of his beer.

"Then what?" they ask. Daddy shrugs.

"Then they lifted up the table, moved fifty feet down the causeway to the next shop and did it all over again." Normal. Everyday. "They went the length of the High Street like that, stopping at every Indian shop they came to. It'll most likely be going on for weeks. It'll be going on down here in Entebbe before long."

"Daddy, who's Major Malyagamba?" I ask later.

"Oh, sunshine, you don't want to know about him. He's not a nice man, that's all you need to know." Later on, at school, I ask my friends if they know who he is.

"Major Malyagamba is a great soldier," says one boy, a year older than me, bigger, and far more worldly-wise. Someone I listen to. "When the President needs to take care of bad men, Malyagamba is the one he sends." *Tek keya off baad min.*

I learn that he used to be an askari, a bank guard, before Amin took over. "A right nasty piece of work," Aunty Ida calls him. Amin promoted him to major and put him in charge of rounding up Obote's men. Malyagamba once gathered up a group of them lined them up for execution, ready to be shot one at a time in the back of the head. But before he got started, he especially didn't like the looks of one of them. So before he started pulling the trigger, he cut off the man's genitals and stuffed them in the man's mouth.

I start to hear stories like this, when nobody thinks I'm listening, and not just about Malyagamba. Like about the officer at Masaka prison who was trying to save bullets, and instead of shooting his prisoners, he put them all in a cell and tossed in a live grenade. The grenade's concentrated blast blew the back wall out of the cell, but the force was absorbed by the first two or three rows of men in front of it, so that everyone else not killed in the blast was able to escape through the hole.

Or like the story of officer who laid captured men across the road and drove his Russian T-55 tank over them, leaving their crushed torsos screaming in the road while their severed legs bled out separate from their bodies. About the men lined up in Makindye prison and killed with a blow to the head from a sledgehammer wielded by the first man in line; it was handed to him and he was expected to walk down the line smashing in the row of waiting skulls, with the promise that he'd be pardoned if he did it. Except that *he'd* then be shot in the head when he was finished. That way, the soldiers only had to use one bullet to kill a large group of prisoners, simply shooting their own appointed executioner when he was done with the task at hand.

And then there're the days that words gets passed among the M'zungus,

"Whatever you do, don't be on the Kampala road tomorrow." On those days, the soldiers stop cars and make the occupants watch the execution of prisoners, who are clad in clean white shirts and tied by their wrists to a high tree limb. The soldiers on the firing squad used them for target practice, and the clean white shirts, it seems, help to make the show that much more entertaining. It certainly made an impact on the spectators.

At first, it had usually just been soldiers loyal to Obote who disappeared. Then it became people unfortunate enough to share the name Obote, whether related or not. But soon something so silly as having a surname that happens to starts with the letter "O", usually meaning that the person so named is from Lango and therefore possibly of a related clan or bloodline. The list of possible crimes grows endless; a careless word, even an overly attractive wife, could earn a man an appointment with the major. Apparently, Major Malyagamba is very good at his job.

Uncle John works for British Airways and has several African assistants. About the Reallocation Committee, Uncle John says this;

"My lads kept slipping out of the office throughout the day," he says, "And coming back with brand new European dress shirts, top quality, very pricey. I asked them where they were getting them and they told me that a chap they knew had been awarded a men's clothing shop in the reallocation, and was selling the shirts at a good price.

"I went down to the shop," he says. "The fellow had never run a business before and didn't know what to charge for his stock. So he was selling these shirts for the amount on the collar tag; fifteen shillings, sixteen shillings, sixteen and a half shillings. He was pricing them same as the collar size. The bloody things were worth three times that amount, but he had no idea!" All the grownups laugh at this. But Uncle John isn't joking, he's quite serious.

"I know what you mean," says Daddy. "There's this chap works for me, he asks me to help him fill in this mimeographed application form for the reallocation of a store. Tells me he wants to start a bicycle repair shop and needs somewhere to do it. Says he doesn't understand some of the words on this form. When I read it, it's just full of spelling mistakes and typographical errors.

'List you assest,' it says in one place. *You assest.* So I ask him what he owns; a house, a car, anything like that. He tells me, all proud-like, 'I have fifty-five shillings, in a bank. I have two wives, six children, and a cow.' So, I itemize his vast wealth on the form, and have him sign his spidercrawl at the bottom, near the X. He leaves happy. Two week later, he comes back to see me. He says, 'B'wana Dave, I am very happy, because the Committee has selected me to get a shop. Would you consider driving me in your motorcar to see it?' *Een yo-ah moto-caah?*

"I'm curious, of course, curious as to what the committee might have awarded him, so I tell him sure, I'd be happy to. So that afternoon after work we drive up to Kampala, and out in front of this shop is a sign saying 'Quality Street Shoes, E. Patel, proprietor.' The chap shows his papers to the soldier from the Reallocation Committee, and they break the padlock off the door with a crowbar and hand him his broom. 'Course, when he walks in, he's disappointed to see that it's still fully stocked with shoes. 'But I asked for an empty shop,' he says, and the soldier just shrugs. 'Sell all the shoes, then you will have an empty shop,' says the soldier.

"So he did, he moved up to Kampala, sells all the shoes in the shop, gave them away to all his friends and relatives, stacked the extras outside the back door, to clear space for his bicycle repair business. One thing he *didn't* do, though, was pick himself out a decent pair of shoes. Last time I saw him, he was still barefoot."

It's like that all over now. Some fellow received a furniture shop, he sells or trades or gives away all his furniture, then once it's empty, he either moves into the space and lives there, or simply abandons it. Hundreds of others like them do the same thing; they sell out of their stock of shirts and bolts of cloth and dresses and television sets, English cigarettes and Belgian chocolate and tins of Vim. It becomes commonplace to see

Ugandans wearing rags one day and new suits, a nice watch, the next, as the contents of shops are haggled over and bargained for.

"They've doubled the price on sugar since *yesterday*," Mummy says to Daddy when he gets home from work. "They don't know how to restock the shelves, and there's nothing to restock them with if they did. So when they run low on something they just double the price."

Sugar is the first thing the shops run out of. Then salt. Powdered milk, tinned milk. Flour. One at a time, items begin disappearing, as everything is bought and nothing is restocked, with no suppliers and no way to get anything into the country more than a car-boot full at a time, coming across the border from Kenya. Shops on the High Street are busy one day, then the next, empty, stripped of fittings and anything else of value by their new owners, and then abandoned. Some don't even bother closing the door behind themselves on the way out.

"What's that awful smell?" asks Daddy, walking out of the kitchen door. "You're not burning something out here, are you?" I shake my head? I know better than to play with matches. It's more than my little arse is worth.

"It's coming from over that way," Mummy says, pointing towards the lake, towards a column of dark, drifting smoke to the southwest. "They must be burning off a cane field or something."

"I've never smelled a cane field like that before," says Daddy.

"Me either," I say.

"Let's go and have a look," says Daddy. We get into the Capri, pull out of the driveway, swing down Bugonga road to the left.

As we get down towards the lake, towards the Smelly Fish Market, towards the beach where the bodies wash in, the smell gets thicker, more acrid. I can see a strange, wavering haze rising up into the air.

"Jesus," says Daddy, "It's the airport. Maybe a plane crashed? Looks like there's rare old bonfire."

As we get closer, I see the sooty black smoke coiling upward in a hard column, its top drifting inland on the breeze off the lake. The smoke smells harsh, more like burning plastic than sugar cane or the grassfires the farmers start to keep the long grass and the snakes out of their cassava patches.

"Jesus, it looks like the airport itself is on fire," says Daddy as we get closer.

"D'you think there's been an accident?" says Mummy. Daddy doesn't answer her. As they get closer still it becomes clearer what it is that's burning. It's not any of the buildings or even an aeroplane that's on fire. It's the heaped mountain of personal effects left by – confiscated from – the departing Asians.

We pull off into the murram car park across the road from the airport, and when the engine stops, I can hear the crackling roar of the flames, like barrels rolling down a hill, like heavy stones tumbling underwater. We get out, walk over to a group of Africans watching idly, hands in pockets as the great banked windrow of personal effects melts and buckles and sags under a shimmering mirage of trees that hang and trembles over the rising heat of the flames. The smell, of burning plastic and Bakelite and leather, is appalling.

Uncle John is there, has come down from the control tower, and he's standing with some other M'zungu airport personnel inside the chain link fence that separates the road from the airfield. Daddy waves, they wave back, and there's a peculiar kind of resigned and puzzled acceptance exchanged in the gesture; *What the hell is going on here?*

"What happened?" asks Daddy, of a reasonably well-dressed African man standing on the murram at the corner of the terminal building, watching the fire bring the top of the pile closer to the cleared red dirt field in which it sits.

"The soldiers," he says. "They came and they poured petrol on everything, and light it on fire." *Thi soljas, they kem, they poe-add, on evarytheeng.* "They had orders from the President." *Oddaz.*

There's nothing more to be said, no way the flames can be put out, and after sitting for so many weeks in the rain and the baking equatorial sun, there's not much worth saving even if the fire *could* be doused. I watch as a sewing machine leans and folds in on itself like wet cardboard in the heat of the conflagration, watch a tape recorder melt and blacken, the heavy black casing of a telephone handset roll down the pile, its flex ablaze while the rest of it save the dial dances behind the waves of heat, seemingly untouched. The column of smoke rises high into the air.

"I bet that can be seen for miles," Mummy says. "What a bloody shame."

Normal. Everyday. Commonplace. After a while, it's remarkable the kinds of things that people can get accustomed to.

It became a game, sort of. How to get things into the country – sugar, salt, flour – the things that everyone needs but nobody can find. Beer. Newspapers. Car tires. All the M'zungus make a point of being friendly with all of the pilots who fly in and out of Entebbe airport, stopping over on their way between London and Nairobi and Dar es Salaam via Cairo and Zurich and Johannesburg. The pilots do a brisk trade in cigarettes and bottles of Johnny Walker, and newspapers brought in from England – the Daily Mail, the Observer, the Guardian, even ones that are weeks out of date are like gold, and get passed around between M'zungus eager to find out what was going on in their own country. The Argus prints what they're told to print, and so these out-of-date English and Kenyan newspapers become the only way a M'zungu can learn most things about what's happening out in the world, even about what's happening in other parts of Uganda. The President decrees that anyone caught with a copy of the Observer will be arrested. And shot too, most likely, which is the implied other half of any threat of arrest in Uganda.

When someone travels to Nairobi, and someone usually does at least once a week or so, they always bring back a car boot full of 2 kilo sugar bags, perhaps a couple of cases of beer. And so life goes on. Normal, commonplace, everyday. When it comes to getting supplies into the country, the M'zungus are nothing if not enterprising. The problem is, the army likes to play too. One morning, Uncle Dave comes over to the house;

"Quick, let's take your car – I've heard there's some fellow with a lorry who's brought in a shipment! Flour, sugar... even beer! It'll be up near Kirefu's this afternoon. We'd better get some while we can!"

The grownups like flour and sugar, but they love their beer, they're mad about it, and every time there's even a rumor of a shipment, they're off, grinning and smirking and joking and planning another party.

When they get there, there's already a line outside the lucky little duka – someone must have known someone who knows someone at the border checkpoint that day, perhaps, who owes them a favor, perhaps. It seems that everyone in Entebbe heard that there's a truck full of supplies on its way, and they're all waiting in line for their share. Daddy and Uncle Dave wait in the queue, patiently. A hour passes, then two. Just when everyone is beginning to think the beer was nothing more than another rumor, a shout goes up; the lorry, it's coming!

The flatbed approaches from the east, from the direction of Kampala, and pulls up with a hissing of worn brakes. The air outside the duka is competitive but festive. The Africans unload sack after white puffing sack of flour, crate after crate of short brown beer bottles, stacking them in tidy rows in front of the duka.

"One crate per customer," the shop owner calls, "There should be enough for everyone!" *Wan cret*, he says. *E'naf foa evary'wan!*

Just as the last few loads are being brought down, just as the first customer is about to buy his allocation, there's the sound of another lorry, and angry shouting from the back of the line.

"Soldiers!" someone yells. *Soljas.*

A squad of men arrive in faded green fatigues, black berets, tin helmets strapped ridiculously to their heads despite the heat, in a big canvas-covered transport. They walk through the crowd, pushing past people, a few with their rifles at held tight into their chests, most with their weapons indolently slung over their backs. They don't ask permission, they don't wait their turn. They simply ignore everyone, like we're not even there, and set up a bucket brigade, handing the full beer crates and heavy sacks man-to-man down the line, setting them on the back of their own truck. One at a time, they work their way down the stacked merchandise, while the shop owner watches, too afraid to say a word. Everyone around looks on in silence.

When they've finished, the soldiers get back into their truck and drive away. None of them thought to pay the shopkeeper. He's crying, open tears streaming down his face as the empty delivery truck too pulls away. The M'zungus, at least, realize that this unlucky little duka will never again be stocked with beer or much of anything after today.

But it's not like we ever go hungry, or want for shoes. The Entebbe marketplace is always there, and we go with Mummy for vegetables pulled from the ground that morning, and maize still on the stalks, still warm from the sun, and meat bled fresh the day before and cut into steaks, wrapped in old copies of The Argus for us while we wait. There's no white sugar, but sugar cane still grows almost wild, and we can chew on it when there're no sweeties to be had, and the Africans make demarera sugar that they'll sell in the market. Mangos and bananas and paupau are free from the trees – everyone has a mango or a guava tree, or knows a friend that does. What we need, we find, and what we can't find, we live without. There's always *someone* coming from or going to Nairobi, and flights come in from England a couple of times a week. What do we need that we cannot find, make, or do without?

Chapter 15

From our driveway, to the right, Bugonga road is very straight, but it undulates up a down as it follows the uneven ground stretching toward the golf course. The tarmac is worn, now, and waves in widely spaced ripples, like the top of the lake on a clear morning. The monsoon ditch still runs its length on the lowland lake side, and telegraph poles, crusty with black creosote to protect against termites, still stride along the other. There are still houses down both sides of the road, but I don't know most of the people any more.

For a variety of reasons, not the least of which is the alarming frequency with which people simply vanish, more and more M'zungus aren't that enthusiastic about renewing their contracts to work in Uganda, and are leaving. Going home to England, some of them, others to Kenya and Nigeria and other, safer African countries. The Danish girl from school who always played Mary in the Christmas play, she left... when *did* she leave? It seems like some families just slip away in the night. Some were asked to leave, by our government or their own, but others have simply packed up and gone home, sad to leave but happy to be going, away from the madness and exhilarating fear that have become so bloody *normal*.

The Danish girl's house, the white one with the stone steps and tiled roof and red painted porch across the street from ours, is supposed to be empty now. It's supposed to be empty, but it isn't; there's an African family living in it. *Squatting,* Mummy says, but they seem to walk normally every time *I* see them.

Daddy's friend Uncle Olaf, with his red rimmed eyes and thick bushy Viking beard – he was from Denmark too – he lived a half-dozen doors down on the right, with the guava tree at the top of his driveway; I lost a baby tooth biting into a guava from that tree, when a tiny stone-hard seed pushed up between my two front teeth and knocked the left one loose with a soft *pop* that I could hear inside my head, like flicking the skin on a pudding. But he's gone now as well, back to Denmark. I wonder if he still keeps jars of special grass on the shelves of his kitchen. Happy Grass and Sleepy Grass and Laughing Grass, it said on the labels. I wonder if he still rolls it into funny-smelling cigarettes and shoots his airgun at the houseboy, calling him in from the kitchen, whooping with riotous Norse laughter as the nervous black face quickly ducks back through the doorway and pellets *zing* dents into the plaster.

At the far end of Bugonga road, where it swings sharply uphill to the left, there is a thick patch of eucalyptus trees, a barrier between Uncle Ray's house and the golf course. There's nothing save a monsoon ditch between the golf course and the road, no fence or wall, just the ditch and some tall coarse grass. The seventh green is right there by the corner, the fairway stretching up next to and in from the road, a strip of rough between the ditch and the smooth rolled grass of the fairway. My friends and I speculate as to what it would be like to get caught under the big steel roller they tow behind a tractor, back and forth across the grass, to squash it down smooth after it's been mowed. From here, the low banks of the bunkers and the well-tended trees along the fairway block the view of all but the roofline of the clubhouse, but I can see the rest of the course stepping away in stages down the hill behind Uncle Ray's house. In the distance at the bottom of the hill, the light gleams off the lake like a puddle of pink-tinged mercury.

Taking the swimming pool off us was one thing, but when the soldiers take over the golf course, that's when the grownups really get cross. But who can they complain to? There's no one to listen; we M'zungus are on our own.

The soldiers, President Amin decided, need a place to relax and unwind, just like the M'zungus. The golf club has a bar, which the soldiers envy greatly, and a stage for putting on plays, and a big roll-down screen for showing films, and some tennis courts, even a swing set for the totos to play on. It's 1973, I'm eight, when it happens – eight, nearly nine, which is almost twelve, which is almost nearly a teenager. Eight! In my mind, I'm practically a grown up.

The army had taken over the M'zungu golf club at Jinja first, but we all thought that it was a long way away from Entebbe and wouldn't happen here. I don't know anyone, M'zungu or otherwise, who lives all the way up in Jinja, but Daddy does. He plays golf – *played* golf – there, from time to time.

"It was a beautiful course," he says sadly. "Pretty facilities, lovely little clubhouse. A shame, really. Bloody army." There are few things Daddy praises in such flowery terms. Since coming to Uganda, golf courses have become one of them. Aeroplanes, and a well-crewed sailing boat, these are some others. But Jinja, the M'zungus decide, is too far away to worry about.

Daddy is the Golf Captain at the Entebbe Club. Not that this is any great office; there are few enough M'zungus left now that they just take it in turns, being captain, treasurer, committee members, just like me and my friends, taking it in turn to be Tarzan or Batman or Georgie Best.

"We're going to pull the archives for safekeeping," he tells Mummy. "If the buggers show up and want to take over we'd best have all the valuables out." The archives are kept in large leather-bound volumes, each like a wizard's spell-book, all written in tidy copperplate script. The books go back to when the club was founded in 1906, signed by Lord this and the Earl of that, Sir Edmund something-or-other, Colonel so-and-so; the cream of British colonial society at the turn of Victoria's century.

"1906!" says Mummy. "My *dad* wasn't even born yet."

"Each of the original members donated money to bring materials and furnishings from England," say Daddy, "By ship, around the Cape of Good Hope, up to Mombasa. Each step of the club's conception and construction is written down in these books. It even describes how they brought the gear up from Mombasa by camel."

"Why didn't they take the train, like we did?" I ask.

"Well, sunshine. I don't think the railway had even been built yet." I think again, of the narrow little ledge on which those tracks had been laid, of the Great Rift Valley stretching out below.

"The building itself, the club house, at least the one we're in now, wasn't designed and built until much later. But look at this," he says, opening the first of the big leather books, like a magician's book of incantations. The handwriting is perfectly even, perfect in spacing and height and proportion – all the things my teachers tell me that my own handwriting *isn't*. He opens another book, rests them side by side. "Look," he says, and it's more of the same, the hand so perfect and even, it could have been done by the same person on the same day, even though the two pages were written twenty or thirty years apart, and by different men. "And see here?" he says, lifting a more recent book. It's not nearly as big, and the handwriting a little less tidy, the spacing a little more sloppy. "Definitely a sign of things to come." He picks up a binder book with pre-punched pages of loosely handwritten minutes, and more recently, towards the back, pages transcribed in a blocky type-written face that skews stiffly across the page in ragged squared-off lines. "This is our latest one," he says, leafing through the pages. "That's progress for you," he says, rolling his eyes. He turns to Mummy. "We've taken the all silver as well, the trophies and whatnot, and put them in a vault at the bank,"

"What about the other things, the furniture, all the props for the theater?" She asks. Daddy shrugs, resigned.

"We can't assure it all, love," he says. "Besides, it's not like they're going to nick the curtains, even if they *are* brand new." They've just been replaced, at great expense to the club, just before the Asians left. "No, we're more concerned with the trophies and silverware, that sorta thing."

Inside the clubhouse, three large glass trophy cabinets line the foyer, on either side of the doors to the bar and at the far end by the auditorium door. The trophies must be worth a thousand pounds, I think, or perhaps a million; bluish silver loving cups with little plaques and brass plates around their heavy ebony bases, and shields engraved with the names of players who had won them going back to before the war. In addition to the silver trophies are other valuables; some heavy crystal ashtrays, ornamental glassware, a big rococo punchbowl with a scalloped lid and filigreed handles. Ornately engraved silver goblets, etched silver platters. Daddy's name is on a few of them, for winning some of the tournaments, and Mummy's too.

There's a knock at the door one evening when we're all at home a few days later. We're not used to people dropping by unexpectedly; a bolt of cold fear goes down my back. Soldiers? Bruno starts barking savagely in the kitchen, but when Daddy opens the back door, the dog goes quiet. I can hear him, slobbering and panting. That's how I know it must be a friend. I look around the corner. It's Uncle Ray.

"Hullo all," he says. "Sorry to barge in on you. But I thought you'd want to know. They've done it. The soldiers are there."

"Where? At the club?"

"Uh huh." He sounds stoically resigned to the fact that once the golf club is gone, there won't be much of anything left for the M'zungus. This is exactly what most people believe the army wants.

"Oh, shit." Daddy sucks air in through his teeth and begins chewing the edge of his mustache in frustration. "Hang on, I'll be right up."

"No, don't bother," Uncle Ray says. "I was up there when they arrived. They herded us outside at gunpoint. They've locked the doors from the inside and posted an armed guard at the gate. None of us can get near the place, and even if we could, we wouldn't want to. By the sound of it, they're well into the booze already. The lights are all on and the place is crawling with jeeps. I can only hope they start on each other, once they've finished shooting all the windows out.

"Oh, they're not, are they?" asks Mummy disappointedly.

"Afraid so. I heard the gunfire, and the sound of breaking glass." He turns back to Daddy. "No point going by until tomorrow. Just thought you ought to know. You got everything out, right?"

"Bloody hell," says Daddy, to himself. It takes him a second to answer Uncle Ray's question. "Yeah, it's all safe. At least, the valuables I was able to get out are. But what about the rest of it?" I know what he means, I think; it's not just the *stuff*. It's the years of memories and history, and the loss that it represents. Daddy looks like he's just been hit with a solid blow to the chest. "The trophies are all in the vault at the bank. But there's our lockers. I didn't clear mine out yet, did you?"

"No, not all of it. My clubs are still in there, my shoes... what do you think? Y'think they'll let us get it out?"

"I don't think we've got much of a choice, do we? All we can do is ask. Let's just hope they concentrate on getting plastered and worry about exploring the locker rooms some other time. Besides, what are they going to do with my sweaty old golf shoes, eh? Meanwhile, I'll get up there first thing in the morning and see what can be done." Daddy thanks him for coming by, shakes his hand.

The next morning Daddy drives up Bugonga road, past the Lake Vic, right on Airport road, right again at the driveway of the Entebbe club. There are two army lorries parked crosswise on the grass sloping towards the practice green, and a Land Rover parked squarely on the lovingly tended green itself. Tire tracks mar the first tee like two stripes of fresh shit down a clean bath towel.

M'zungus mill about at the bottom of the stairs, some arguing with the soldiers who bar the way with rifles. There's a good deal of swearing going on.

"God, Dave, you should have seen them," says Uncle Stan, walking over to Daddy from where he's been standing next to his car, waiting for answers. "They just came stamping in, no warnings, started pushing everybody outside with machine guns. It's bloody disgraceful, disgraceful is what it is!" Everyone is furious; those not arguing with the soldiers stand in little knots, talking quietly and earnestly amongst themselves. They wave to Daddy, but nobody is smiling.

"Has anybody seen them hauling anything away? I mean, is all our gear still in there?" Daddy asks. "Our clubs and what-not?"

"Not clear," says Uncle Stan. "At least as far as I know. I've not seen anything going out this morning. That's why we're all here. But the buggers have been in there all night. We didn't have any warning or any time, and now they won't let us back in. So we've no way of knowing 'til the bastards let us go in and have a look." It's a horrible thought, what the place might look like on the inside, and no one wants to think about it. Thousands of pounds worth of property had been considered safe and secure, locked away in sturdy metal cabinets. Now... well, who can tell?

"Fuck," says Daddy. "I've got *cases* of the club's new balls for sale locked up in there, and all those boxes of Roland Ward crystal, as well as my own bloody clubs." Roland Ward is a famous artist from Nairobi who does beautiful engravings of African animals on crystal beer mugs. The club gives them as prizes in the competitions, since the players don't actually get to take the trophies home with them if they win, they just get their name engraved on the base. Daddy won a couple himself, an elephant, a giraffe, a rhino, deeply and beautifully etched into the clear polished glass.

"Nora Headly managed to get her things out, but she was the only one. They started pushing her around, but the old bat pushed back!"

"Was this this morning?" asks Daddy.

"No, last night after they first got here. Shoved her finger in the bugger's face, told him that she wouldn't be pushed about by an ignorant, dirty soldier, and started shouting at him, first in English then in Swahili, that she wasn't going to leave without her clubs and he'd have to shoot her if he wanted to stop her. The chap was so shocked he didn't know whether to take her at her word and knock off a round or click his boot-heels and salute her. She pushed his gun aside and strode back to her locker, got her clubs and walked outside as regal and dignified as you please. She's the only of us who's been in there since, and certainly the only one who's got anything out."

"Well, good for old Nora," says Daddy. "If anyone could get away with it, it'd be her." He looks at the soldiers standing guard, searching for the officer. "Who's in charge in there?" Uncle Stan grimaces when he answers.

"Who do you think?"

"Malyagamba? Christ," says Daddy. "Everybody's favorite major. Things keep going from shit to even shittier." He starts walking toward the clubhouse, greeting other members as he passes, trying to assure them they'll get their belongings, that everything will be taken care of.

In addition to the armed soldiers at the foot of the steps, there are others loitering around by the door, their grubby rifles leaning against the wall, and more out on the lawn, smoking and smirking and sneering at the M'zungus. As calmly as he can manage, Daddy approaches the guards.

"We're here to see Major Malyagamba," says Daddy quietly. The soldiers look at each other. They can't be more than fourteen or fifteen, he sees, with dark black skin and wide flat noses. They're young and scared, more likely than not illiterate village boys conscripted from up north in Kekwa country. Though *conscripted* might be too polite a word for it – they'll have been picked up from their villages and given a sound summary pre-disciplinary beating, before being handed a rifle, a rudimentary uniform, and told that they are now soldiers. They'd have been given a simple choice, of military service or a ride to the lake. Obedience to a superior is all they'll ever know, and at the name *Malyagamba*, they flinch visibly as though struck.

Daddy watches them intently while they decide what to do next. One gestures with his bottom lip, using it rather than his finger to point at the door, looking towards the other. The message is clear; *you go, I'm not going*.

"Wait here," the boy says. *Wet hee-ya*. Daddy waits. When the young soldier returns, he beckons brusquely from the top of the stairs. "Kuja," he says. Uncle Stan follows, several of the others. Men tell their wives to wait while they walk up the steps behind Daddy. The soldiers are nervous, having expected only Daddy to go inside, not all of them. The commander's instructions to the boy can't have been too specific, as he doesn't try to stop them all from entering.

Inside the door, Daddy stops. The others fan out behind him, and they all stop too, shocked into immobility at what they are seeing. Of course, they were expecting the bar to have been pilfered, and a certain amount of damage. But the sight that greets them turns their stomachs.

Every container from behind the bar, every bottle, every potato crisp packet and cigarette carton, every beer crate, is lying empty on the floor. Judging by the sheer numbers of empty bottles, every single drop of beer, of whisky, of gin, of everything, has been drunk. All of the crates and crates of booze from the bar and the store room, acquired and accumulated through dozens of shady arrangements with the BOAC and EAA pilots and the occasional trip to Nairobi, are empty. The bottles have simply been left where they were dropped, or more often, are scattered where they were smashed.

The large photograph of Queen Elizabeth II from the main wall is lying face up on the floor, its glass shattered. Cigarette butts have been ground out into the picture, and there's a suspicious looking brown pile smeared across Her Majesty's face. There is litter scattered everywhere, sheaves of papers from the office tossed around on the floor, empty cigarette packets and sweet wrappers and crisp bags crumpled and tossed without concern for where they might land, every flat surface scorched with cigarette burns. The only thing not taken off the wall and smashed is the portrait of President Amin.

And Mummy was right. Even the new curtains have all been removed from their railings, permitting the damage to be viewed in brilliant unhindered sunlight streaming in through the now naked windows. Bullet holes pock the ceiling and walls, and several windowpanes are smashed, the shards of glass in the frames like grinning crystal teeth. All this, in one night.

"This way," orders the soldier. The members pick their way through the broken glass and empty bottles and other takataka towards the dining area, where Major Malyagamba is waiting. Up close, he's not the monster you'd expect from the stories about him. He is short, very dark of skin, his peaked cap on the table in front of him. He's not a particularly attractive man, with small eyes, a wide nose and pursed meaty lips. His unpleasant features are made even less attractive by the big beaming smile that spreads over his face as Daddy and the others approach.

"Hello, thank you for coming today. How can I help you?" he says cheerfully. There are a few soldiers still leaning drunkenly against the bar, rummaging in the coolers and cupboards for anything they might have missed. They watch contemptuously over their shoulders, not even bothering to turn around. Daddy surveys the mess and the damage in the bright morning light pouring through the bare, shattered windows. Arguing, making demands, statements of outrage and indignation, all of these would be useless, he knows. There would be no point. There's only one thing he can hope for.

"We would like to get our belongings," he says, "...Please," he manages to choke out.

"*Your* belongings? What belongings? This is now an officers' mess," Malyagamba says cheerfully. "This facility has been ordered into army custody. These are now *our* belongings." *Odd-add into Ah-mi costadee. Ah-wa bee-longins.* He smiles warmly as he gestures around the room.

"No," says Daddy, "I mean our personal belongings, our *personal* property, from our *private* lockers." He indicates the changing rooms against the far wall, under the lavatory sign.

"Oh, there are lockers? I had not realized you had not yet completely vacated the building. Of course, since these are your *personal* items, you may take them with you." *Va'kated thi bilding. Lokkas? Ay hed not re-hillized. Tek theym, off kos.* Daddy is taken aback at the Major's air of cooperation. "Come, come with me," says the officer. He leads the way towards the men's locker room, followed by the boy with the rifle who had led them in.

Once inside, all the members are surprised to see that the row of lockers appear to be intact. The padlocks are still in place on all the doors, the hinges and hasps secured. "Please," says Malyagamba, "You are free to remove any belongings you find that you have left behind." He smiles again, his teeth framed by the meaty flaps of his lips like segments of some plump brown fruit.

Daddy approaches his locker, tugs on the padlock. It's still clinched tight, not a mark on it. He tugs at a few others down the row, tests the doors. They seem secure, all of them, no sign of forced entry. He nods to Uncle Ray.

"Looks like we're all right," he mutters softly, his mood momentarily buoyed by this unexpectedly positive development.

"Small miracles, and all that," replies Uncle Ray. Both men pull out their key rings, turn their keys, open their doors.

"*Jesus Christ!*" Daddy says, looking into the locker. "Jesus..." he turns angrily to Malyagamba. "Christ! Look at this! You..." The muted beginnings of several choice profanities form themselves on his lips, but he manages to get a hold of his tongue before saying anything he might regret.

"What is it?" says one of the other members, walking over to have a look. "Oh, dear," he says. "Oh, dearie me."

The back of the locker has been cut away – *all* the backs have been cut away. Uncle Stan goes around the row to have a look from the other side. The line of metal lockers, from behind, looks like an opened tin of sardines, the bracing rudely hacked with an acetylene torch, the rivets smashed off with a chisel, the sheet metal peeled back like tinfoil, battered and buckled, and propped against a wall like a badly creased playing card. Each individual stall has been emptied out – from behind. Everything is gone, even unlaundered golf socks, worn down nubs of scoring pencils, broken tees. Through the open hole, Uncle Stan watches as Daddy addresses the major.

"You're in charge here, what the bloody hell do you think you're doing! This is theft, pure, unadulterated robbery, and you let it happen!" Malyagamba doesn't move, but continues smiling his wide grin.

"What a terrible shame! I had nothing to do with this. I know nothing about it. But I will look into it, immediately." *Terribal! Ay know nathing.*

"How could you *not* know about it! Look at all this, our golf clubs were in here; somebody had to have carried them out, somebody had to have seen it! What the bloody hell are you going to do with golf clubs, for Christ's sake? And how could you not see someone bringing a torch in here? Not to mention the pounding they must have done on the rivets! You're trying to tell me you know nothing about it?" Malyagamba shrugs.

"Perhaps it was kondos. Perhaps you should not have been so careless with your belongings." *So kelless wyth yowa belongings.* He has lost his smile, and is beginning to sound much less friendly. "I know nothing of this."

"Kondos? But you're in charge! You're responsible, and you should have known. You should have bloody well stopped it, and you know bloody well who the Kondos were," snaps Daddy. "How could you not know? Tell me that, how could you not? This was full last night, these were all full last night, not with your belonging, not with *effing* Government property, but with *our* things! With *my* property! We're British subjects, damn you. We're here, we're all here, at the invitation of *your* effing government! How dare you!" The major says nothing, just stands looking into the lockers with a blank unconcerned expression of absolute impunity, guaranteed him by two dozen well-armed soldiers and a mandate from Amin.

"Your complaint is duly noted." His voice turns suddenly ice cold. "Now, since there is nothing of yours here for you, I think it is time you left." *Na'think of yoas.*

There's nothing more that can be done. There is no way to find out who had done this, and all the M'zungus standing there know it.

"Come on," says Daddy to the others, contemptuously ignoring the Major. "I don't know why we even bothered."

After that first night of drunken revelry, none of the soldiers seemed to have any further interest in seeing that the whiskey bottles got replaced, or the cooler chests were refilled with Tusker and Fanta and Pepsi. They knew that the M'zungus weren't in charge anymore, so they took down all the photographs and portraits of Lord this and Lord that and Sir Edmund somebody-or-other that lined the wall above the bar, but only after first smashing them with their rifle butts. They pissed in the corners, they pissed on the walls, and the stale ammonia smell hovered around the building long after the beer and the soldiers were all gone.

The soldiers may well have liked the golf course, but even with all the shiny new clubs they found themselves in possession of, they didn't seem to play much, and if they weren't going to play, there wasn't much point in mowing the grass. Within a month, the fairway is only slightly less ragged than the rough had been a week before the takeover. The bunkers become choked with weeds and broken glass, the greens shaggy and breaking out with spindly stalks of elephant grass sprouting up in feral clumps. After a week, even the few soldiers who had been going there to legitimately socialize stop showing up, and the lights stay off. The club, gates chained and off-limits to M'zungus, is abandoned. By us out of necessity, but by the bloody Ugandan army by sheer lazy choice.

Chapter 16

By way of escape, Mummy and Daddy start going to parties at different M'zungus houses almost every other night. Sometimes, they all come over to ours. They're just like the parties they used to have after we first arrived, except now, unless someone's been able to smuggle beer or whiskey across the border, or a pilot friend has brought something in on a recent flight, the booze is all locally distilled bush-waragi, which comes in rinsed out pop bottles with corks in. It tastes like one part banana juice, three parts petrol, is clear as water and flammable as jet fuel.

There is an air of exuberant desperation at these gatherings. Human life trades cheap in Uganda these days; the normalcy of just how crazy things are in the country catches up with everyone only occasionally. Surrounded by it, one or two more bodies every day doesn't seem that big a deal. But then you read, in the smuggled English and Danish newspapers, stories about what's happening – what's *really* happening – elsewhere around the country, and no one can believe it's actually gotten this bad. A body here and a shooting there, after three years, starts to add up into corpses by the *thousand*. The place, both the surroundings and the ex-pat community itself, is the same, but everyone understands, now that it's too late, that there's something just not right anymore and no one knows what to do about it.

And so the grownups, including Mummy and Daddy, get drunk nearly every night now, and stay drunk longer. The curfew, and the increasingly filthy, ignorant soldiers with freely waving weapons which they have only the most rudimentary idea how to operate, and the more frequent sounds of machine gun fire in the night; they all seem to make the waragi more and more appealing to the grownups.

"I tried to talk to this chap at the airport, this young soldier standing guard duty in customs," says Uncle John. "I commented on his rifle, a Fabriqué National that looked like it had seen better days. There was a crust around the muzzle, looked like he'd shoved it up a baboon's arse. I asked him what caliber the rifle was, and I kid you not, he shook his head, didn't know what the hell I was talking about. So I asked him, 'What size are the bullets?' You know what he said to me? He held up one hand with his thumb and forefinger yea far apart and said, *'Ebawt thees beeg'*." Everyone roars with laughter, and drinks some more of their waragi.

The M'zungus take great delight in stories like this. They have to find humor in something, what with the bodies piling up on the beaches, disappearing within a few days as though melted into the sand, only to reappear the next week, a fresh crop, bullet-ridden and bobbing in the surf. These parties are all that the M'zungus have left which is theirs, save the sailing club.

"It's not *if* they'll take it, but *when*," says someone.

"But what would they do with it?" say another.

"*Do*? What did they *do* with the Golf Club? Sweet bugger all, that's what. They take because they want. They're stupid, ignorant bastards and they *do* what they fucking well please because they've got the guns. And because Amin wants, he *needs*, to keep them happy, because he so fucking shit scared of someone doing to *him* exactly what he did to Obote. Kill the buggers before they kill you, or keep them drunk and occupied, that's his way of dealing with things. If the army's happy, Amin can take what he wants and do whatever he sodding well pleases." Had they not been M'zungus, were there anybody not M'zungu around to hear them, whoever said this would most likely have been arrested by the SRB, most likely have been shot.

210

Commonplace. Everyday. But a bottle of waragi often lubricates the tongue.

"What we need to do is clear it all out. At the Entebbe Club, they saw the bar, all that lovely mowed grass, and said, 'Ooh, we want some of that,'" says Mr. McGowan.

"True enough," says Uncle Anthony. "It never occurs to the silly sods that somebody's been *taking care* of all that lovely mowed fairway. This country was just open grassland 'til we got here. They haven't got a clue, the lot of them." Lately, Uncle Anthony doesn't sound nearly so glad to be helping the poor dear unfortunate Ugandans as he once did.

"It's the booze they want more than anything," says Mr. McGowan. "We've got to make sure that if they ever come by and have a look, there'll be nothing around that they could possible want. They're like fat greedy children, put away anything shiny that might catch their eye, and they won't be interested."

"Good idea," says Daddy. "But what about the boats?" Mr. McGowan thinks a moment.

"I don't know. But have you ever seen one of them interested in boats all that much? Except for the fishermen, and there're not many soldiers who're fishermen." This is true. Amin made sure that soldiers never served in areas near their families, made sure that like-minded tribesmen never had kin in the local garrison; that kind of familiarity and fraternization is how coups get going. Nearly all the soldiers in Entebbe and Kampala are the deep blue-black of the Kekwa and Lugbara, brought down from the dry country up north and west of the Nile. They are not known as fishermen, or even to be particularly fond of the water. Soldiers of the Baganda, conscripted from around this area, are generally stationed east of here, near the Kenyan border, or over by Lake Albert and the Congo, away from any bases of tribal support. Just in case any of their officers decide to get ambitious and secretly start rallying for popular support, just like Amin had once done himself.

211

"Just because they're afraid of the lake doesn't mean they won't try to make a bob or two off the boats," says Daddy.

"Well, where else would we keep them?"

"My best suggestion is out at their moorings, so if they want one, the buggers'll have to swim for it." Everybody laughs, but there's a nugget of truth in this. They decide, in the course of these discussions, to make sure there's never anything of value left in the club house. The beer, the food, it's all removed from the bar and the big storage room and refrigerators each Sunday night, and the gates locked after the last car leaves. Then, hopefully, there will be nothing the soldiers want if they do come around for a look.

I don't really notice the fact that Mummy and Daddy seem to be drinking so much more until the shouting starts. It happens more and more; Mummy wants to leave, to go home to England, but Daddy wants to stay. In the night, their voices in the living room and through the cinderblock wall from their bedroom gets louder and louder, and when the swearing starts, I just want to pull the pillow over my head and be somewhere else.

They're fighting because more and more people are leaving the country, getting their papers in order and catching a plane for England. I notice Uncle Dave and Auntie Ida's going most of all. They've been our neighbors for four years. Uncle Dave doesn't want to go back to England, he wants to stay in Uganda and keep working at the newspaper. But it's his own fault he has to leave, or that's what the President says.

The reason he has to leave is because he broke his collarbone. Quite a long time before, actually, and I'm not even sure what a collarbone is – I think it's something to do with shirt collars and mango flies. All I know is, it must have hurt a lot, but all the doctors at the Entebbe hospital did was bandage his arm to his chest and gave him some aspirin. These were the African doctors, or Africans who claimed to be doctors, because since all the

Indian doctors who had been teaching and supervising them had been deported in '72, there was no way to tell any more. Uncle Dave was *very* cross with the hospital for not being able to take better care of him, and he said so. He told all the doctors that he'd be better off in England, that if he was in an *English* hospital they'd have known how to take better care of a broken shoulder. He told quite a lot of people about how bad it could be here if you got hurt; he was quite upset indeed. And it's not just Uncle Dave who is unhappy. Things have been getting uncomfortable for a lot of M'zungus, and they've been complaining about it, to the newspaper, to their government, in letters home to England. Some are people who lived near Jinja, who had their golf club taken away from them too, and other people who have had aiyas and shamba boys picked up in army trucks one day and never heard from again. Some people are unhappy that they can't buy sugar or salt in any of the shops, and when they can the price is double or treble what it should have been. People begin to complain, to say bad things about President Amin and his government, to ask for change.

President Amin doesn't take criticism well, and takes care of the problem in his own inimitable style.

"Anyone," he says one evening on the radio, "Who is unhappy with their lot in Uganda, or who has expressed a wish to get out – you are free to leave the country." Well, actually, no, that's not really what he says, not exactly. What he says is, anyone who has ever publicly expressed a desire to leave the country or who has publicly criticized the government in any way, you have two weeks to leave the country or you will be arrested and imprisoned. And shot, most likely, except he doesn't say that. He doesn't have to.

And so Uncle Dave has to leave.

"Why?" says Daddy. "Whatever are you talking about?" Uncle Dave shakes his head.

"Don't you remember when I fell? You remember how unhappy I was about those so-called wog doctors at the hospital? You heard me," he says, "Going on about them. Christ, everyone heard me. The nurses, half the buggers at the Argus. Shit, even our shamba boy got an earful. Too many people know what I said when I got hurt, about this country getting itself out of the bloody stone age."

It's true. The risk to him of being denounced to the SRB, of being turned in for a reward as a traitor, is just too great. So he has to go.

"God, if only I'd kept my mouth shut!" he moans. "It's my own fault, I shouldn't have said anything, I should have just gone back to England, had my shoulder set, and come home again. But I didn't. With this latest decree, staying's not worth the risk. Amin doesn't muck about," he says. "All it takes is the wrong person saying the wrong thing about me, and..." He makes a sickening *crrrunch* sound, draws a thumb across his throat. There's an uncomfortable pause. "Y'know, Davie, there's other options for clever lads like us. The Agency is always looking for people in Kenya, Nigeria... I've written to them, just curious, like, and I'm hoping we won't have to be in England for very long. You'd be wise to start thinking about packing it in as well." It's obviously not the first time the thought has crossed Daddy's mind.

"Yeah, we've talked about going home for a while now, especially because of the kids." He doesn't mention that these *talks* have been at full drunken, angry volume. But we're still under contract here," he says. "I renewed mine after we got back from England, and I've got over another year to go. They're going to be a bit reluctant to offer me anything in Kenya if I go trying to wiggle out of this one."

"The British government is *already* talking about pulling out, stopping all aid, and cutting off assistance and support like us," says Uncle Dave. "Wouldn't surprise me at all if the Ugandan government doesn't stop paying us altogether before the year's out." Daddy nods.

"Yeah, but at this point it's not about the money, is it?" he says. "We're getting paid a fortune, but I'd stay on even if they only paid me half that. God, I love it here, don't you? I mean do you *want* to go back to soddin' England after this?"

"Of course I bloody well don't! Besides, even if I did chance it and stay, that's fine for lads like you and me, but like you say, there's our wives to think about. And your kids, my granddaughter... Amin's decrees are getting more and more peculiar, and when it's not carrying out his last crack-pot order, the army does as it bloody well pleases. How long d'you think it's going to be before things start affecting *our* families, eh? What happens then? And by then, it'll be too bloody late, mate." Daddy nods, understanding his point. "It's just getting too dangerous out here," Uncle Dave says. "Christ, you have no idea how disappointed we are, me and Ida both. I've lived here nearly seven years. This is my home. But it's just not worth it anymore."

At least Auntie June and Rebecca will be staying. Auntie June met a man, who I've been told to call Uncle Lars. He owns a big construction company in Kampala and is very rich. She and Rebecca moved up to Kampala with him, so we don't see her as often. But they'll at least be staying.

Mummy and Daddy come home from Uncle Dave's going-away party at the Lake Vic, and I can hear them shouting in the driveway before they're even in the kitchen. It wakes me up, and at first I think the soldiers are coming. My door is open a few inches, the hallway light is on, and I see them standing in the living room, shouting at each other. I can tell they've been somewhere special, because Daddy is wearing the trousers of his safari suit and Mummy is carrying her new white handbag. I can practically smell the waragi on their breath from my bedroom.

"What's it gonna take, eh!" Mummy shouts. "How many more times d'you think we're going to get away with being pulled out of a fuckin' car at gunpoint for a packet o'biscuits? I'm sorry, but I've had enough! I'm not going to spend another night worrying about you not coming home because some soldiers have dragged you off into the bush and shot you for your soddin' watch!"

"Don't be so daft, woman!" Daddy shouts back. "We're not out in the middle of nowhere here! Look, nothing like that's going to happen, I promise. When the contracts up, we'll look at going somewhere else. But this is our home! I love it here, don't you?"

"Of course I do, you silly bugger, but I'm don't want to end up chatting with fuckin' Malyagamba inside the bleedin' SRB, and I'm certainly not going to leave my kids orphans just because I like a bit o'sunshine!" I see Mummy start to say something, then stifle a scream of exasperation. She turns, walks down the hallway, towards my room, pushing the heavy white door closed behind her. It's dark in my room; I know she can't see me, propped up, watching them.

Suddenly she turns as though she's though of something else she wants to say, walks back towards the door. As she does so, Daddy shoves the door from the living room, obviously cross, following her. The door hits her in the side of the face with a loud *Smack*! and she reels away from it, dazed, dropping to one knee in the hallway. In one hand, she's still clutching her handbag, like she's forgotten it's there. Daddy comes over to her, shocked, bends down to help her, and in pain and anger she flares and shrieks at him,

"GERRAWAY, YOU!" I see her, crouched on the floor, hear her starting to cry, and I jump from the bed, run up behind him, start smacking my fists against his back. In a rush, I know exactly the outrage the Indian doctor who treated my burns must have felt, believing that Mummy or Daddy could have done that to me.

"Stop it!" I shout, "Stop hitting my Mummy!" I'm crying, angry, afraid, confused. "Stop hitting my Mummy!" I scream again. Daddy looks stunned, Mummy's mascara is running down her cheek, she's holding a hand against an angry red mark just by her right eye; I want to kill him and help her and make all the shouting stop. Daddy is murmuring,

"I'm sorry, I'm sorry, love," over and over, though I'm not sure if it's to me or to her. Mummy doesn't move for a while but then slowly gets up, and tries to smile at me. With her tear-stained face and smeared makeup and red cheek, the effect is not reassuring.

"I'm okay," she says to me, between sobbing gulps of air. "I'm alright, lovie. Y'Daddy didn't hit me, it was an accident. I'm okay," she says again. She puts her hand on Daddy's arm. He stokes her back, looking at her face, but she won't look at him, not yet. "G'back t'bed, love," she says to me. "G'back t'bed. Everythin's alright." She squeezes Daddy's arm, finally glancing at him. "It's alright," she says to him. "Put 'im to bed." She turns, walks slowly away. Daddy puts his hand on my head, guides me down the hall. The smell of waragi is strong on his breath, like bananas carrying a panga. He stands in the doorway while I get into bed. He's about to turn away, but then turns back.

"Y'er a good lad," he says, finally. "Get some sleep."

"Dad," I say, as he walks away. He turns back

"Yes, sunshine?"

"I don't like waragi." What I really mean is, I don't like them drinking it, I don't like them fighting, I don't like the uncertainty of wondering if they'll make it home when they stay out drinking after curfew. After a pause, he says,

"Neither do I, sunshine. Neither do I."

Within a month of Uncle Dave's leaving, an African family with about twenty children has moved into their old house. His meticulously tended lawn has been tilled under and a variety of crops planted; cassava, of course, and ground nuts, as well as long green loofa plants, and brightly-colored beans that grow on a trellis. They've started cutting down sections of the hedge that separated our gardens, and at night, we can smell it burning, fuel for their cooking fire in the back of the house, and smell the sour corn smell of pombe simmering away.

It's Sunday, a clear blue morning like any other at the sailing club. The lake is still flat and calm; the wakes of the speedboats pulling skiers around the bay haven't set up too much of a chop yet. The wind the sailors will use for the race this afternoon is still just a puff of breeze occasionally stirring my hair around.

"Shit," says Mr. McGowan. "Would y'looka that." Me and the other kids all look up; that's an event worth noticing, someone saying the *S*-word out loud in front of us without trying to disguise it. At the moment, though, none of the grownups notice us totos watching them. They're busy looking down from the concrete deck of the clubhouse, up the murram road leading out through the gates, under the dusty overarching eucalyptus trees shading the road.

"Oh, balls, here we go." It's an army lorry, and a jeep. The jeep is leading, and there's an officer riding in the back seat, his hands folded in his lap as he looks with interest at the beach. He looks out over the sailing boats at rest on the sand with their sails drawn down, at the cabin cruisers bobbing on their mooring buoys. The Mummies on the sand prop themselves up on their elbows, begin pulling the straps of their tops back into place, covering themselves with towels and kitangis. The men up at the clubhouse stand in front of the blackboard they use for planning race strategies, silently looking down on the lorry. The soldiers in the lorry don't immediately dismount, which, at least, is promising. They sit still, the butts of their rifles between their boots, waiting for orders.

"This is it for the old sailing club, then," mutters someone pessimistically.

The officer looks around a little, nods politely to the women before noticing the men watching quietly from the clubhouse. He begins climbing the steps up to the deck. He walks without looking where he's going, his attention riveted on the figure of Linda Radkey in her tiny purple and white stripped bikini, skimming along behind a little red Fletcher speedboat, Daddy's boat, being driven by Uncle Chris. The *burr* of the engine, the *skkksh* of the skis over the water and the perpetual *skreeeee* of the grasshoppers around us are the only sounds; all the M'zungus have their eyes glued to the officer, and the truck full of armed soldiers.

"Hello," he says, in a friendly tone, to the quiet gathering of M'zungus waiting for him in the shade of the open-sided apron of the clubhouse. The men nod cautiously in greeting. "I have seen the boats out here from up on the road," he says, "And I wanted to take a look for myself." *Tek eh look*, he says, *foa maiysel'f.* It sounds funny to me, the way he emphasizes the wrong words of the sentence; *take* and *for* and *my*. The M'zungus aren't sure how to respond. He doesn't notice. He's still staring out at the pretty young woman on skis.

"Tell me," he asks them, not taking his eyes of the lake, "How do they do that?" Dad looks out to where his gaze is fixed, tracking along with the figure slicing across the water behind his boat. He wonders if Chris has noticed the soldiers yet.

"Do what?" Daddy asks.

"Walk on the water like that." *Wok on wotta.* Dad thinks he's kidding.

"Eh?"

"He is walking on the water, yes? You can do this also?" Apparently, from this distance he doesn't seem to have noticed it's a girl who is being towed. And he's not kidding, Daddy sees.

219

Skiing is not a concept the man is familiar with. He looks at Uncle Stan, Uncle Anthony, Mr. McGowan.

"No, you see, they're not..." Daddy begins. Mr. McGowan steps forward.

"May we offer you a beer, Major?" The officer, from his uniform and cap, is obviously a captain. But he beams with bright yellow-white teeth and does not correct the M'zungu.

"All right, yes, perhaps I shall."

"Davie, see if y'canna scrounge up this fine soldier a drink, will ye?" He nods knowingly at Dad, indicates the little portable polystyrene coldbox on the floor next to the bar. He's turned up his jovial Scottish charm a notch for the officer's benefit. Daddy offers a bottle, the second to last one in the cooler. He sees the officer looking pointedly at the dusty, unoccupied shelves of the bar, the empty wall brackets where the whisky and gin bottles might otherwise have been mounted, the big empty beer cooler with its lid open and the bare aluminium interior dry and warm, the plug and cord laid obviously and uselessly across its top. "Cheers," says Mr. McGowan jovially.

"This is a very nice place you have got here," the officer says, trying to sound as M'zungu as he can, but emphasizing *nice* and *got* more than he should. *Eh nyce ples.*

"Och, this ol' dump? I dinna know why we bother showin' up, m'self," says Mr. McGowan. "But, y'know, the women and the kiddies, they like to play in the water, so I reckon we put up with it. Y'won't catch me in that lake though." He taps his nose, knowingly. "Too many bloody crocodiles." He leans in conspiratorially towards the officer. "You know how it is. There's nothin' to drink but the few beers we can scrounge up ourselves, and there's no' even a comfortable place to sit down," he says, pointing to the mismatched folding metal chairs scattered around, the oldest and saddest of the barstools stacked up in the corner. He looks away, shakes his head. "Honestly, I don't know why we bother." He sips his beer, looks out over the water, innocent and wide-eyed.

They explain to the officer about skiing, that it's done with two boards on your feet, that no one is actually walking on the water. They make it sound precarious and dangerous, especially the part about having to avoid the crocodiles, then cautiously ask him if he'd like to have a go. He declines.

It hasn't escaped anybody's attention that the other soldiers are still down below, though it's taken as a good sign all around that they're all still in the back of their lorry, rifle butts still sitting harmlessly between their feet.

The officer's eyes dance repeatedly over everything in the sailing club – the empty trophy shelf, the dry bar, the handwritten Out of Order sign on the cigarette machine, the open door of the vacant storage room. He has no clue as to the effort that has gone into making the facility look disheveled and uninviting.

When he leaves, he shakes everyone's hand cheerfully, salutes, then walks down the steps. Once in the jeep again, he gruffly indicates to the driver to turn around. The lorry follows.

"Och, that w' a close one," says Mr. McGowan. He's still laying the Scotsman on thick.

"They might still come back, y'know. A scouting party for Malyagamba, in advance of him and his sodding Reallocation Committee." Everyone knows that this *is* still a possibility.

"No, he got a good look at the bar, he saw that there's no' a bloody drop t'drink... he'll nay be back."

The next weekend when we arrive, Daddy seems almost surprised; the gates to the sailing club are unlocked and open, and there are no army trucks blocking the entrance. It seems, after the captain's reconnoiter, that the soldiers have decided they're not interested in the club; there's no booze, and nothing of value for them to cart away.

Daddy pauses before entering the gates; as he does, I look out the back window of the car, I see the white trees behind us, and I have to ask him a question that has troubled me since the day my friends and I poked the body on the beach.

"Dad," I ask, "What's down that road?"

"Which road's that?" he asks.

"That one, the one going the other way." I kneel on the seat, looking back up the murram track leading out to Entebbe, and the side-road running off it.

"You mean the tip?" He looks puzzled. "You know what that is, we've even driven down there, remember? And we've passed it, hundreds of times! It's just the rubbish dump." I shudder involuntarily. It's true, I do remember one day that we'd driven down there, so Daddy could photograph the birds. It was a strange, nightmare landscape, of white trees, stark and dead, their branches heavy with fat crops of carrion birds, vultures and hideous, rottenheaded, sausage-wattled marabou storks, ugly creatures like leprous undertakers, with nasty pointed hooks at the tips of their wide bills. The birds were fat and quarrelsome, though there always seems to be plenty to go around, in the heaped piles of garbage. I knew there was something horrible about the place, but the *real* truth of it was something I wasn't sure I that really wanted to know. But I had to ask. Dad sees there's something more to the question.

"What is it that you're asking me?" he wants to know. I hesitate, in case he laughs at me.

"Well... one of my friends once told me that that's where they... where the council men... where they take the bodies after they come to get them from the lake. He said... he said those big ugly birds *eat* them." Dad pauses a second, looks at me, chews on the question a minute. After a while, he nods.

"Well, it's true that they do that with a lot of them. The council workers use disinfectant so they don't catch any diseases off them, and to keep the truck from smelling, and they toss them on the tip with the rest of the rubbish. When no one else will claim the bodies, that's where they'll end up. And the birds eat the rubbish. I don't know if they eat the bodies too, though…" I'm silent, knowing that he's trying to shelter me from the obvious truth. "Bloody horrible things, them storks, aren't they?" I nod and cringe at the thought. He pulls a puzzled face, and I know he's about to make a joke, to change the subject, to lighten the mood. "I wonder what a vulture tastes like?" he says, laughing, "Roasted, and stuffed with sage and onion?"

"Yuck!" I laugh, "I think I'm gonna spew!" I turn back from the window, thankful for something to break the moment.

That's what you do, I suppose, when things becomes too horrible to contemplate; you laugh about them, you tame them, you use humor to cut them up into pieces small enough to digest. You can do it with anything, I've learned, if you can think up a joke big enough and sharp enough to slice them with.

Chapter 17

The going-away parties, like the one for Uncle Dave and Auntie Ida, are happening more and more often; Mummy and Daddy don't come home fighting anymore, but still sometimes slip into my room to kiss me goodnight stinking of lipstick from all the goodbye kissing, and nasty banana waragi. All over Entebbe, M'zungus are getting to be less and less of a common sight; there are a dozen other families left, maybe, a few Danish bachelors. But other than the occasional American tourist, the odd pilot and flight crew that might stop over for a couple of days on their way down to Cape Town or up from Nairobi, we're about all that's left..

It's 1974, and the M'zungus leave for lots of reasons. While some M'zungu families have lived in Uganda for years, since after The War, even, most of the men are here on contract, just like Dad's. The British government hired them to come and teach the Africans how to run their country; how to operate and repair the power plants, the hospitals, the telephone systems, the airport, the printing presses. They were hired as teachers in the schools, and professors at the colleges. They came in to teach nursing, to teach medicine, as electricians to teach wiring; political independence was accomplished with the stroke of a pen, but there were a hundred other jobs that need to be done in order for true financial, economic independence to ever happen.

But when their contracts are up, many can't wait to get out. Everyone has heard the stories, of bands of drunken soldiers raiding the homes of the more well-off Africans, of robberies, perhaps, or women, alone, passed back and forth between a band of soldiers; rape, as sport and entertainment. And by now

224

everyone knows about Robert Siedle and Nick Stroh, the American reporters who went missing. After they disappeared, an army officer was seen regularly driving Stroh's bullet-ridden car; shortly thereafter, its burned-out shell turned up in a garbage dump. The bodies had not yet been found. The Argus gave a full accounting of the Government inquest – Amin's inquest – into their deaths; it was determined that a traffic accident was the official cause of death, and naturally, this was how the Argus had to report it.

And everyone has heard reports by now, secondhand, about M'zungus in remote locations being pulled from their cars by soldiers, beaten with rifles, robbed. Pulled from their cars, stuffed into the boot, their shoes left at the side of the road, never to be seen again. It's commonplace. It's everyday. A pair of shoes, left at the side of the road, becomes a calling card, a warning. A pair of shoes left at the side of the road was another person who would never be seen alive again, if at all. Policemen, farmers, soldiers, Government ministers, lawyers, bishops and priests; none were immune. Even judges in their own courtrooms were not safe from the army and the State Research Bureau. If a person happened to be in the wrong place when the wrong people showed up, a pair of shoes left at the side of the road was the only trace anyone would ever find. Through the shoes, it's as though Amin himself is laughing at us, laughing at the world, laughing at the idea of civilization itself. *Look,* it said. *I can do any fucking thing I like.*

Amin's censorship is such that the Argus can make no mention of any of this, but the English newspapers smuggled in by the pilots say that the British Government has lost patience with President Amin. It has lost patience with the killings, the expulsions, and with the great river of international aid monies seen flowing into Uganda, but which seems to evaporate overnight every time the President gets anywhere near it. We know Her Majesty has just about had it with Amin. We just don't know yet what She's planning on doing about it.

At night, I hear the muffled voices of Dad and Mummy, talking from down the hall. Even Daddy has started to have his doubts about staying. At first, it was easy for him to think that the killings and reprisals had nothing to do with us. Now, with roadblocks everywhere, a wife and two children to think about, even he's starting to question just exactly what is going to have to happen before what's going on around us becomes too much. About what it means to stay, about where we'd go if we were to leave. Somewhere else in Africa, perhaps, or Australia. Or America. Daddy shows me a letter he'd received from his brother, in a country far away called Disneyland. There's a garishly printed brochure from this place, where they have giant mice and spaceships; hippos and elephants too, apparently, judging by the picture. *Maybe,* he says, *we'll go here, someday.* But Africa is all I really know or care about, and America seems so crowded and exotic and foreign that he may as well be taking about going to the moon.

Mail comes in intermittently now, and with the exception of scratchy, distant telephone calls that have to be scheduled well in advance and patched through upwards of a dozen different operators, there's nothing in the way of telephone service to England. So when Dad brings letters home from the post office, it's an event. This time, in addition to the thin blue aerogrammes from Drandrad, there's an unfamiliar white envelope, Dad's name and address typed, not written, on the front. *The Crown Agency,* it says in fine script across the top of the letter.

"What's that?" I ask.

"It's about Daddy's job," says Mummy.

Dad reads the letter several times. He chews on the ends of his mustache, deep in thought while he reads.

"Is that what I think it is?" asks Mummy, after his third or fourth reading. Dad answers, almost to himself,

"They're saying if we try and stay 'til the end of my contract, they can't guarantee the Ugandan government will pay their portion of my salary." He starts reads again, stops, looks out of the window.

"And..." says Mummy. He looks back at her.

"And for our safety, if we voluntarily get out now, the British government will pay us in full for both governments' shares, plus a bonus for all leave due through the end of the contract."

"So what does that mean?" says Mummy. He hesitates, staring out of that same window. It is a very long pause.

"I suppose," he says slowly, "It means we're going home."

Home? What, England? Not to *that* place. Not that cold, miserable, wet, sad place with the awful food and rain all the time and never ever any sunshine. With the miserable cruel children who can't speak English *or* Swahili properly, and small-minded people who think it adventurous to even cross the bloody road. But it looks like that's where we're going.

I find myself in the bathroom once again, standing on the step-stool, looking in the mirror for the little Ugandan boy who I know should be there. I want to ask him who I'll be when I get back to England, whether he'll remember that I'm really African. I want to know if he'll stay here, at least a part of him, in this, the place that he loves. But I don't see him. All I see is a fair haired M'zungu looking back at me, taller now, older, skin tanned the color of beef gravy, nose perpetually burned and crusted with scabs and freckles from the sun, but underneath, still white. He's crying, but for all his tears, the whiteness still hasn't worn away.

We all have to go to the hospital, and get injections and inoculations against all the horrid diseases that the English think we might be bringing home with us. Those same posters are up on the walls, showing all the awful diseases you can catch if you drink from the lake or eat spoiled food or get bitten by the wrong kind of insect. I wonder for a moment, if I caught one of these diseases, would they'd have to let me stay?

I remember all at once and with sudden clarity, being here before. Sitting on this same bench, looking up at that same picture, of the young African boy with white, puss-filled sores all over his chest. I hear the same toilet-roll hospital sounds echoing up the corridor, metal instruments clattering in metal kidney-pans, plimsolls squeaking on polished concrete floor. I smell the Dettol and the boiled bandages, and I scuff my flip-flops against the rail of the same wooden bench where I'd once sat waiting for the Indian doctor to look at my sunburn. My legs didn't even touch the ground, then.

The door across from me swings open and I look up, startled, expecting for a moment to see that same Indian doctor waiting in the doorway. But of course, these days there are no Indian *anybodies*, let alone Indian doctors. Instead, it's an African in black trousers and a white coat, a silver reflector dish on a white band around his head. He *looks* like a doctor, at least, though with Amin around he could have been a taxi driver until last week for all we know.

Lulu walks past him unwrapping a boiled sweet, a brownish orange patch on her arm where she's just had her injection.

"Your turn now," says the doctor. *Yoah tan.*

Walking back to the car, each of us with a mercurochrome smudge on our upper arm, I look out towards the lake and remember the slimy sunburn medicine the dispensary had given me, and the salad cream bottle it came in. For a brief moment I can feel the tingle of that old sunburn on the hairline at the back of my dark brown neck, like chlorinated pool water in a cut that hasn't healed. Down the hill, I can see the lake, the roof of the Lake Vic hotel, the buoys that mark the bay where the sailing club sits overlooking the beach, and all I can think about is how I just can't wait to get back out into the sunshine, back into the water, one last time.

228

Chapter 18

"Where are you going, Dad?" I ask.

"Up to Kampala. I've got to get some papers looked at so we can go back to England." As much as the President seems to want to be rid of us M'zungus, going back to England is no easy task. Getting ready to leave has become almost a full time job, for most of the M'zungus in fact. There are forms to be filled out, documents to be stamped, and as this is Uganda, there are bribes to be paid.

"The tax clearance alone is going to be several days, shuffling backwards and forwards to Kampala, going to all the different government offices," says Uncle Chris. He's leaving, too. "Make sure you bring a few extra ten bob notes with you," he adds, laughing.

Dad has to go to the bank and get statements for the last two years. Everyone leaving the country has to account for every transaction over two hundred shillings in the last four years. The President doesn't want anyone smuggling out more than their fair share of his Uganda money.

"Make it out for sixteen thousand," he says to Uncle Anthony. "Put down that it was for a new engine for the boat or something."

"But I don't own a boat," says Uncle Stan.

"Yeah, but these buggers don't have to know that, do they?" A veritable equatorial snowstorm is going on around us, as friends write worthless but necessary receipts to each other for all sorts of things that they didn't buy, so that everyone can account for money that has been withdrawn from Uganda banks and converted into pounds on the black market, sent back to their various banks in England.

"Y'don't think they'll get a bit suspicious?" says Uncle Stan. Uncle Anthony laughs.

"Suspicious? This receipt'll be read by some semi-literate paper-pusher who earns about a hundred shillings a week. Slide it across the table with a twenty shilling note folded inside it and I could have sold you the Mona Lisa and the left bollock off the wooden horse of Troy for all he'll care."

"Changed your tune a bit, haven't you, Tony?" Uncle Anthony looks up from the table where all the grownups sit, writing bogus receipts to each other. For boats, cars, hi-fi sets; everyone who is leaving is making out receipts to everyone else, back and forth, thousands of shillings worth of paper that will be slid across some official's table as gift-wrapping for an ever-growing stack of ten shilling bribes. Commonplace, everyday. It is just how things get done.

"What do you mean?" Uncle Anthony says.

"Well, what happened to changing the world, righting the wrongs perpetrated by colonial Europe?" Uncle Anthony shakes his head.

"Yes, well, I'm afraid you have me there. I thought I could make a difference, I really did. But these ignorant fuckers… Jesus, it's like they *want* to live like animals or something. Christ, I've never met people so eager to kill each other over nothing!"

"Come on, Tony," says Uncle Chris, "They're not all like that."

"No, of course they're not," says Uncle Anthony, softening slightly. "Just the army, and any of the crooked bastards who works for the government. It's got nothing to do with what's in the best interest of the people, or the country. Every one of them is only interested in how they can best line their own pockets, even if it means turning someone else in to the SRB. God, I've loved it here, but it's certainly cured me of any illusions I'd had about just why it was that Europeans were able to colonize Africa and not the other way 'round."

"He's a good lad, this one," says Dad later, looking straight at me when he gets home from Kampala. He's very happy, with a great big smile on his face. "You did me a real good turn today, son," he says to me. "Normally takes at least three or four rounds of sitting in that tax office!"

"What happened?" says Mummy.

"Well, I get into the tax stamp office, and this chap starts shuffling through all the papers, slipping out the ten shilling notes and dropping them into his desk. When he opens up your passport, though, he says, '*Samahani*, what is this?' He was polite, but God, he looked annoyed." I can just see him, sitting in an office painted the curiously tinted institutional beige of all Ugandan schools and official buildings, with flakey brown wainscoting half way up from the floor. The official, I know, would have been sitting at an old desk with varnish worn thin, its legs in little dishes of paraffin to guard against termites. I can almost hear the wire-covered fan spinning over a filing cabinet in front of a high, pebbled-glass window.

"He lays the passport down on the table in front of himself, and turns it around. He stabs his finger into the space below your photograph, pointing to that picture he drew, the one he scribbled in there when he was a kid.

"I thought, *oh, hell, here we go*. I said, 'Sorry, it was my son, he's only little, he was concerned that since he was traveling on his mother's passport you might need to see what he looked like. I'm really very sorry.' He kept staring at it, but then all of a sudden his face breaks into a great big grin.

"He starts calling other people over from his office, 'Kuja, kuja hapa!' come here, come here. He looks at me and says, 'This is just what my own son would have done.' All these other guys see the picture, they all start laughing as well. People were

231

coming in from other offices just to see our artist's self-portrait." He looks at me. "Now they all know what you look like, sunshine," he says.

"Are you in trouble?" I ask.

"Well, normally getting all that tax stamp approval is a right old pain in the backside," he says. "You normally get shuffled off to the other side of town for a different form, another stamp, another tenner slid inside the passports. They're all in it together, and will keep on trying to milk the same cow for as long as they can. But this chap, he was so amused with the picture you drew, he issued me the clearance right then and there!" He holds up a form, which obviously must be very important, because it's covered in rubber stamps and signatures. I'm not sure what milking cows has to do with anything, but Dad seems happy enough. He shakes his head, turns to Mummy. "Chap was nearly in tears when I left his office, he was laughing so much. He says to me, 'What are we going to do, when all you M'zungus have left us?' He must be getting a lot of customers these days."

Dad puts an advertisement in the Argus for the Jensen. An African man comes to the door, unusually well dressed, in a dark Savile Row suit and shiny polished shoes.

"There it is," Dad says. The car is washed and buffed and looks like a sleek blue leopard ready to pounce. The man's eyes dance over the gleaming car.

"How fast will it go?" he asks.

"Oooh, she's fast enough. I took her out to the runway at the airport," he answers, "And got the speedo up to 150 mph with power and runway left over." He shrugs in a self-effacing way. "Then I chickened out."

They take it for a drive around Entebbe, and when Dad comes back, he doesn't have the Jensen with him anymore.

"He was pretty enthusiastic," he tells Mummy.

"Who was he? Y'don't usually see Africans that well dressed, looking at a car like that?"

"There's a story there," says Dad. "I asked him what he did for a living. He told me he was a bank manager. He says, 'I manager the Kampala branch of the Bank of Uganda.' Said he was buying the car for his wife.

"She's going to have a hell of a time finding petrol for it," Mummy says.

"Well, that's his problem now. Besides, I fibbed a bit and told him how it just barely sipped at fuel." He smiles a cheeky smile.

"Did you tell him about the stuff you've had done to it?"

"I just told him that it had new brake drums." He smirks at her again.

"Rotten bugger." He'd neglected to mention that only *one* of the brake drums had been replaced, as well as the reason. On the way back from Kampala after having new tires mounted on it – Land Rover tires, because that was all that was available – Dad kept on hearing a sharp metallic *Zing!* sound from outside the car. Thinking he was being shot at by kondos or soldiers, he'd ducked down in his seat and tried to accelerate. All of a sudden he noticed a wheel rolling down the road next to him, like a kid playing with a hoop and stick right next to the driver's side window. As soon as he'd tapped the brakes to see what was going on, the front end dipped over and the car slid to a screeching, sparking halt on the front brake drum. The tarmac wore the heavy cast iron cooling fins flat and flush to the drum. Turns out, the man who'd mounted the tires had only cinched the lug nuts finger tight – the gunshot sounds he'd heard were the wheel studs sheering off one at a time and shooting off into the banana fields like chrome-plated bullets.

"Yeah, well, listen to this. He said he wanted to buy it anyway, so we stopped in at the Lake Vic to sign the papers and finish the deal. Meanwhile, I buy him a drink, he buys me one, then another. I kept mentioning to him just how much his wife will love the Jensen, and before long the beer is making us great friends. He asks me about what I do, I ask him about the bank. After a bit, he leans in close to me, and says, 'Do you remember a few weeks ago when the president went to the conference of East African leaders in Mogadishu? Well, Field Marshal Amin came in to see me, in my office. Shortly before he left…'"

"*Field Marshal*?" Mummy interrupts, amused. "When did *that* happen?" Dad shrugs.

"He's also awarded himself a Doctorate now, from what I understand. Field Marshal General Doctor Idi Amin Dada, V.C."

"Gosh," says Mummy sarcastically, "He must be very brave to have won the Victoria Cross as well."

"Hmm," says Dad, "I think he's also got a Distinguished Flying Cross, and he's never even sat in a cockpit. But anyway, this bank manager tells me that Amin came into the bank and told him to give him all the hard currency they had – American dollars, British pounds sterling, Deutschmarks, Krugerrands. Amin said he may have 'incidental expenses' that might need covering. I asked the bank manager, 'What, all of it? Can he do that?' He said, 'He is president for life, He can do whatever he pleases." *Whateva hi plizes.* "Anyway, when Amin came home, he brought back what was left over; the fellow said it was perhaps a quarter or less of the initial amount he'd taken out."

"That doesn't sound too bad," says Mummy. "How much did he take out to start with?" Dad answers slowly, with emphasis.

"All totaled? Just under eight million pounds."

"*Million?*" Mummy says. "Eight million?" Dad nods, and repeats, calmly,

"Eight *million* pounds."

Normal. Commonplace. Everyday, at least for a Field Marshal.

"So how much did this guy give you for the Jensen?" asks Mummy. Dad starts laughing.

"Not nearly as much as it's worth, that's for sure. I just hope he can take care of it is all. It'd be a shame if anything..." he doesn't finish. Dad loved that car.

I come home from school one day and Dad is reading a book, very thick, with very small print in it. He's been reading it for days, and I'm not very happy about it at all.

"What about this one, sunshine?" Dad says. "What do you think of this? They've got judo, a swimming pool, gymnastics, a woods where you can ride bikes, and you'd be close to Drandrad. Doesn't that sound good?" No, thank you very much, it does not sound good, it does not sound good at all. I can't see it yet, but I know there's a catch in there somewhere.

"Is it a boarding school?" I ask.

"'Course it is," says Dad, holding the book-cover up, marking the page with his finger. "See?" *A guide to English Public Schools*, it says. "They're all boarding schools, that's what a Public School is. We've talked about this before. You'll be near Drandrad, he'll come and visit you every Sunday. You'll stay with Nannan and Drandrad for a weekend every month or so, and at the end of term he'll come and get you and they'll put you on a plane to come to stay with us for the holidays." I'm nine, for God's sake, and I don't *want* to go any school where they make you sleep there while your family lives somewhere else, even if it *is* close to Drandrad. And no, We haven't talked about it, *He's* talked about it, *He's* told me about how I won't be able to get a very good education if I say in African schools for much longer, that there are no good African secondary schools. I want to cry. Stupid judo. Stupid gymnastics.

"Ooh look, it's near Sherwood forest," he says. "Maybe you'll see Robin Hood." Dad always tries to make jokes like this to lighten the mood, that I'd laugh at if they were about somebody else. I can't even manage a smile, though, when they're for my sake, especially when I know that's what he's trying to do.

"Will you be living near Sherwood forest as well?" I ask archly. I can tell by his tone, the jokes, the shiny distractions he's tossing my way, that I'm probably not going to like the answer.

"No, sunshine," he says, "Probably not."

"Where will you be then, *probably*." He hesitates.

"Well, y'Mum and I will stay in Sheffield with y' Drandrad for a bit, until you're all settled into school, but then..." he hisses air in through his teeth, looks pained, sad, wishing there were something else he had to tell me. "...After that, I think we'll be coming back to Africa, maybe to Nigeria, but probably to Kenya..."

"Kenya!" I shout, horrified. "What, and just leave me in Sheffield? No! You can't just *leave* me there!" Brick-stained memories of that awful, cold, sad, funny-sounding place leap to mind, red buildings and bullying children and rain, rain, drizzling icy rain every sodding bloody day. I make one last gambit;

"What about Bruno," I ask. "Will he be coming with us?"

"No, lovie, but your Uncle Ray will look after him until we get to Kenya. Then once we're settled, y'Daddy'll drive back across the border and fetch him.

Bugger. I was sure I'd out-thought them on that one; there was no way they were going to leave me *and* my dog behind. But it turns out even the dog is going to Kenya, while I stay in bloody rotten England. Memories of the place are made twice as dreadful knowing that my family will be a million miles away in Kenya, lying on a warm beach in Malindi, perhaps, swimming in the warm bathwater sea while I shiver and freeze in the bitter English winter.

"We don't want to leave you at school there," Mummy say, "But we've got to, lovie. You want to have a good education, don't you?" *Tsk*. I'm nine, for Christ's sake, I could care less about my education, especially if it means living in England, sodding bloody miserable bloody England.

236

"We want the best we can give you. There're no suitable schools in Nairobi, so this is our best option." At least if my family are in Nairobi they won't be basking in the perfect sunshine at Malindi, I think. But just when I think it can't get any worse, it does. Dad says, "And in a couple of years, when Lulu is old enough, she'll be going away to school as well..."

"Lulu's going *with* you?" I shout, incredulous. I can't believe this is happening. "You're gonna come back to Africa with Lulu and leave me in *England*? No, you can't do it, no, please don't... I'll never go!" I scream, and Mummy, in her own grief and sadness, snaps and screams back,

"Well, never bloody go then!" It's a silly and meaningless thing to say, because I know I'll be going anyway, no matter what Mummy says when she's angry.

I cry and cry and keep on crying until there's nothing left in me. Nothing I can do or say will change the fact that this is what's been decided, and the best I can hope for is to prick them with the weapon that hurts them most; the hate they have for the idea themselves. At every opportunity, I mope around, I turn my eyes away from them when they speak, stare in martyred silence at the furthest corners of the room. I speak in African accented English at home more and more, clinging to the hope that doing so will make me somehow less British, which will in turn, somehow, let me stay.

But I can't keep it up for long. There are loofas to be plucked and dried from the viney shrubs in the new neighbor's garden. There are sunflowers heading out, that I grew from seed in the servant's garden, between the dining room window and the hedge. There are weaver birds and mouse birds to watch, bobbling on branches, and cockamanders to chase and chameleons to find in what's left of the hibiscus bushes. There are banana trees to *thwock* and hills to be ridden down on my bicycle, *Look Ma, no hands*, to which Mommy always answers, *look Ma, no teeth!*

The promise, or threat, of our impending return to England begins to become unreal, after a time. It won't ever happen, I tell myself. There is only the eternal African *today*. It makes it impossible to see us ever leaving; *that* day will never come, the day they drive me to the back door of the imposing Edwardian manor house in my stiff new wool blazer and grey flannel shorts, grey wool socks, itchy grey shirt, striped school tie.

That day will never come, when I'm escorted up the back stairs to a cold dormitory room with ten other boys, introduced all around by a hale and cheerful headmaster and shown to a narrow iron bed under which is the heavy wicker basket where I'll keep my clothes and other personal effects until the end of term. The day will never come, when I'll be known only by my surname and first initial, or worse, as R423, my school number, and live with boys I know only by *their* surnames, and have *Masters* instead of teachers and *Matrons* instead of Mum.

I'll never see, I tell myself, the trunk set out at the foot of my bed, with my last name and school number stenciled on it, and unpack the grey weekday uniforms and blue Sunday uniforms, the crisp, gilt-edged Holy Bible and its twin, The Book of Common Prayer. I'll never have to fold away gym clothes and cricket boots and football kit, and dungarees for going into the woods. That day will never come, when I will stand sobbing wretchedly in the arched stone doorway next to a stern-faced Matron, while Mum and Dad drive away. I will never have to stand in the drizzling rain of a darkening Sunday night after chapel, after singing those sorrowful, aching Anglican hymns, like *In The Bleak Midwinter* and *Abide With Me*, Mum and Dad waving and crying as much if not more than me. That day will never get here, I tell myself over and over, until the African boy I have become almost – *almost* – begins to believe it.

Chapter 19

We'll be leaving Entebbe in a few days, and for a change, we'll all be traveling together. The house is nearly empty of all our things. Most of the furniture is staying – the settee, the dining table, Dad's big flowered armchair. But the hi-fi has been sold, the beds, most of the kitchenware. My clothes, what few I have or need, are laid out ready to pack away in suitcases.

We'll be moving to the Lake Vic hotel for a couple of nights before we go, while Mummy and Dad finish boxing up the carved wooden elephants and Massai shields, the zebra-skin drum and the plaque that was presented to Dad by the employees of Government Printing as a going away present. The batik prints Mummy collected, the antelope hides and beaded flywhisks and all the other treasures we've accumulated in the years we've been here; all will go into wooden crates to take with us, to be shipped on behind us.

The walls of the house are bare. The African paintings and carved masks are already packed away, the leopard skin rug wrapped up and tied in brown paper, the photographs and the large mirror over Dad's chair wrapped up in old copies of the Argus and stacked against the walls ready to go. Dad's books are gone, given away to other M'zungu friends. The only things still up on the walls are the paintings in my bedroom, the paintings I did years ago in art class. Head and shoulders, of Mummy with her golden yellow hair and a flowered dress, and Dad with his thick black beard and a neat white shirt, me and little Lulu standing outside our house, a child's portraits daubed on course pulp paper in thick, chalky tempera paints. I was still just a little boy when I mixed flour and water and pasted them proudly over my bed.

"I'm sorry lovie," says Mummy, "But I told you they wouldn't come off. You'll just have to leave them here. But never mind, because now, whoever lives here next will know exactly what we all looked like, won't they?" Yes, I think, but will they know that despite my sandy blond hair, I'm secretly really an African?

Jeliati and Powlino walk around sad and hangdog at our going; the shamba boy wears his grief at our family's leaving in a slack expression of dejected resignation. Jeliati weeps openly, sitting on the back step, sobbing. She holds us tightly, the M'zungu boy that she's known since he was five, the M'zungu girl she's known since she was nearly a baby, and sobs.

"Will you remember me?" she asks. *Weil you rimemba mi*? My chin quivers and I nod and bury my face in her smooth black bosom, and sit in her lap as she rocks us and says over and over, "*Bas, bas, bas.*" Quiet, quiet, little one, cooed over crying babies and the grieving.

Mum and Dad give them each gifts, of clothing and money. But still, when they leave the little dutch-doored rooms in the rusty building that has been their quarters for more than four years, neither of their belongings fill more than a single battered valise and a cloth bundle tied up in a square of bright kitangi. A suitcase and a bundle, and an oil lamp, ingeniously folded from scraps of old tin cans, soldered together at the seams.

All the other M'zungus fête us at the Lake Vic hotel the night before we leave, just as Mummy and Dad have helped to say goodbye to all those other M'zungus who have left before us. All the Uncles and Aunties, they come for one last party with Mummy and Dad out on the hotel's patio, and everyone laughs a lot and talks a lot about how much they can't wait to get back to proper English weather. They talk too loudly though, and laugh too hard until their faces are shiny and red and they are crying. Everyone hugs us tight and tells me to be a good boy; they squeeze Lulu and kiss Mummy on the cheek and shake Dad's hand, promising to write and keep in touch.

The next morning, the pool is quiet and it's cool outside, and the sun hasn't yet warmed the air or set the grasshoppers screeching. I watch the hotel staff in white shirts and black trousers, arranging the deck chairs by the pool and checking the ashtrays on the tables. There's a combi pointed in zebra strips sitting under the porte cochére, our taxi, waiting to take us to the airport.

The driver, in shirtsleeves and rubber sandals, leans against a pillar smoking a cigarette. He beams a smile at me as I approach.

"Jambo, M'zungu mtoto. Habari yako?"

"Habari musuri, asanti." I answer, smiling back at him. I am indeed a child, a stranger; despite how African I may feel. But in spite of this, yes, thank you – I am well.

Chapter 20

The signs hanging over all the shop windows along the concourse are completely incomprehensible to me; were they in French, I'd most likely be able to stab a guess at a few of them, possibly. Since starting the term at boarding school – *Ramsby House Preparatory School*, as it says in gilt letters on the discrete blue sign by the gate, on the quiet road heading east through the rolling Nottinghamshire countryside – I've been thrown right into the deep end of the French language. That's the English way, pitched in and expected to catch up to the other boys, *tout de suite*, and on my head be it if I don't.

But the signs in Frankfurt airport – why, not only can't I read the language, but on some of the blasted things I can't even read the *letters*; a bulbous capital B that doesn't quite touch at the bottom, unreadable symbols slap in the middle of silly words, nonsense words, like six words cramped together without any spaces and not enough vowels to go around.

This liberty, to freely walk the airport concourse, is peculiar after these, my last few months at school. Now, I'm wandering Frankfurt airport alone, waiting to board my Lufthansa flight for the next leg of my trip home to Africa, in my Sunday uniform of black shorts, grey socks, white shirt, blue blazer, and striped school tie. Around my neck is a clear plastic pouch with the letters "UM" – Unescorted Minor – which contains my passport, tickets, and money.

Ramsby is a place of routines. We rise each morning at six, wash and brush-up, dress and stand for bed inspection, line up silently for breakfast at the rectory tables by half-past. Headmaster leads the prayer, our heads bowed;

"For what we are about to receive, may the Lord make us truly grateful, Amen." Or in the words of my fellow school-mates,

"What we are about to receive, the pigs have just refused." Ramsby School, hilariously to us at least, is less than a mile from HM Ramsby Prison; farms on the land between the two serve both school and prison and, at least in the mind of the boys who board here, there's very little difference between the two establishments.

A hand bell rings; we sit, still silent. It rings again, and we may talk. Two boys are assigned, by their surnames and first initial, to go up from each table to bring the food back from the kitchen, scoured steel chaffing dishes of bacon and scrambled eggs, or greasy wrinkled pork sausages and fried tomatoes, and tea, already milked and sugared, poured from a great two-handled pot in the middle of each table. We get what we're given, we eat what we get; greasy rashers of bacon, eggs like crumbled rubber, fried bread, dry toast, and jam from a jar on the table. If we don't like it, we can just bloody well lump it.

Ramsby was once an elegant Georgian manor-house, with heavy stone walls, battlements, oak paneling and tall fireplaces, broad main staircases, dark servant's stairs. The outlying buildings get ever more modern the further from the main hall one gets; the chapel and gymnasium are brick, from the turn of the century; the classrooms are brick, from just after the war. The main dormitory rooms are upstairs, in the main hall, but the New Dorms – built ten years before, and still the newest part of the school – look like a pre-fab concrete office building, circa 1960. We eat in the rectory, built in the '30s as an annex to the main hall, joined to it by along, ugly umbilical tunnel, with what had once been garden greenhouses now serving as the kitchen.

From breakfast it's straight on to class, all morning until lunch, history and geography or arithmetic, English or science and art. Lunch is the same routine as breakfast, except it's shepherd's pie, meat gristly – stewed sheep's hearts, or boiled pig

243

gizzards – with lumpy mashed potatoes, string beans boiled pale and flaccid as dead men's fingers, and stewed rhubarb with custard for afters. To drink there's tea, plenty of it, already milked and sugared, poured from the great two-handled pot in the middle of each table.

After lunch, it's classes again until mid-afternoon, history and Latin or arithmetic, geography or divinity and French. Sports in the afternoon of course, that effective Victorian device to keep a boy's mind off all things carnal; football and rugby played full-tilt on a muddy paddock, cheeks pink, tingling with cold, and dull, numb fingertips warmed pathetically with our steamy white breath. Field hockey in drizzling rain only two shades this side of snow, in dying daylight, with wicked hooked sticks, an old sprung cricket ball, and no elastic left in the tops of my socks to keep them pulled up over my bare white shins. Showering afterward in the tiled locker room, under the watchful gaze of the Master on duty, each boy casting sidelong glances to see if anyone has sprouted their first pubes yet.

We have our evening meal, our tea, at six – stew, perhaps, with scraps of meat that even the sausage-makers would not take, and vegetables tortured limp and grey as an English sunrise, and harsh powdery cocoa for afters, good only because it's hot. And tea, a milky, sugary ocean of vile English tea, poured in steaming brown gouts from a great two-handled turd of a teapot in the exact geographic center of each sodding rectory table, like some comical tin prop from a pantomime performance of Alice in bleeding Wonderland.

Then it's time for prep – homework, in a place where we don't go home, another hour reviewing the day's assignments, looking at my own reflection in the window, the sky outside already pitch dark since four o'clock. The coming English winter is already implicit in the weak and feeble heat rising just a few inches off radiators that try to, but don't quite, warm anything beyond themselves. We study and review what we've learned that day, under the stern, silent and eager gaze of the Prefects, mature older boys of thirteen, fourteen, who love to crack down and mete out discipline whenever given the chance.

An hour of free time after prep, to watch *Six Million Dollar Man* on the tele in the oak paneled Great Hall, under the names of the old Captains of School hand-lettered in gold around the walls, the honor-roll listing the Ramsby boys who gladly gave their lives for their country in World War II, and in the Great War before that. Or to build model gliders from balsa wood and smelly glue in the modeling room, or play table tennis or billiards in what was once the Front Room of the old manor house, off the Great Hall, just next door to the Master's lounge where they can drink tea and smoke their cigarettes in peace. Or perhaps read a book, in the library next door to the Headmaster's office, the ancient oak paneled walls stacked floor to ceiling with books surrounding a heavy claw-footed table, polished like a black monolithic mirror in the middle of the room, covered in the day's folded newspapers.

The bell rings for bedtime; we all move off up the back stairs, stopping at Matron's cart in the cloakroom for our cocoa or orange squash and two arrowroot biscuits before bedtime. We brush our teeth, bathe if it's bath night, in the tiled institutional bathroom smelling harshly of carbolic soap, Colgate toothpaste and Dettol. In bed before lights-out, the Master on duty comes around and reads off names of boys due for their monthly haircut; if it's my turn, I'll be led with a dozen or so other boys to the Matron's supply room, where we can joke and laugh without the Prefect's stifling presence. There, the ancient bespectacled barber, who has been cutting the Ramsby boys' hair for about the last hundred and fifty years, sets up his chair. There are men buried at in Normandy whose hair had at one time been cut by this same man, when they were boys, just like me, in this same room. He cheerfully calls every boy *Gooseberry*, and everyone gets the same blunt-scissored, pudding-bowl cut, with a short-back-

and-sides and a fringe chopped straight across and each stray
cowlick clipped off close to the scalp. If you don't like it, lump it,
both the nickname *and* the haircut.

Thus shorn, we all look equally defaced and dreadful, so
nobody really notices. Back in the dorm, under my single blanket,
I read in my dressing gown, trying to keep warm until lights out.

There's Chapel three times a week after breakfast – singing
from the dour Church of England hymn book, and reading aloud
together from the Holy Bible and the Book of Common Prayer,
each of us, as we file in, praying silently for a seat close to the hot
water pipes that run the length of the wall. Even though the
crucified Jesus looks down on me from the ornate wooden altar,
I'd gladly sell my soul to the devil if I thought he'd keep my bare
white legs warm, since the short trousers all boys have to wear
for their first three years do so little to help against the chill of a
bleak English winter.

Lining up for chapel on a Sunday morning, we're each
handed our fivepence piece for the church collection; I drop my
shilling in the collection plate in chapel, while Father Theodosius
offers Holy Communion to the boys who have been confirmed.
While he mumbles and chants and passes out the bread and the
wine, the little falsetto angels of the choir sing hymns to God and
to the Masters through the ruffled collars of their crimson robes,
accompanied by the full-throated trills of Doctor Smythe playing
his huge, many-stoppered pipe organ, which takes up the
chapel's entire back wall.

Lord, have mercy upon us,

Lord, have mercy upon us,

Christ, have mercy upon us, they sing, and He to whom they
direct their devotion looks down from His cross under the
covered wooden altar while I hold the embroidered kneeler
cushion a little closer against my lap for a bit of extra warmth.
Mercy isn't exactly what I'm praying for. The heat of a little
hellfire would be a much more welcome comfort.

But it's the Christmas holidays now, and I'm in this middle kingdom called Frankfurt Airport, somewhere between England and Africa, waiting for a plane. I'm standing on the airport concourse with a small overnight case in one hand, my duffle coat in the other, wearing my Sunday uniform, looking in the window of the funniest shop I've ever seen.

In the last term I've learned so many new words, aside from the French ones, and new meanings for some of the words I already knew. The boys at school take great pride in teaching cheeky new-bugs like me all of the polite, accepted words for everyday things, like *Masters* instead of teachers and *Court* instead of the vulgar *toilet* – but also a whole crop of new words for things that one *does* in such places. I learn a raft of new words for parts of the body, both mine and those of the few Day-Girls who attend the school, being driven in from Retford and Worksop in their father's Jaguars and Mercedes, and picked up again at night.

Here, stood in the concourse of Frankfurt airport, all those new words take on vibrant new meanings as I stare wide-eyed and fascinated in the window of a kiosk, right here out in the open, encased in glass in the middle of everything – *Mr. Martin's Sex Shop*, the sign says.

I assume it *must* be English, since it's the only sign I can read save the numbers over the gate where I'm supposed to meet the Lufthansa lady who'll help me catch my plane. And *sex shop* would seem to be an accurate description of the place – wide garish ties with pictures of naked ladies printed on the back side, and packets of playing cards with a different nuddie woman on each, posed in vapidly lustful anticipation, fanned out in the glass display case. Novelty toys, like a gun that that has a man and a woman on top who *do it*, who, y'know, *fuck*, when you pull a little trigger. There are luridly colored photographs of entangled naked couples wearing expressions like they're having trouble moving their bowels, and bottles of what looks like Nivea hand-cream, called *Motion Lotion* and *Moregasm*. There are magazines, racks and racks of magazines, showing vividly colored pictures of naked women, men, some others it's hard to tell what they are, all lettered heavily in German and Swedish and French. There are life-sized blow-up rubber dolls with vivid pink lips and nipples and a triangle of teddy-bear fur glued between their sticking-out legs. Weathervanes that look like a farmer and a fat farmer's wife; when the wind blows and the propeller turns, he pokes his willie up her bum. After the Christmas holidays, when I get back from Africa for the Spring Term at Ramsby I'll be ten, but as I walk around Dr. Martin's Sex kiosk looking at everything they've got, not one single person in the entire Frankfurt airport says a single word to stop me. The liberty is delightful.

Drandrad had picked me up from school yesterday at the end of term, driven me to Manchester airport this morning, put me on the plane for Africa.

"Just do what she says," he'd told me, of the pretty German woman in the stewardess' uniform, with the little Mickey Mouse pin on her blouse. "She'll take care of you 'til you get to your Mum and Dad on the other end."

"Spreken sie Afrikaans?" She'd asked me, before Drandrad gave me one last kiss good-bye. I looked at him, hoping he knew what she just said.

"No, love," he told her slowly, as though she might be a bit simple. "He's English, he's on his way to Nairobi." *Ny-roe-be*, he said, slowly, with emphasis.

"Ah," she said, in accented English. "Ve hope you vill have ze pleasant flight on Lufthansa." She sounded a bit like an advert on the tele.

Once the Mickey Mouse lady gets me seated on the plane, a stewardess asked,

"Would like perhaps the game or some comic?" *Perhips*, she said, gargling on her *R* like it was mouthwash. "Be bick here at this room in one hour," the Mickey Mouse lady had said, after the

248

plane debarked in Frankfurt, after she'd led me up the concourse to a waiting area for other Unescorted Minors like myself. I'm the only one today, apparently, in this whole crowded airport. "I shall come and see that you may be properly seated for your flight on to Kenya." Then she'd smiled brightly and turned down the corridor back towards the plane. And so I, a boy just a month shy of his tenth birthday, with a suitcase in one hand and grey wool duffel coat in the other, spend an hour wandering around Frankfurt airport, alone. A Minor, Unescorted, just like it says on the front of the clear plastic pouch around my neck, the one containing my passport and ticket and spending money.

The plane will take off from Frankfurt and fly on to Geneva, which will be snow-covered and clean, and white as a wedding cake. Then on to Cairo, which will be hot and gritty, with air the color of gravy. I will sleep a while, as the darkness of Africa passes beneath me, and eat a meal of dense black bread and a fat sausage that must be slit open and spread with a knife, like potted meat.

The plane will come in low over sweeping expanses of tawny grass, cut over with knife-straight lines of tire tracks disappearing into the distance, and snow covered mountains rising straight up off the plain, far off at the edge of the world. Compared to the short, nearsighted foggy landscapes of England, my heart will dance to see so much *space* again.

The wheels will skip on the runway, as we taxi past the berm laid out with bright colored flowers spelling *NIAROBI* in large, candy-sweet letters. I'll descend the stairway, gasping in grateful sweaty recognition at the heat and humidity seeping through my blue wool blazer. I'll walk across the tarmac toward the crowd of people waiting at the gate, following the lady with the Mickey Mouse pin.

And there they'll be. Mum, with her white-blond hair loose past her shoulders, holding Lulu's hand, she all freckle-faced and gap-toothed and giggling. Dad, with his coal black hair and squinty, grinning eyes, and arms as thick as axehandles.

"Bloody hell," Mummy will say through her smile, "You scruffy bugger. Who's been at your hair?" I'll grin and beam and walk faster when I see them waiting for me.

I'm a M'zungu, certainly, but this is Africa, and I'm home again.

Epilogue

Except for my own family, most of the characters in this story are composites of several different people. Most of the names have been changed, and the chronology streamlined here or there for dramatic effect, but everything else – "Nora Headly's" Karamujong houseboy and his abbreviated trousers, the money under the carpets of the Capri, the fried ants, the sunburns, the iridescent ocean at Malindi, and the bodies, most especially the bodies, all of it – is honest-to-God true.

I really did go to school not just with one, but with several of Amin's children, which was no great accomplishment, since he was rumored to have over forty of them. Though I confess, the ones I remember were bullies and not exactly friends of mine. I remember my mother coming to the school to complain about one particularly unpleasant girl, and, upon hearing her surname, advised us to simply avoid the girl, since the school was pretty much powerless in the matter. Amin really did dress his favorite younger sons in miniature versions of military uniforms and parade them about with him at official functions; and yes, the parent's day races at Lake Victoria School were, ridiculously, given full ceremony, pomp and circumstance.

In a drawer in my desk are photographs taken with my father's Hasselblad, of our lives in Africa. Bruno going nose to nose with a big cockamander lizard; Lulu and I playing in the garden; sunset over the lake; Jeliati standing next to Dad as he carves a Christmas turkey; and the bodies, lots and lots of pictures of the bodies. Bodies on the beach at Bugonga fishing village, of patchy white dead men under trees alongside the Kampala Road, of corpses washed ashore at different locations

251

around the lake. I can remember standing next to him while he took many of them, just another everyday sight in an African childhood.

He really did work for Uganda Government Printing. He really was hired by a British government agency to teach the printing and photography trades in Africa, and as such took hundreds of rolls of film, both as an interested Englishman in a new and wild place, and as the official photographer for Uganda's tourism ministry. He took pictures everywhere; at the golf and sailing clubs, in the various game parks and places of natural beauty around the country, of the people in their villages, around the lake, across the equator. The brochures that the tourism bureau sent to travel agents around the world in the 1970s were produced by my Father and the men who worked for him at Uganda Government Printing, using his own pictures. And he really did meet Amin outside the darkroom one day, and the President really did tell him that he was friends with Her Majesty the Queen. What Amin *didn't* say was that he'd actually only *dreamed* he'd had tea with her; with the Queen, and with Hitler, and Napoleon, and a few others. Amin was a big, physically imposing man; he was funny and canny and vicious, and nuttier that baboon shit, due, it's been speculated, to syphilis. He put a great deal of stock in his dreams, especially ones where world leaders sat down with him to tell him what a marvelous job he was doing.

Amin's regime continued for nearly five years after we left, the country spiraling deeper and deeper into insanity. There were tribal skirmishes and military power-plays between the various army commanders, back and forth, until it wasn't safe anymore even to drive the main Kampala Road, even for a M'zungu. The man I've called Uncle Lars in this story was a family friend, a Dane, who married my Mother's best friend, here called Aunty June. He was killed about a year after we left, in the crossfire of a battle. A rocket propelled grenade was fired directly into his car as he drove down the road, and his body was found in the burned-out shell. At least that's one version of what happened. No one knows for sure; he was white, he was wealthy, he was the owner of a large private company. Uganda had become a dangerous place to be any of those things. The various army sub-commanders had by that time become like feudal barons, and they were no stranger to appropriating people, property and businesses, and setting up their own semi-autonomous fiefdoms. The man named Malyagamba in this story is based on a real officer in Amin's army, and many of the atrocities listed were the hallmarks of this man. But there were many others like him. So who knows? "Uncle Lars'" death was simply another death among thousands, hundreds of thousands, and at some point, finding out the *why* of any particular one of them simply becomes impossible. Even the details of deaths as public as those of Nick Stroh and Robert Siedle are sketchy at best; it is my understanding that their bodies have still never been recovered.

Amin didn't really gain worldwide popular notoriety until 1976, when he allowed hijacked Air France flight 139 from Tel Aviv to Paris to land in Uganda. The aircraft, carrying nearly 250 passengers and crew, was given personal permission by Amin to land at Entebbe. While Israeli commandos planned the rescue operation that would free the passengers, "Field Marshal Doctor President Idi Amin Dada" used his position as chairman of the Organization of African Unity to pose for the television cameras, offering to mediate between the Israeli government and the Palestinian hostage-taker. Basking in the world's media spotlight, Amin railed against England, France and Israel, and while ostensibly "negotiating," he secretly allowed additional German and Palestinian terrorists to enter the country and reinforce those already on the ground. Showman that he was, with the cameras of the world's news outlets trained on him he was able to keep the media distracted, proclaiming himself "The white man's burden" and having himself paraded around Kampala in a litter carried by a few of the remaining M'zungu businessmen. These men had previously been ordered to literally kneel before him and swear an oath of allegiance in order to avoid execution.

The fact that Israeli engineers had designed and built the airport, and thus had all the technical specifications and blueprints on file, certainly didn't hurt the Israeli commandos' chances at success; it was only afterward, when the rescue was complete, that it became clear that Amin's role in the drama had been pre-scripted with the aid of the hijackers themselves. Of the forty-odd Ugandan soldiers and terrorists killed, and the one Israel soldier and the three hostages who died, no death is sadder than that of Dora Bloch. Bloch, a 75-year-old Jewish woman with health problems, was given Amin's permission to be transferred to hospital shortly after the plane landed. Later, however, as one by one the Israelis picked off the hostage takers and the Ugandan army's complicity in the charade was revealed, she was dragged from her hospital bed by the army and executed, on Amin's personal order.

In 1979, former members of his own government and military finally drove Amin from the country. The opposition was led, politically, by Milton Obote, and his own loyal soldiers who'd been able to escape the country in the days and weeks after the coup, and aided by the army of Tanzanian president Julius Nyerere. Until Amin finally died in 2003, the self-proclaimed "Conqueror of the British Empire" lived a life of relative luxury in Saudi Arabia, as an honored guest of the Saudi royal family.

No one knows how many people died at the hands of his army and under "interrogation" by the SRB, and even by Amin's own hand personally. But it's been estimated that the number is in excess of 300,000. The final resting places of the majority of these men and women may never be known; Uganda has its own killing fields, though they're not nearly so well publicized as those in Cambodia or Bosnia or Rwanda. The few brutal examples detailed in this book are just some of the cases more well known to those of us who lived there.

The Indian citizens of Uganda, all sixty-odd thousand of them, were never permitted to return to their country during Amin's reign. This Asian diaspora relocated mostly in England; northern towns like Bradford and Manchester absorbed a large influx of deposed Indians, though several thousand sought refuge in places as disparate as Kenya, Malawi, Canada, Pakistan and West Germany. Those who did return, after Amin's ouster, found the country much changed from when they'd left. Their businesses were gone, their houses were ransacked ruins, and all title to their former possessions was null and void. They were never compensated for the loss of their homes, their personal assets, or their businesses, which totaled into the hundreds of millions, in whatever currency you chose.

All that being said, I hope it does not sound cold of me when I say that as a child, none of *that* part of the Uganda experience ever seemed truly real to me. The deaths, the expulsions, were all *other*; they were as foreign to the European expatriate community as we were to Uganda. They were a minor inconvenience, an interesting if shocking and unusual conversation point.

Instead, I remember Uganda as a beautiful place, and the *memory* of the place, if not the place itself, will always be a part of me, a part of what has defined who I am as a man. As a boy I had no contact with the politics, and no real point of reference against which to judge the events that went on around me. The killings and the brutality that I've touched on in this story truly were, in a sense, perfectly *normal*, at least in the eyes of a child. What looks brutal and awful in the benign light of a comfortable American living room really can become, when one is surrounded by it every day, surprisingly commonplace and acceptable. Everyone's childhood, everyone's *life*, usually is.

What I remember most is the light; the light of Africa had a quality that's hard to define, a clarity, a brightness, a brilliance, a texture that made the place seem almost like it had somehow been magnified through crystal. There are moments frozen in my mind like photographs; of the almost edible magenta-purple of bougainvillea in the afternoon; of the shocking yellow brilliance of a weaver bird; of the feel of the thin salt crust on the sand at Malindi; of the sharp, bumpy rind of freshly fallen fenai, and the combined meaty, curried, and not entirely unpleasant smell of decay in the open Entebbe market. I also remember our aiya, Jeliati. Looking back now, I realize that I never knew this woman, who was almost half a mother to me. Though barely twenty, she had children of her own, a man who loved her, a life and a family in her home village, wherever that was. We were so close, and yet she had a whole other life that I never saw and never even thought about, until now. All these things I have tried to convey to you, the reader, in order to paint on the canvas of your mind the vivid reality and wonder that is childhood, and the brilliant, brutal miracle that was the Africa I knew.

I recently, and for the first time, "Google Earth-ed" Entebbe, and zoomed in on my old house, number 22 Bugonga Road. There was a recent major motion picture about Uganda and Amin's excesses; scenes of that movie, as best as I could tell, were filmed near or even in front of my old house. I followed the road, down past where Bugonga fishing village used to sit, past the swimming pool, the remains of which are still discernible, and which I imagine was never used again after the army's blunder with the artillery piece mentioned earlier. The beach, where my friends and I found and played among not just the one but dozens of bodies over the course of several years, has been covered with real sand and is now part of a large hotel complex. It extends up the hill towards my old house, a beautiful resort grounds in what was once open cassava and banana plantations owned and worked by the women of Bugonga fishing village.

The golf course is still there, as is the sailing club; in photographs tagged to the satellite image, the golf club looks exactly the same, while the sailing club is completely unrecognizable to me. Lake Victoria School looks little changed, with red murram stains still running up its walls, but the hedge I remember is long gone, replaced instead by a wire and concrete fence. And with the exception of a man on a blanket selling wood-carvings in front of the port cochére, the Lake Vic Hotel still looks exactly the same as it did the day we arrived… and the day we left.

When my family did leave, we weren't able to take a whole lot with us. Except for a couple few dozen slides and prints, the thousands of pictures Dad took of Uganda were left behind, in long narrow drawers in a purpose-built wooden cabinet at the Government Printing offices. There, they most likely moldered into paste or were destroyed in the many wars that have wracked the country since we left.

We had no real choice about leaving, but Africa had become our home. So we moved to Kenya, where we stayed for another few years while I traveled back and forth to boarding school. After Kenya, Dad moved us to the island of Mauritius, about six hundred miles off the coast of Madagascar. This is where our African travels ended; the business in which he had sunk all his savings from Uganda and Kenya went bankrupt, and we eventually returned to England, quite literally penniless, much to the smug satisfaction of those who thought Dad too proud for having strived to improve his lot in the first place. But it was fun while it lasted. And, it eventually brought us to America. This story ends with my arrival in Nairobi after my first term at boarding school; perhaps there's another story there, in everything that happened afterwards.

Uganda was, and is, a beautiful country whose people have suffered war and tragedy on a scale that we M'zungus can't even begin to imagine. I have never been back there. Someday, perhaps I will.

Made in the USA
Lexington, KY
14 April 2013